The Lost Music of the Holocaust

francesco lotoro

THE LOST MUSIC OF THE HOLOCAUST

Bringing the music of the camps to the ears of the world at last

Translated from the Italian by
Katherine Gregor

HEADLINE

Originally published in Italy as *Un canto salverà il mondo. 1933-1953:
la musica sopravvissuta alla deportazione* by Feltrinelli in 2022.

First published in the English Language in 2024 by
HEADLINE PUBLISHING GROUP

1

Cataloguing in Publication Data is available from the British Library

Hardback ISBN: 978 1 4722 9779 2
Trade paperback ISBN: 978 1 4722 9783 9

Typeset in Adobe Garamond by CC Book Production

Printed and bound in Great Britain by Clays Ltd, Elcograf S.p.A.

HEADLINE PUBLISHING GROUP
An Hachette UK Company
Carmelite House
50 Victoria Embankment
London EC4Y 0DZ

www.headline.co.uk
www.hachette.co.uk

To my wife, Grazia

Contents

One
From Budapest to Prague

Two
In Search of Lost Music

Three
A Testament of Talent

Four
KZ Musik

Five
Ghettos

Six
Concentration Camps

Seven
Heil, Sachsenhausen!

Eight
Poland

Nine
Italian Military Internees

Ten
The Steamroller

Eleven
With Chains on their Feet

Twelve
Deep Connections

Thirteen
Music Lives in the Air

Fourteen
A History that Needs Rewriting

Fifteen
Maestro

Sixteen
New Encounters

Seventeen
Globe-trotting

Twenty-one
Gulags

Twenty-two
Aliens

Twenty-three
Roads that Separate and Unite

Accompanying Music

In 2011, Franco Bixio, president of the record company Musikstrasse in Rome, published the 24-CD record encyclopaedia KZ MUSIK, directed and recorded by myself. KZ MUSIK includes a selection of the music featured in this book. I am both personally and professionally grateful to Franco and Musikstrasse.

Please scan the QR code to listen to this music:

Foreword

'Music,' as the Polish composer Leonard Krasnodębski wrote while interned in Sachsenhausen, 'is a spontaneous human act that matters for ever.'

Undoubtedly, making music gave comfort and purpose, and an outlet for their talent, to those incarcerated in twentieth-century concentration camps. Millions lost their lives, but the music they left behind provides us with a unique and vital opportunity – it serves as a testament to those who suffered, those who died.

Despite everything, somehow their human dignity never failed when faced with imprisonment and deportation. Where lives were lost, oceans of music have been salvaged out of the horror. This music, created in captivity, reaches us like a wonderful bird that has escaped from its cage and headed to safety, a messenger from the darkness.

As Jewish violinist and Treblinka survivor Jerzy Rajgrodzki attested: 'In the camp, songs had a revolutionary purpose for us. They encouraged us to keep up our fight for survival and to find a way to salvation.' In the midst of tragedy, the *melos**

---

* Melos – the succession of musical tones that constitute melody.

of those who feel compelled to create music, even when faced with physical extinction, elevate us. Music marked the triumph of common humanity over the destructive ideologies of the twentieth century.

The music that survived the camps is incalculable, both in quantity and worth, and the eight thousand-plus scores found so far may represent but a fragment of what was produced over the twenty or more years between the opening of the Dachau concentration camp in 1933 and the closing of the Kolyma gulag in 1953. This book gives a mere glimpse.

Music, it is claimed, is the cultural element most widely shared among humans. It possesses the rare power to fill the gaps between doctrines and religions, allowing it to bring even the shadow world of concentration camps under the banner of its language. Throughout the history of humankind, all momentous tragedies, from the destruction of the Second Temple in Jerusalem to the fall of the Roman Empire in the West, to give but two examples, have inevitably sparked a musical response. Whether this music was recorded by Talmudic *savoraim* or Benedectine monks or some other equivalent, their shared aim was to save, codify, find and pass on this evidence, this repository of human knowledge – these spiritual treasures of a nation or an entire generation.

It falls to modern-day musicians and academics – just as it did to monks, amanuenses or transcribers of sound into marks and writing – to preserve the immense musical literature from the camps. We have given these musicians their dignity back. We have saved this most beautiful and fascinating dimension of who they were. *Music.*

The Lost Music of the Holocaust comes out of decades of research into 'concentrationary music' – that is the music that emerged from the death camps. While I am a pianist, conductor and piano teacher at the "Niccolò Piccinni" Conservatory of Music in Bari, Italy, I have made it my life's work to research, recover, perform and publish the music that so many talented individuals produced in the most horrific of circumstances. While the corpus of concentrationary music is thought by many to have emerged with the opening of Dachau concentration camp, in 1933, ending with Joseph Stalin's death in 1953, my research dates back much further. I begin in 1919, with the first gulag on the Solovetsky Islands, and end in 1956, with the liberation of the Latvian composer Jānis Līcītis from the Vorkuta gulag coal mines: that is thirty-seven years of musical output in prison, deportation, internment and extermination camps. Here though, I focus on the lost music of the Holocaust during the rule of the Nazis.

While thousands of talented artists were killed during this period, their music allows us to save them in a metahistorical, metaphysical sense. While paintings and artefacts were purloined from museums and private collections, stolen, confiscated and, at times destroyed, music – the most intangible and immaterial of arts – cannot be bartered, confiscated or destroyed. It lives on. History may belong to the human race, but music, I believe, belongs to the soul.

ONE

From Budapest to Prague

Beginnings

In 1988, when I was twenty-four, I was accepted as a student at the Franz Liszt Academy of Music in Budapest. At first, I had no definite idea of what I would be doing in the Hungarian capital besides studying the piano with eminent teachers. Hungary at that time was still part of the Warsaw Pact, although it was by then the twilight of Communism. I did not have a scholarship, but I had free access to the archives and libraries and was given three hours of piano lessons a week.

I did not know then that I was in the birthplace of Sándor Kuti, who wrote Communism-inspired choral pieces, children's music, songs, three poems to texts by Sándor Petőfi for chorus and orchestra, two string quartets, and a Suite and Sonatina for piano. In 1940 he was arrested and sent to an unidentified forced labour camp in the Carpathians; in July 1944 he wrote a Sonata for violin on two small sheets of paper sent to him by his wife Amy. Transferred to another unidentified punishment camp in the Reich's metropolitan territory, he died in April 1945. Many of his works were lost.

Likewise, Sándor Vándor, director of the Sopron theatre and choir master, who was also arrested in 1940 and who was sent to an unidentified forced labour camp in Ruthenia; a polyglot, during his three months of imprisonment he learnt Ruthenian and collected Ruthenian songs. In 1944 he was moved to Szentendre, near Vác, and in November 1944 to a camp opened by the Hungarian militia in Sopronbánfalva. He died in January 1945, killed by torture and abusive treatment.

But in those libraries, I caught the research bug: the desire to know everything. Though, in hindsight, perhaps the source of this omnivorous instinct lay with my father, Giuseppe, a tailor by trade, who had bought me encyclopaedias rather textbooks as a child. I would pretty much devour them whole and often memorised vast tracts of text. I think he wanted me to acquire the knowledge he had been denied.

Soon after, during the fall of Communism, I moved from Budapest to Prague, which is where I was first introduced, by librarians and fellow scholars, to the scores and documents of twentieth-century captivity, as well as to the survivors and witnesses. Unlike Budapest, where I had arrived unprepared, I now had more knowledge, having devoured the entire *Musical Encyclopaedia* in Italian – every single volume and appendix. When I arrived in what would soon cease to be Czechoslovakia, I started to study the biographies of all the professional musicians of that region, from the early twentieth century until 1950. I was rapidly discovering that, for this kind of research, your brain must work first and foremost as a huge database.

The secret of good research, I find, is knowing not only what you are looking for, but also the where and when of it all. I arrived in Prague on a Friday and spent the Saturday and Sunday trying to work out where I would have to go, and when the libraries, document centres and bookshops were open. Saving even a couple of hours or a day was essential for financial reasons, and in order to win the race against time in locating the witnesses, many of whom were ageing or frail.

In Prague I came to understand the capital importance of human resources. Some of the people who by now are part of history were still alive. That shifted the parameters entirely. I figured I would still be able to find a book or an archive document in the same place a year or five from now, but when it came to the survivors, there was the anxiety of being too late. When you find a score written in a concentration camp, you must immediately ask yourself if its composer is still alive, if their relatives are reachable or if they have fled elsewhere. It is a time-sensitive quest that runs in parallel with, or rather has priority over, the hunt for books and archives. Human beings are the best possible resource, able to fill in detail and history, and it is in this particular quest, we start in Theresienstadt.

Theresienstadt

In 1941, Theresienstadt (present-day Terezín, in the Czech Republic) was chosen by high-ranking Nazis Reinhard Heydrich and Adolf Eichmann to be an internment and transit camp, as part of the 'Final Solution' to eliminate the European Jewish population. This former military citadel, situated just north of Prague, had been built in the late eighteenth century by Emperor Joseph II, in memory of his mother, Empress Maria Theresa of Austria, but had been abandoned by the Habsburg garrison around 1880 and assigned for civilian use. It proved to be inadequate for Heydrich and Eichmann's plans, however – the deportation of some 140,000 people over the next four years. Problems of overcrowding and hygiene quickly ensued, which encouraged the spread of scabies, dysentery and typhus. Tens of thousands died of disease or starvation.

The Third Reich's propaganda machine portrayed Theresienstadt to the international community as a kind of enclave, self-governed by a *Judenrat* (Jewish Council), at the heart of Europe, attempting to legitimise it as a successful experiment in the precautionary relocation of the Central European Jewish population. An appropriate number of deportees enjoyed 'prominent' status, among them First World War veterans, scientists, entrepreneurs, artists, renowned intellectuals and musicians, members of the Nazi party who had occupied important positions before falling from grace and women formerly married to Nazis. All enjoyed moderately preferential treatment in terms of family quarters and food. University courses and Talmudic studies, schooling, sports tournaments, libraries and handicrafts were organised and a ghetto currency even minted.

Until 1942, musical activity was all but forbidden, but after local civilians were finally evacuated that July and Theresienstadt was remodelled into a camp, well-structured musical and theatrical activity developed. This was partly encouraged by the uncommon availability of musical instruments brought in from Prague or confiscated from music shops in towns bordering Terezín. Despite its circumstances, in Theresienstadt, great musicians thrived, not only reaching absolute peaks of creativity, but also forging new ways of musical thinking, outlining original paths and languages that turned the town into a crossroads of contemporary music.

Theresienstadt, however, is essentially an anomaly in the deportation phenomenon and the musical landscape of the camps; its form as a town reinvented as a civilian internment camp, with a high density of Jewish population, cannot be used as a standard, arguably, in the general logistics of the Nazis' death camps. And yet, within the context of the tragic events of the war, artists, musicians and theatre people there engaged with the possibility of sharing idioms unconditioned by everyday life, in an unprecedented explosion of creativity against the backdrop of the humanitarian devastation of war and the deportation crisis. Theresienstadt could even be considered the last bastion of great Central European music in the first half of the twentieth century.

In the autumn of 1942, the SS set up the *Freizeitgestaltung* (literally, 'leisure activities') for the development of artistic programmes in the camp. In addition to providing musical instruments for individual study and practice, chamber and symphonic concerts, there were cabarets and poetry readings. If accepted into the scheme, individuals could fully engage in the camp's cultural life. They were also given special lodgings, extra food rations and reduced heavy labour.

Deported to Theresienstadt on 30 November 1941, Rafael Schächter encouraged the musicians in the camp, organising concerts and directing operas, including Smetana's *The Bartered Bride* and *The Kiss*, working with the singer Karel Berman, as well as staging Hans Krása's opera *Brundibár*. He formed a mixed choir with over a hundred and fifty members. From 1941, he undertook the mammoth task of putting on Verdi's Requiem with them. The performances continued until early October 1944, when the Requiem was performed to piano accompaniment only and with sixty singers before members of the International Red Cross and SS officers, including Adolf Eichmann. Schächter was moved to Birkenau on 16 October 1944. He died on the Death March following the evacuation of Auschwitz in January 1945.

The violinist Egon Ledeč, whose grandson I met, was taken to Theresienstadt on 10 December 1941. There, he performed as a soloist with the pianist Alice Herz-Sommer and the accordionist Wolfgang 'Wolfi' Lederer, and formed a quartet with the violinist Adolf Kraus, the violist Viktor Kohn and the cellist Robert Dauber. After being transferred to Birkenau on 16 October 1944, he was one of the many people gassed, it is believed, the day after his arrival.

The paraplegic Czech composer Rudolf Kende (Rudolf Kohn) was also sent to Theresienstadt, along with his parents.

Despite the Nazi tendency to eliminate people with disabilities, Kende received help and was kept safe. Unable to use his hands and feet, his manuscripts were most probably written down by his students and friends. In 1943 he wrote *Návrat*, two songs for soprano, baritone and piano with lyrics by Moritz Hartmann.

From June 1944 onwards, plans to transfer the Jewish population to the Nazi death camps in occupied Poland gathered pace. Most Theresienstadt musicians, theatre people and librettists were transported to Birkenau on 1, 12, 16, 23 and 28 October 1944, respectively. Kende's parents died there. As did Austrian pianist and composer Franz Eugen Klein, who had written the one-act comic opera *Der gläserne Berg* to a libretto by Otto Brod in the Theresienstadt (we have the piano score of the introduction).

Records show that Franta Goldschmidt, Pavel Haas, Bernard Kaff, Petr Kien, Franz Eugen Klein, Gideon Klein, Viktor Kohn, Hans Krása, Egon Ledeč, James Simon, Carlo Sigmund Taube, Viktor Ullmann and František Zelenka, all of them Theresienstadt residents, were either among those killed in the gas chambers on arrival at Birkenau or who died in the sub-camps. An entire generation of musicians, composers, orchestra and theatre directors and piano virtuosi, a whole Central European Jewish musical élite, perished over the span of just a few days. Yet others like Czech-Jewish composer Hans Winterberg arrived at Theresienstadt on 26 January 1945, where he wrote *Suite 1945* for piano and went on to survive the war.

Perhaps realising what lay ahead, earlier that same year Viktor Ullmann wrote, in his essay 'Goethe und Ghetto', that the conditions in Theresienstadt *acted as a stimulus rather than a hindrance to my music and in no way did we sit on the banks of the rivers in Babylon, weeping; our respect for art was equal to our desire to live. I am certain that all those who, in life as in art, fight to establish order in the chaos will agree with me.'*

Unlike the Babylonian Exile of the Biblical Jews, in Theresienstadt Jewish musicians did not hang their harps on fir trees, as in Psalm 137. Instead, they clasped them tight and played on.

Gideon and Eliška Klein

Blanka Červinková, musicologist and library science expert at the Prague municipal library, had a clear vision of the musical, historical and human genome of Theresienstadt. In addition to her work as a librarian, she founded one of the first publishing houses devoted to the musical output of Theresienstadt. When we met, she gave me a large quantity of sheet music, as well as a list of addresses of survivors and other people who might help me in my research.

One day, Blanka invited me to the Divertimento bookshop, a few steps away from the monumental clock in the Old Town Square. She was waiting for me inside, in a room that had been turned into a library, separate to the main public area. She gestured towards an elderly lady who sat hunched over some scores and, in impeccable English, murmured softly, 'That's Gideon Klein's sister. Let me introduce you.'

Before being interned in Theresienstadt, the pianist and composer Gideon Klein had been one of the most brilliant musical minds of his generation, as well as one of the most fascinating characters in the Czech musical landscape. He studied piano with Vilém Kurz and composition with Alois Hába at the Prague Conservatoire, and musicology at Charles University.

Forbidden from performing in concerts after the German occupation in 1939, he was arrested on 4 December 1941 and transferred to Theresienstadt. He was one of the promoters of the *Studio für Neue Musik*. In the short film *Theresienstadt 1942*, directed by Irena Dodalová and commissioned by *SS-Obersturmführer* Herbert Otto, he appears for a few seconds in the camp *cafehaus*, looking directly into the camera.

On 19 October 1944, two days after his transfer to Birkenau, Klein was redirected to the Fürstengrube sub-camp. On 19 January 1945, with the Red Army at the gates, German soldiers evacuated it and the majority of prisoners set out on one of the infamous death marches of that period. Gideon Klein disappeared.

His (assumed) untimely death is a gap in contemporary musical thinking and leaves unresolved a number of steps in Hába's microtonal technique, in Leoš Janáček's and Vítezslav Novák's musical idiom, as well as in the pro-European imprint on the Moravian *melos* adopted by Klein. The latter was a profoundly Czech music, intoxicated by the Prague of the Clementinum, which looked to the past while turning its back on it, and which, as early as 1943, made twelve-tone technique obsolete, recreating it in new linguistic formulae, flexible structures connected to languages and tonal combinations that were thought to have been abandoned. Just listen to his two madrigals for two sopranos, contralto, tenor and bass, setting poems by François Villon and Friedrich Hölderlin to music. These are highly experimental works based on an old vocal form, which signal a new musical Renaissance, of which, sadly, no traces remain in post-war music.

Some of Klein's other works composed in Theresienstadt — the song cycle *Die Peststadt* for contralto and piano and *Dva Horra tance* for mixed chorus, for example — seem to have been lost. Yet others have been salvaged, such as the trio *Variace na hebrejskou lidovou píseň* (incomplete) for violin, viola and cello, the fantasy and fugue for string quartet and the three-movement piano sonata. Among Klein's originals kept at the Terezín Museum, shockingly, I found the beginning of a 4th movement to the sonata.

When I saw Gideon Klein's sister for the first time, she was interacting with a young pianist from Barletta.

After introducing me to Eliška Klein, she left the room. Eliška, who was also a musician, addressed me in German, thinking I understood; I did not dare interrupt her even though my German is passable. She gave me a precious, printed copy of her brother's original piano sonata, written in Theresienstadt, and provided his various metronome indications.

I took the sonata and promised Eliška that I would study it and record it myself within a few months. When I returned to Prague, some time later, and met up with Eliška again, I was able to give her a CD of my performance. I showed her on the score how I had interpreted passages I thought contained errors that had occurred during the transcription from the manuscript. Eliška liked my input very much, which was gratifying. Still, when I finally consulted the original, many years later, I was relieved to discover I had correctly interpreted Klein's intentions.

Accounts of Gideon Klein's death in Fürstengrube differ. According to the British musicologist David Fligg, Klein and his theatre director friend, Gustav Schorsch, stayed behind in the sub-camp with over two hundred other deportees who were too ill to manage the evacuation march. On 27 January 1945, an SS patrol returned to the camp – already abandoned by the

Soviets – and incinerated the bodies of the remaining prisoners, including, it is thought, Klein. The documents at the Auschwitz Museum archives, the enquiries led by the researcher Jacek Zając and the mass grave discovered in the wood adjoining the sub-camp confirm this theory.

However, to confuse matters, other witnesses reported that a young man called Klein* was still alive after the Soviet troops' tumultuous attempts to liberate Fürstengrube, and that a certain Klein was spotted in a column of former deportees rounded up by the Soviets in order to escort them to the nearest shelter. During a toilet break, this Klein was seen withdrawing behind some bushes, but reports say he did not reappear when the Soviets summoned everyone to rejoin the column.

I spoke to Eliška about these conflicting reports. 'He could be alive,' she said. Blanka did not need to translate; that was perfectly clear to me. She felt convinced that in some way her brother *was* still alive. That I can understand, in as far as I am, even now, certain that the identity of people like Gideon Klein and their suffering outlives physical life – that they live on in their music.

I met Eliška again, sitting in the front row at the Festival of Jewish Music that took place in Prague every year and at which they performed her brother's music. She spent her life championing her brother's works and is the main reason why his work is known. She died in 1999.

---

* It should be noted that the surname 'Klein' is very common in Eastern Europe, so it is not unlikely that this was a namesake.

Rudolf and Ivan Karel

One of my favourite piano composers is Rudolf Karel. I both devoured and recorded his Theme and Variations, op. 13, having found the 1910 manuscript in Prague's Clementinum. Karel was born in Plzeň, in 1880, and studied composition with Antonín Dvořák, as his last student. From 1923 to 1941, he taught composition at the Prague Conservatoire, and he was arrested by the Gestapo in 1943 due to his membership of the resistance. Imprisoned in Pankrác prison for two years, he underwent harsh interrogation and torture, and was forbidden from using any conventional methods of writing. Suffering from dysentery, Karel spent long periods of time in the prison infirmary.

Despite his dire situation, Karel remained prolific: he wrote the lieder 'Pìseň svobody', op. 41a (setting a text by Stanislav Falta and other fellow inmates), and 'Žena-Moje štěstí', op. 41b (text by Josef Remta), for baritone and piano, *Pankrác March*, op. 42a, for piano, with a religious text in the trio intended for a chorus (dedicated to Navara, a doctor who, like Karel, enrolled in the Czechoslovak Legion during the First World War), *Pankrác Polka*, op. 42b, for violin and piano (dedicated to Veruska Müllerova, the daughter of the prison warden, a friend of Karel's), and *Pankrác Waltz*, op. 42c, for piano.

Karel also drafted the five-act opera *Tři zlaté vlasy děda Vševěda* (*Three Hairs of an Old Wise Man*) to a libretto inspired by Karel Jaromír Erben's book, with 240 sheets of piano reduction and vocal and choral parts; the keyboard texture was written by his cellmate, Stanislav Falta. Karel wrote in pencil and vegetable charcoal on handwritten music paper or ordinary paper expressly prepared by his fellow inmates. Müller, the warden, would secretly take these musical scores out of the prison and either hide them at home or get them to Karel's family members or to Zbyněk Vostřák, Karel's pupil. On being discovered, Müller was later arrested and tortured.

On 7 February 1945, Karel was transferred to Theresienstadt, where he finished drafting the piano score of Nonet, op. 43,[*] dedicated to the Czech Nonet ensemble founded in 1923 by the violinist Emil Leichner. The draft of the first movement pre-dates his move there, dated 1 February 1945. At Theresienstadt, Karel's already fragile health deteriorated further and he contracted pneumonia. We know he wrote *Terezínský pochod* and *Terezínský valčík* for piano around this time, although both are now lost. We do have *Pochod Höftlinku* for piano, however, dated 25 February 1945, written shortly before his death. Just over a week later, on the night of 5–6 March 1945, a feverish Karel was left outside the cells while they were being cleaned and disinfected. He died, presumably from hypothermia, along with nine other prisoners.

On 21 December 1945, Czech radio broadcast a live perfor-mance of Karel's Nonet, as reconstructed by František Hertl, but it was not authentic. In 1984, Václav Snítil, first violin of the Czech Nonet, made a new reconstruction that was more faithful to the original and it was performed on 5 May 1985

---

* Nonet – a group of nine musicians

in Beroun on the fortieth anniversary of the liberation of Czechoslovakia. This reconstruction was then published in 1995 by Carus Verlag in Stuttgart.

Rudolf Karel's great theatrical work, the opera *Three Hairs of an Old Wise Man*, had its world première on 28 October 1948 at Prague's National Theatre in a brilliant reconstruction by Zbyněk Vostřák. In 1947, the Prague publishing house Melantrich published *Skladby z vězení*, op. 41 and op. 42, written by Karel during his time in Pankrác.

I met Rudolf's son, the ophthalmologist Ivan Karel, in Prague. Ivan and I have become good friends over the years and that has been a blessing. I have watched him age – he is now older than his father, who died aged sixty-five – and yet still retain his old-style gentlemanly ways, and his help has been invaluable. Always ready to assist me and provide information and material, he has written to museums and archives, hoping his recommendation might give me access to otherwise inaccessible documents.

Whenever I went to Ivan's home, his wife would cover the living-room table with dried fruit and slices of bread with salami, gherkins and mayonnaise. It was wasted on me. So focused was I on Ivan that all I would partake of was their *caffè lungo* – I wished for nothing more than to listen to my friend.

Once, when I was with my writer friend Thomas Saintourens, who wrote the book *Il Maestro* about my research, Ivan handed me the bulky volumes – 660 pages – of the piano and vocal draft of his father's final work, *Three Hairs of an Old Wise Man*, so that I could photocopy it. He explained that it was not a reduction for voice and piano, as is customary in opera. The work was composed for a piano line but there was no orchestration because Rudolf Karel had died, so these volumes are considered the score.

I promised to return these precious volumes within a couple of hours, so Thomas and I rushed to a photocopying shop in the Anděl district. We walked in at ten in the morning and left at sunset! On our way back to Ivan, we worried he would be concerned, but there he was, waiting for us on his doorstep, with open arms. I was glad when I recently gave him the piano score of his father's masterpiece, the Nonet I had reconstructed, and asked his permission to publish it in the *Thesaurus Musicae Concentrationariae*. Ivan readily agreed.

A few years ago, I recorded the Nonet in its original piano version. It is a gigantic score and very difficult, steeped in modernism and with harmonic solutions that echo Schoenberg's Chamber Symphony, op. 9. It's practically impossible to play on the piano, of course, as it was not devised for it and is technically a piano score awaiting arrangement. Still, I played it. And thought of the man who had penned it, in such horrific circumstances, almost eighty years ago.

Pavel Haas

Pavel Haas is another influential musician who was murdered in the death camps. Before that, he wrote the music for the films *Život je pes* (*Life is a Dog*), *Mazlíček* (*The Little Pet*) and *Kvočna* (*Mother Hen*), directed by his brother Hugo, also an actor. Haas also wrote *Scherzo triste*, op. 5, for orchestra, *Fata Morgana*, op. 6, for tenor, piano and strings on a text by the poet Rabindranath Tagore, String Quartet No. 2 '*Z opičích hor*', op. 7 ('From the Monkey Mountains'), with ad lib percussion, Psalm 29, op. 12, for organ, baritone, female chorus and chamber orchestra, Suite, op. 13, for piano, performed in 1936 by the Czech pianist Bernard Kaff (who died in Birkenau in October 1944) and Suite, op. 17, for oboe and piano. He created the tragi-comic opera *Šarlatán* (*The Charlatan*) to his own libretto in three acts and seven tableaux, staged in Brno in April 1938.

In 1935, he married Soňia (Sofia) Nikolaevna Feldmann, who had previously been married to the famous Russian linguist Roman Osipovič Jakobson, and their daughter, Olga, was born in 1937. Having been assistant conductor at Brno and Saarbrücken operas, Haas tried in vain to emigrate after the German occupation in 1939. Brother Hugo was more successful and took refuge in the United States, where he embarked on a steady film career.

Prior to his arrest, Haas formally divorced his wife (who was not Jewish) to save her and her daughter from the same fate. In December 1941, Pavel was moved to Theresienstadt. In the camp, after an initial period of emotional isolation, he wrote *Al S'fod* for male chorus to a text by David Shimoni. His *Four songs on Chinese poetry* for baritone and piano, to texts by Wei Jing-wu, Wang-wei, Tchang Tiou-ling and Han I, and translated into Czech by Bohumil Mathesius, was dedicated to the singer Karel Berman, who, on 22 June 1944, performed them at the town hall (with Rafael Schächter at the piano). Berman, also interned at Theresienstadt, managed to protect an original copy of the score and bring it back to Prague following the liberation of the camp. *Study* for string orchestra was conducted by Karel Ančerl in Theresienstadt. You can hear *Study* in the 1944 film *Theresienstadt* and see Haas himself receive the final applause.

After the war, the Czech composer, poet and musicologist Lubomir Peduzzi – a former pupil of Haas, as well as responsible for rescuing a large number of his musical works in Theresienstadt – reconstructed and completed his works based on instrumental parts kept by Ančerl. *Three Pieces* for mezzo-soprano, tenor, flute, clarinet and string quartet, Variations for piano and orchestra, *Partita in olden style* for piano, *Fantasy on a Jewish Melody* for string quartet and Requiem (for unknown forces) appear to have been lost, however.

According to Ančerl's testimony to Hugo Haas, the composer saved his life. On 16 October 1944, Haas was taken to Birkenau and during the selections for the gas chamber, Josef Mengele, the SS officer and physician nicknamed 'The Angel of Death', was picking Ančerl when Haas started to cough, so Mengele choose Haas instead.

Hans Krása

Hans Johann Karl Krása grew up in Prague in a family of German-speaking assimilated Jews. His works include the cantata *Die Erde ist des Herrn* for soloists, chorus and orchestra, the two-act opera *Verlobung im Traum* (*Betrothal in a Dream*) and *Kammermusik*, for harpsichord and seven instruments. His musical idiom, influenced by the French avant-garde of *Les Six*, gradually shifted towards a Mahlerian aesthetic. He met the writer and caricaturist Adolf Hoffmeister, for whom he wrote the incidental music for the play *Mládí ve hře*. After the German occupation of Czechoslovakia, Krása's musical life became limited to just a few concerts at Prague's Jewish orphanage. In 1941, he was arrested by the Gestapo and taken to Theresienstadt on 10 August 1942. There, he wrote Three Songs for baritone, clarinet, viola and cello, to a text by Arthur Rimbaud, *Tanz* and Passacaglia and Fugue for string trio, Overture for small orchestra and piano and the reconstruction of his Theme and Variations for string quartet, originally composed in Prague. He was transferred to Birkenau on 16 October 1944 and died the following day, it is thought in the gas chamber.

Brundibár

Hans Krása's name is linked above all to the short opera in two acts and sixteen tableaux for children and orchestra, *Flašinetár Brundibár* – just *Brundibár* in the handwritten score. It takes its inspiration from an Aristophanes play, with a Czech libretto by Adolf Hoffmeister (who took refuge in London before the war broke out), and was composed in 1938 for the inauguration of Prague's Jewish orphanage. It was entered, in 1939, into a competition announced by the Ministry of Education and Culture, which did not take place due to the German occupation. The short opera was performed, however, in December 1941 at Prague's Jewish orphanage, with the musical accompaniment of only three instruments. Krása himself reconstructed it in 1943 in Theresienstadt (he took the chorus parts and the arrangement for voices and piano with him).

Besides differences in texture and tonality from the Prague version and the reduction for voices and piano, the Theresienstadt version omits two episodes: 'Captain Novak's Song' (included in Act I, Scene 8) and the episode involving the pursuit of Brundibár (Act II, Scenes 6 and 8), the latter being essential to the understanding of the plot.

It was performed in a new orchestral arrangement on 23 September 1943 at the Magdeburg Pavilion and had at least fifty-five performances (mainly with harmonium accompaniment), conducted and arranged by Rudolf Freudenfeld with musical coordination by Rafael Schächter, and decor by the Czech set and costume designer František Zelenka. According to Anita Klingsberg, who performed in *Brundibár*, Krása was a very distinguished man who enjoyed dressing smartly and was of a shy nature; she saw him only once in the auditorium, watching the rehearsal of his opera in Theresienstadt. The main character in the opera, the evil fiddler Brundibár, was played by fourteen-year-old Honza Treichlinger, who died in Birkenau. Only a few of the children who appeared in the opera survived the war; the majority were decimated by starvation, infectious diseases or transferred to Birkenau.

In 1995, I recklessly decided to stage *Brundibár*. The production costs were extremely high: I spent 15 million lire – borrowed from a friend and paid back over two years – on preparing the orchestra, the chorus and the recording. I wanted to stage an Italian version translated from the original Czech, so I had the libretto translated. All I had was a terrible photocopy of the manuscript, in addition to the material obtained from Blanka Červinková and Ricordi, the rights holder in Italy. The recording session at the Sorrisi studios in Bari was organised meticulously, the role of evil Brundibár played by the brilliant Paolo Candido. On the same record, I also included Viktor Ullmann's Piano Sonata No. 7 and Lullaby by Gideon Klein.

Viktor Ullmann

Viktor Josef Ullmann was born in the Silesian city of Teschen, then part of the Austro-Hungarian Empire. The child of Jews who converted to Catholicism and moved to Vienna in 1909 – his father was a career officer in the Habsburg army – Ullmann studied piano with Eduard Steuermann, theory and composition with Josef Polnauer and counterpoint and orchestration and the theory of form at Arnold Schoenberg's composition seminars. In 1920, thanks to Schoenberg's recommendation, Ullmann became assistant to Alexander von Zemlinsky at Prague's New German Theatre, a position he occupied until 1927, and thanks to which he conducted many works, including his own Symphonic Fantasy (lost).

During his time at the New German Theatre, he wrote Seven Putty Songs with Piano, op. 4, incidental music for the comedy *Der Kreidekreis* by Klabund (the pseudonym of Alfred Henschke), the Octet for piano, wind instruments and strings (these are also lost), as well as the first version of his Variations and Double Fugue on a Piano Piece by Arnold Schoenberg, based on the composer's op. 19, no. 4. Its orchestral version was to earn Ullmann the 1934 Hertzka Prize, one of the most prestigious prizes in contemporary music.

During the 1927–28 opera season, he became artistic director of Aussig opera house in (present-day Ústí nad Labem, in the Czech Republic), where his repertory was impressive: Wagner's *Tristan und Isolde*, Strauss's *Ariadne auf Naxos*, Mozart's *Marriage of Figaro* and Křenek's *Jonny spielt auf.*

After returning to Prague in 1928 and being appointed Kapellmeister at the *Schauspielhaus* in Zurich, where he stayed for three years, he experienced a deep change in ideology, triggered by his visit, in 1929, to the *Goetheanum* in Dornach (Switzerland), an international centre for Rudolf Steiner's Anthroposophical Society. Ullmann embraced anthroposophy so radically that he suspended his artistic career to run an anthroposophical bookshop in Stuttgart.

With the rise of National Socialism in Germany, in 1933, his bookshop was closed down by the authorities. He returned to Prague and, with some difficulty, resumed his career as a full-time musician and composer. He worked at the music department of Czechoslovak radio, wrote music books and reviews and, in 1935, composed the monumental opera *Der Sturz des Antichrist* (*The Fall of the Antichrist*), op. 9, to a libretto by the anthroposophical writer Albert Steffen. It won Ullmann his second Hertzka Prize, in 1936.

From 1935 to 1937, he studied microtonal music with Alois Hába, composing as his final thesis the Sonata for quarter-tone clarinet and quarter-tone piano, op. 16 (we have only the clarinet part today). His works during this period include his first four piano sonatas, op. 10, op. 19, op. 28 and op. 38, Six Songs (Steffen), op. 17 for soprano and piano, *Slavic Rhapsody*, op. 24 for obbligato saxophone and orchestra, Piano Concerto, op. 25 and the opera *Der zerbrochene Krug* (*The Broken Jug*), op. 36.

After the Nazis' occupation of the country, Ullmann tried in vain to obtain an exit visa for his second wife, Annie Winternitz, from whom he had separated in 1941, and their three children, Max, Johann Marcus and Felicia – the latter two were sent to Britain in summer 1939, thanks to the International Red Cross. On 15 October 1941, he married his third wife, Elizabeth Frank-Meissl, and on 8 September 1942, he was arrested and taken to Theresienstadt, along with Elizabeth and Max.

At Theresienstadt, the *Judenrat* gave Ullmann the task of coordinating musical activities, which meant organising and reviewing stage productions and concerts. In the camp, he was prolific. He wrote *Drei Lieder*, op. 37, for baritone and piano (started prior to his deportation, then revised), the libretto for the two act opera *Jeanne d'Arc* (we have a fragment of the piano score, entitled '30 May 1431', ascribable to the opera), *Der Mensch und sein Tag* for baritone and piano, *Chansons des enfants françaises* for voice and piano (we have one song, 'Little Cakewalk', from it), 'Chinese Songs' for voice and piano (we have two of the songs), Piano Sonatas no. 5, op. 45, no. 6, op. 49 and no. 7, String Quartet no. 3, op. 46, 'Autumn' for baritone (or contralto) and string trio, two 'Songs of Consolation' for baritone. He also penned a string trio or piano, thirteen traditional Jewish songs (which we have from a copyist's text) from the *Jüdische Makabi Liederbuch* (a sign of his return to Judaism), incidental music for a play by François Villon for violin, clarinet, guitar, percussion and harmonium (performed on 20 July 1943, we have a violin fragment of the *Seeräuber-Ballade*). There was also 'Wendla im Garten' and three Hölderlin Songs for baritone and piano, the cantata *Immer inmitten*, to a text by Hans-Günther Adler for mezzo-soprano and piano (we have the first song complete but only the texts for the other two), an Overture to the opera *Don Quixote tanzt Fandango* (we have the piano version), *Die Weise von Liebe und Tod des Cornets Christoph Rilke* for narrator and piano (we also have the first two passages for narrator and orchestra) and cadenzas for Beethoven's piano concertos (we have the cadenzas for op. 15 and op. 37). Finally, Ullmann produced the one-act opera *Der Kaiser von Atlantis oder Die Tod-Verweigerung* (*The Emperor of Atlantis or Death's Refusal*) to a libretto by Petr Kien.

Der Kaiser von Atlantis

The Emperor of Atlantis is one of the most disturbing operas of the twentieth century, a touchstone of the most advanced modernity, on a par with Schoenberg's *Pierrot Lunaire* and Stravinsky's *Soldier's Tale*, thanks to its use of several musical idioms with non-symphonic formations, as well as its Brechtian inspiration. Ullmann wrote it in Theresienstadt between 1943 and 1944, reworking it until shortly before 16 October 1944, when he was transferred to Birkenau, where he died, gassed, it is believed, on the following day.

The opera was due to be staged at the Theresienstadt *Sokolhaus* in the summer of 1944, under the baton of Rafael Schächter, and featured, among others, Walter Windholz (Kaiser Overall), Bedrich Borges (Loudspeaker), David Grünfeld (Soldier and Harlequin), Marion Podolier (Bubikopf), Karel Berman (Death), Hilde Aronson-Lindt (The Drummer); with Pavel Kling as first violin in the string quintet. It was never performed, however, because, during rehearsals, German censors intervened, sensing in the principal character, Overall, a clear caricature of the Führer.

Shortly before being moved to Birkenau, Ullmann entrusted the manuscript of *The Emperor of Atlantis* to Theresienstadt's librarian, Emil Utiz. After the liberation, he gave it to Hans Günther Adler, former president of the Theresienstadt *Judenrat*.

Adler moved to London after the war and gave the opera and other materials by Ullman to the Goetheanum in Dornach.

On 16 December 1975, at the Bellevue Centre in Amsterdam, *The Emperor of Atlantis* was staged for the first time, a production that was reprised in 1976 in Brussels, and in 1977 in San Francisco and New York. Other reconstructions of the manuscript were carried out by Michael Graubart and Nicholas Till in 1981, and by Ingo Schulz between 1992 and 1993. Thirteen years later, in 2006, I decided to create a definitive reconstruction of the opera and entrusted this task to the conductor and composer Paolo Candido, a lifelong friend and colleague. In March 2010, we performed the definitive version of the *Emperor* in Barletta.

'*Hallo, hallo!*' is the motto uttered by the loudspeaker at the very beginning of *The Emperor of Atlantis*. It is the humanisation of a 'sentient object': the Emperor does not speak 'through' the loudspeaker but 'with' it. The loudspeaker never appears on stage and its '*Hallo, hallo!*' is based on two tritones of the Death Theme from Josef Suk's symphony, op. 27, *Asrael* (the name of the exterminating angel), music used at state funerals during the First Czechoslovakian Republic (1918–38).

How can we forget another dramatic '*Hallo, hallo!*' modern history has bequeathed to posterity? The '*Hallo, hallo!*' repeated twenty times on 21 December 1989 by the last President of the Romanian Socialist Republic, Nicolae Ceauşescu, from the presidential balcony in Bucharest, to a crowded square shouting against the last Emperor of the last Communist Atlantis in Eastern Europe.

In the epilogue to Ullmann's opera, Death asks the Emperor for his life to make up for its violated dignity. Just before he walks through the mirror that separates the world of Atlantis and the astral world, the Emperor sings one of the most heart-wrenching arias, a piece of unparalleled beauty we cannot hear without being moved; in doing so, the final message he leaves us of that crazy, cruel being gets as close to perfection as is possible.

As in the opera, in his final words at his military tribunal, Ceauşescu continued to pontificate about himself and his regime as though the world around him had not changed. The Emperor and the Loudspeaker became one, just before death caught up with Ceauşescu and led him, dismayed, to the firing squad.

In *The Emperor of Atlantis*, Death has ethics, however. In its own way, it is fair and wise. It admonishes us against wishing our enemy's death, even when they wish ours, because only Death, not humans, can decide who will die. It is a kind of upside-down commandment: *Thou shalt not speak the name of Death in vain ('Du sollst den großen Namen Tod nicht eitel beschwören').* Whoever offends Death dies.

How very poignant, given the context in which the opera was created.

Originally inspired by Mahler and by Schoenberg's formal structures, Ullmann was gradually heading towards a wider polytonality in parallel with his rediscovery of his own Jewish roots. His idiom constituted the third way of the post-twelve-tone technique started by Eduard Steuermann and would have influenced contemporary musical thinking. The use of voice in his works was a precursor to Krzysztof Penderecki and Gian Francesco Malipiero's early experimentalism. In the piano sonatas Ullmann wrote in Theresienstadt, we can sense the formal and aesthetic break which the contemporary piano sonata tackles in Sonata No. 2 by Pierre Boulez and the *Concord* Sonata by Charles Ives.

In an infernal microcosm managed by people 'born human but turned into animals' – words uttered by chief prosecutor Gideon Hausner about Nazi Adolf Eichmann during his closing argument at his 1961 trial in Jerusalem – musicians were drafting the manifesto of a new civilisation. What they wrote was no longer connected only to art; it was an affirmation of beauty as an absolute value. Among them, Viktor Ullmann was a musician with broad horizons, a genius who looked far into the musical future.

TWO

In Search of Lost Music

The paradox of creativity

The music written, created and experienced in the camps passed along sometimes unthinkable channels of transmission. Through their creativity, musicians brought the world into the camp, and today, the music that is left brings the camps to the world. Writing music soothed the omnivorous instincts of the mind and provided a sense of lightness, compared with the unbearable heaviness and brutality of where these men and women were. It was an individual and a collective survival strategy.

The phenomenon of music developed in captivity and during deportation is so complex that some have argued it suggests two strands running in parallel: one, a Europe able to support creativity and concerts despite the war; the other a form of music thriving in confinement. These parallel strands were not only unconnected, but also may have developed their own idioms, opened new but distinct frontiers in musical thinking and original applications of avant-garde compositional techniques. Paradoxically, these two dimensions of music coexisted without ever touching.

Why was it so important to write and play music in the camps? Émile Goué, a brilliant French composer and prisoner of war who died a year after the liberation from an illness contracted in a camp in Nienburg/Weser, Lower Saxony, probably provides the best answer: 'Music wasn't entertainment or a game, but the very expression of our inner lives. We made music in earnest, without any humour. It was impossible to do great things without conviction, and the conviction an artist has to bring to their work is only the belief that what they're writing is necessary.'

Musical work produced in civilian, political and military captivity from 1933 to 1953 cannot be separated from the biographies of its composers, their relatives or those who contributed to saving it and transmitting it. But it has not always been easy to get in touch with survivors or those who knew the musicians, the majority now dead.

During my research, I have met survivors who experienced many different types of captivity – from Jews and partisans and other groups who were held in camps built by the Nazis to former prisoners of war who were held in internment camps set up by the Allies. It is interesting to note, time and again, how many often evaded my questions, skipping over that period with annoyance. Perhaps they simply wanted the past to be the past? To survive such brutality required them to block it all out. And that same impatience and reluctance to talk was particularly evident in relation to the music of the camps. There is often an understandable wish to erase memories of imprisonment and deportation, even when that entails eliminating the fruit of one's own talent. Fortunately, however, in the vast majority of cases, I found cooperation and willingness.

I feel privileged that I almost always became friends with the people I met or interviewed for my research. It was particularly important to me to try to instill trust, so that the people I spoke with would not only share with me the precious scores lying on the shelves in their homes or secreted away in their minds, but also, in some ineffable way, could become reconciled with those energetic young musicians who still live inside them.

As well as somehow trying to define the parameters of my research, I had to come up with a correct definition of 'concentrationary music', or music created in captivity or conditions of partial or extreme deprivation of fundamental human rights. It made for a supremely delicate research topic and required stepping out of libraries and archives and turning from a scholar into an explorer. For this research to have meaning, I felt strongly that I had not only to be credible but beyond criticism. And there is nothing more scientific or mathematically provable than music.

Photos and film clips can be doctored and manipulated; but, in answer to those who deny the Holocaust and the horrors of the gulag, music produced in captivity cannot have been purpose-made. It is totally impossible that, in the space of twenty years, thousands of people could have conspired to create thousands of fake scores. The most immaterial of arts is also, it appears, the most tangible.

To my mind, a civilisation only merits the name in as far as it protects its own artistic, architectural, cultural and musical heritage by doing its utmost to shield stones, pillars, parchments and scores from earth, wind, water and fire. And from the evil that people themselves perpetrate against others, as the National Socialists showed after they came to power in 1933. For that reason and for a thousand others, we *must* hand this music over to future generations. It is our duty. In celebrating the past through staging the sonatas, operas, lieders, opuses that these musicians created in such heinous circumstances, we also *remember* it and perhaps go some way possibly to preventing it from happening again.

Tel Aviv

In 1992, my research took me to Israel for the first time. Almost as though I was heading to the front, my mother stuffed crackers and tins of tuna into my suitcase. Back then, of course, booking a room remotely was not at all straightforward, so I spent my first day in Tel Aviv roaming around in search of the most affordable lodgings.

At last, I found a shabby guest house. The door to my room wouldn't close, so I shifted the bed and slept with my foot pressed against the door to keep it shut. I was supposed to be travelling around Israel, looking for material, documents and people, and this, clearly, was not conducive to concentrating.

Research trips require a different kind of preparation to more usual kinds of travel. I had a huge list of names and works to locate, so I went around libraries and spent my days at the coin-operated photocopier at the Hebrew University of Jerusalem, copying like crazy.

I did not find much that trip but I learnt a lot, adopting a method that went beyond obsessive research and a ravenous frenzy to study on the piano everything I discovered. It was necessary to take a significant quality leap as a musician and researcher, sailing with no metaphorical lifeboat in deep, unfamiliar waters. I realized if I wanted to fathom the phenomenon of music created in the camps, my research could not be limited to the Second World War; I had to include a much longer timespan. It was at this point that I decided to extend the parameters beyond 1939–45, the war years, to at least 1933, when the Dachau camp was first opened, and beyond the end of the war to 1953, and the beginning of the closure of Kolyma gulag, following Stalin's death in March of that year, and the period of mass amnesties that followed.

Back from Israel, I gradually created a network of friends, based on trust and my travels in search of witnesses and scholars. Meeting the survivors, however, presented the very unprepared researcher I was then with new challenges. Although it was essential that the survivors tell me as much as possible, some questions might trigger delicate mechanisms in both the brain and heart. How could they not? An almost surgical procedure was required on the tissues and membranes of their musical memories: I needed to ask questions that would stimulate the appropriate sensibilities and make them feel comfortable gathering their life experiences and sharing them with me. Yet straying from my purpose was all too easy. I also learnt by observing other people's errors: for example, some time ago, a television journalist, who had only one camera and wanted a selection of angles, asked a survivor to repeat the same distressing story over and over again. The survivor ended up bursting into tears. Others turned up with an army of engineers, photographers and technicians and inflicted endless make-up sessions on the survivor before feeding them to the cameras. Result: the survivor went into short-circuit mode, confused events in 1943 with those of the previous year, and remembered being in a concentration camp even though they couldn't possibly have been there at that time, and so on. Despite everybody's good intentions, what was left were tapes bursting with technically impeccable but historically unreliable interviews.

I didn't need these people to tell me about being deported: that was not the focus of my research; besides, other people had already done that brilliantly before me. What I was trying to do was get to the bottom of their musical experience while imprisoned or deported.

With this in mind, I arranged two meetings a day at most, would stay for lunch or dinner, when possible, and spend time with my interviewees, without necessarily interviewing them. When the floodgates of their memory finally opened, I took care not to assault them with questions, instead monitoring their silences: when a survivor suddenly falls silent, it means they're in distress.

The survivor can do what they like: it's up to us to wait and accept what they want to give us.

Ilse Weber

In addition to being a poet and the author of songs and plays for children, Ilse Weber, *née* Herlinger, sang and played the guitar, the lute, the mandolin and the balalaika (a Russian folk triangular stringed instrument). A Moravian from Witkowitz (now Vítkovice, Ostrava), she married Vilém Weber in 1930 and settled in Prague. Following the German occupation of Czechoslovakia in 1939, the Webers sent their eldest son, Hanuš, to Britain on the Kindertransport to keep him safe. In February 1942, they were arrested and interned, with their other son, Tommy, in Theresienstadt, which served as a way-station for those destined for the extermination camps. Ilse worked as a head nurse in the hospital's paediatric wards and wrote some sixty poems while there, setting many of them to music, often accompanying herself on her guitar.

When Vilém was transferred to Birkenau in October 1944, Ilse and Tommy accompanied him. Before they left, Vilém concealed Ilse's poetry and music in the Theresienstadt stables. From Birkenau, Vilém was sent to the sub-camp Arbeitslager Gleiwitz I; he survived. Ilse and Tommy, however, were gassed on 6 October 1944. After the war, Vilém later returned to Theresienstadt to retrieve Ilse's work.

Vilém Weber kept his wife's songs and poetry in his Prague home in the years that followed, but, in 1968, during the occupation by Warsaw Pact troops, a Soviet soldier confiscated most of the material. Vilém decided to leave Prague, but died of a heart attack in 1974 while changing planes in Copenhagen on his way to see his son, Hanuš, in Stockholm.

When I spoke with Hanuš, a former Swedish national radio journalist, he was reticent when it came to talking about his mother – it's a painful subject and yet her music deserves to be remembered.

'You know that in Theresienstadt your mother wrote another song on top of the eight that are already published?' I told him. 'Some people in Israel still remember it.'

'I've heard of it. I'd like to go to Israel, but I don't feel up to making the long journey,' he replied.

'I can do it, if you like,' I offered. 'I'm going there soon, I'll look for this person and bring you back your mother's song.'

A couple of months later, in Kiryat Ono, a city in the Tel Aviv district, I met Aviva Bar-On, née Winkler, a sweet lady who had been deported to Theresienstadt with her parents when she was ten years old. I asked her about Ilse's song, and she sang me 'Když jsem ležel v Terezín', a nursery rhyme in Czech about a doctor who one day, in Terezín (where Theresienstadt was located), examines a child, and then tells him sternly that he has . . . terezinitis. Aviva also remembered three other unpublished songs by Ilse. One, in German, is about the Hamburger-Kaserne, or barracks, where many of the children in Theresienstadt were kept.

Aviva's brain was encyclaepedic, so I asked her one question: I knew another of Ilse's favourite song had been performed, one with lyrics she'd repurposed from Johann Friedrich Anton

Fleischmann's 'Schlafe, mein Prinzchen', called 'Schlafe, mein engelein' ('Sleep, my angel') and I asked Aviva if she remembered it. She opened her eyes wide, looking at me with disbelief: 'How do *you* know about that song? Nobody's asked me about that in sixty-five years.' Then she fell silent, lost in her memories for what seemed an age. I could see her tears. She cleared her throat and quietly sang three times, sang 'Schlaf, mein engelein', to a melody as angelic as its name suggests. Some moments are beyond words.

After the adults had been sent to the gas chambers, it was the children of Theresienstadt who were left to tell their history. To the beat of music, *allegro ma non troppo* – fast, but not overly so.

Arie Ben Erez Abrahamson

The year 2014 found me searching for the relatives of the Jewish cantor Arie Ben Erez Abrahamson. I was attempting to track down the chants he wrote while interned in Saint-Cyprien, in the Pyrénées-Orientales.

Born in Habsburg Hungary and brought up in Pressburg (Bratislava), Abrahamson became a rabbi but never practised. In 1939, he left Bratislava for Belgium, where he worked in the diamond trade. In 1940 he was arrested by the Gestapo in Antwerp and sent to Saint-Cyprien, which was under the authority of the Vichy government.

I was initially getting nowhere until friends from the Italian Jewish community in Jerusalem came to my rescue and tracked down his daughter, Hannah. We eventually located her in Ramat Gan, an exclusive satellite town of Tel Aviv.

Hannah Abrahamson had taught at the University of Bar-Ilan, and so we arranged to meet at the music department she had helped set up there – a wonderful centre, complete with harpsichords and an auditorium. It was winter and she came towards me, wearing a fur hat, in the company of her friend, Bathia Churgin, perhaps one of the world's most eminent Beethoven scholars. Hannah's elegance made her look like she'd stepped out of a Flaubert novel or a De Nittis painting. Introductions out of the way, she began telling me about her father's internment.

'In the Saint-Cyprien camp, Jews were allowed to worship and observe the Shabbat, but, as a chant written by my father says, there was no kosher wine and you couldn't make a *challah*. One Shabbat afternoon, my father listened to Jewish prisoners at the other end of the camp singing the Mizmor l'Dovid [known to Christians as Psalm 23, "The Lord is my shepherd"]. Because writing on the Shabbat is forbidden, he couldn't jot down the melody, so he learnt it by heart. For some reason, that song sounded very familiar.

'Some time later, he was transferred to the Rivesaltes camp, but he managed to escape, taking with him everything he'd written in Saint-Cyprien, including "*Yah Ribbon Alam, Yom Zeh l'Israel*" (setting a text by Isaac Luria), and his notes on that Mizmor l'Dovid sung by the prisoners.

'After a few days, he finally reached Marseilles, on the eve of Yom Kippur, just in time for the Kol Nidré. At the end of Yom Kippur, my father told the rabbi about his internment and sang him the Mizmor he'd heard in Saint-Cyprien.'

As Hannah told it, the rabbi suddenly looked pensive, as though trying to remember something. 'Come with me to the archive,' he said. He rummaged through his papers and books until he found a score for the Mizmor l'Dovid her father had heard in Saint-Cyprien, and there, at the bottom of the score, was the signature of his father, Hannah's grandfather. That was why that melody had sounded so familiar on that Shabbat afternoon in the camp, even though her father had long forgotten it.

The piece had been written by Aharon Ze'ev (known as Erez, an acronym of his two names) Abrahamson, also a musician and the composer of chants left in Marseilles, where he had been a rabbi many years earlier. Someone in Saint-Cyprien had obviously been teaching Erez Abrahamson's Mizmor to the prisoners.

It was an extraordinary story, but, ever on the hunt, I was hoping Hannah had something more for me, and I was not disappointed. From a large bag, she produced her father's scores, photographs and notebooks.

Prague again

It was probably my hyperactivity and dedication to the subject that led Blanka Červinková to advise me not to limit my research to Jewish output. The gates opened on a dizzying world: ethnic groups, cultures, political dissidents, gay people, deported for a variety of reasons. My research was expanding, but I still had no inkling how much it would take over my life. I came across people like poet, singer, composer, playwright and stage director Emil František Burian. Interned in Theresienstadt, then Dachau and Neuengamme, he organised a wealth of clandestine theatrical events and wrote 'Song von der Kuhle' and *TBC-March 'Walter Neff'*. He survived the camps, and the British Air Force's bombing of the German Navy ship *Cap Arcona*, onto which prisoners of Neuengamme and Fürstengrube camp were forced by the Nazi's who planned to sink it with the prisoners on board.

Responding in a material way to Blanka's encouragement was much like realising I had to redraft a novel, three quarters of which had already been drafted, or nothing would make sense. I was certain this was the right path, but at the same time I knew I would be devoting myself body and soul to a life of far from pleasant research. Widening the scope meant multiplying by ten, a hundred or a thousandfold the work I had yet to do.

In 1998, I recorded piano and chamber works by Alois Piňos-Simandl, Petr Pokorný, Petr Eben, Miloslav Ištvan and Milan Knížák, censured after the occupation of Czechoslovakia on 20–21 August 1968 by troops of the Warsaw Pact. The piano scores were very difficult and I quickly realized that studying them was not enough: I had to relate to them and memorise the auditory materials even in the case of very bold contemporary music.

Among the most dramatic testimonials of the Prague occupation, the most striking were from those from people who, thirty years earlier, had experienced the Nazi occupation of their country: alien soldiers were once again shouting in German at the Czech population. While these were GDR soldiers, a language doesn't lie, and there was no escaping that it was the same as that of their previous brutal occupiers.

Guido Fackler and Bret Werb

When, at the end of the last century, I wrote to university researchers and lecturers in the US, Germany, France and Israel with a view to giving my research new opportunities, I was gratified to discover that they were already aware of my work, that my CDs were in their music libraries. My work is so complex, and funding it had proved to be problematic, that hearing this news encouraged me. I had by this point started toying with the idea of finding a home for all the works I was discovering. I pictured a library or something similar that would prevent the material I was gathering from getting scattered and possibly lost again. With this in mind, I contacted two giants of concentrationary music research: German Guido Fackler and American Bret Werb.

I met Guido Fackler in Würzburg, where he teaches at the Julius Maximilian University, and we spent an entire day talking about the musical output of the political camps, opened by the Nazi regime between 1933 and 1936. It's a specific field of research in which Guido is the leading expert. He is deeply knowledgeable about musicology, philology and history: an academic mind in the truest sense of the word. His monumental book, *Des Lagers*

Stimme (Temmen, 2000), has been instrumental in shaping research into concentrationary music, and is an inexhaustible mine of research – names, works and dates. After that initial meeting in Würzburg, I saw Guido again in Dolo, near Venice, where he was writing a thesis on the canal system in the Veneto. He gave me a mountain of material, quoting by heart every document, source and connection to survivors.

We then met again in Rome, when Franco Bixio's record company Musikstrasse presented the DVD of the documentary *Musica Concentrationaria*. Many years before, I had recorded with them the twenty-four-CD encyclopaedia *KZ Musik*. Subsequently, there were frequent, systematic updates by phone and online, although, sadly, we were unable to complete the two large projects close to both our hearts: writing the score for the entire soundtrack of the propaganda film *Theresienstadt* (1944) and publishing the 2,200-page bible of concentrationary music *Muzyka i Piesni w hitlerowskich obozach koncentracyjnych 1933–1945* by Aleksander Tytus Kulisiewicz, the pioneer of the subject.

The other great scholar, as I've mentioned, influencing the road map of my research was Bret Werb, a musicologist and the recorded sound curator at the United States Holocaust Memorial Museum (USHMM) in Washington DC. Bret also knew about me and my research, a fact made clear when I emailed him to ask for materials from the Kulisiewicz Collection at the USHMM. We have enriched each other's work ever since – I would update him on materials I found on my travels, while Bret, in turn, would correct, suggest and send more material.

We've managed to meet up on several occasions: once, he joined me in Atlanta and, in 2013, I opened up for him the boxes of materials I kept at home in Barletta. Bret, in particular, favours the music created in captivity by the Romani: it's my homework for future trips to find more for him.

Bret's office, not far from the USHMM, is the Eldorado of concentrationary music and Bret knows about every book's origin and contents. It means an enormous amount to me that he has often spoken about my research, as his esteem is essential to my credibility as a researcher.

However, Bret, Guido and I owe a huge historical debt of gratitude to the aforementioned Aleksander Kulisiewicz, one of the greatest minds in concentrationary music literature, himself a survivor of the camps.

Aleksander Kulisiewicz

A Pole from Kraków and self-taught singer and guitarist, Aleksander Kulisiewicz was arrested by the Gestapo on 23 October 1939 because of the anti-Fascist views expressed in some of his newspaper articles, denouncing Silesia's alleged political sycophancy towards the Reich. Imprisoned in Teschen, he was transferred to Wrocław in 1940 and on to Berlin Police Headquarters and, subsequently, on 30 May 1940, to Sachsenhausen. While there, Kulisiewicz performed, alone and with musicians such as tenor André Laboissière and the Moravian composer Jan Vala, in secret recitals that provided strong psychological support to his fellow inmates.

Kulisiewicz spoke fluent Polish, German, Czech and Hungarian. He survived medical experiments related to diphtheria that partly damaged his vocal chords, and, as a modern troubadour of concentrationary music endowed with an extraordinary memory, used singing to translate the camp's life and suffering into historical storytelling, employing at times macabre, aggressive and grotesque idioms, as well as the art of parody to do so, and also including in his repertory nostalgic songs inspired by patriotism. He performed and memorised many songs written by other prisoners, including 'Chorał z piekła dna', based on a text by Leonard Krasnodębski, 'Żywe kamienie' and 'Wir sind die lebenden Steine', based on texts by Włodzimierz Wnuk (originally written in Mauthausen-Gusen, but which reached Sachsenhausen), and 'Kołysanka Birkenau', based on 'Wenn ich groß bin, liebe Mutti'. He also created suggestive parodies, such as 'Czarny Böhm', based on the Ruthenian folk song 'I szumyt, i hudyt', 'Heil, Sachsenhausen', based on 'Madagaskar' by Mieczysław Miksne, and 'Muselmann-Kippensammler', based on the Circassian melodies 'Shanghai' and 'Zulejka' by Menashe Oppenheim. The latter's 'Muselmann' initially referred to Jews who had a darker complexion and more Semitic traits, then to deportees in such physical degradation and psychological exhaustion that they were in an almost vegetative state that foreshadowed death.

He became friends with Aaron Liebeskind, a basso profundo in Rosebery d'Arguto's clandestine male choir. Liebeskind told him of the tragic events in Treblinka and dictated a song in Yiddish, which Kulisiewicz translated into Polish and called 'Kołysanka Dla Synka W Krematorium'. Transferred to Birkenau in 1942, Liebeskind died in 1943. Kulisiewicz repeatedly sang 'Kołysanka' in the musician's memory at his concerts in Sachsenhausen, and after the war.

After the liberation, Kulisiewicz was hospitalised in Kraków for tuberculosis and, with the help of the staff, wrote down on paper 716 songs and poems in four languages, which he had memorised over his five-year imprisonment in Sachsenhausen. Having survived, he devoted the rest of his life to recovering the huge output of songs and poetry by Polish deportees in all the Nazis' concentration and extermination camps. Moreover, as editor and journalist of various Polish newspapers, he documented his countless trips within Poland and to other East European countries in search of musical material written in captivity, as well as the musical testimonials of former deportees.

Today, the importance of his collection is beyond measure, representing one of the greatest private archives of poetic and musical literature from the concentration camps.

Accuracies and errors

An error is generally considered a bump in the road, going off course, a wrong turn; in music, an error can be the solution to a gridlock of structural lines that are too perfect, the point of escape in overcrowded counterpoint, the uncalculated rush that reveals unexpected views of the landscape of a sonata or symphony.

The world of concentration camps begins with an error in June 1940 – the 'b' in *'Arbeit macht frei'* ('Work sets you free'), which the Polish blacksmith and prisoner Jan Liwacz fitted the wrong way round over the entrance to Auschwitz I; a reversed consonant that almost seemed like an urgent request to humanity for help. A paradoxical association of ideas leads to a much more rewarding 'b': the first letter in the Book of Genesis, i.e. *'Bereshit bara Elohim'* ('In the beginning'); the universe created by Him who is there from the beginning is literally and dramatically overturned in the camp anti-universe of a back-to-front 'b'.

The music written in captivity performed a work of reparation and recomposition that was both silent and extraordinary: it took the flipped-over 'b' of Auschwitz and straightened it.

*   *   *

In Theresienstadt, Viktor Ullmann wrote the cadenzas for Beethoven's piano concertos for a mostly incomplete project with the soloist René Gärtner-Geiringer, who died in Birkenau in October 1944. In the original, '5 Cadenzas' was erroneously noted, and was corrected by Ullmann to '4' when he remembered that the 'Emperor' concerto doesn't have space for an external cadenza.

We have recovered only the cadenzas for the first and third concertos, and this, too, looks like a mistake at first sight. As the late and much missed musicologist Robert Kolben demonstrated, however, Ullmann himself wrote cadenzas only for those concertos where Beethoven had not composed original cadenzas (specifically, the first and third concertos), drafting from memory the remaining two original cadenzas by Beethoven.

In turn, the definitive version of Ullmann's opera *The Emperor of Atlantis* was not completed by its composer in Theresienstadt: the final parts date from a few days before he was transferred to Birkenau. Following extended reconstruction work by Paolo Candido, the version is now complete.

On the postcards Alexander Kulisiewicz sent in German from Sachsenhausen, there are letters and syllables written in bolder lettering, which are grammatically incorrect; the Sachsenhausen mail censor would have put it down to the language errors of a Polish deportee, but these letters were musical notes in German notation – *A, B, C, D, E, F, G, H, Des, Es, Ges, As, Bes* – of songs written in the camp and assembled after the war by their composer, who survived.

The copy of Beethoven's lieder handwritten by the singer Karel Berman and kept in Theresienstadt, meanwhile, also contains a few errors. Berman did not have the score with him, so had to transcribe both the vocal and piano parts from memory.

It often seems that composers extended an imaginary bridge towards future researchers in order to enable us to discover the snapped golden threads of their music and carry them on by extracting their essence to the very last particle, and performing a historic and artistic repair job on the huge, incomplete human history represented by concentrationary music.

Guido Fackler and Bret Werb's lesson is that concentrationary music needs to be shared in order to be enriched. Its impact and benefits are then a hundredfold. Technically, this music belongs to its composers, but morally it belongs to the whole world; nobody can be motivated by selfishness or individualism.

Music literature is strewn with typos in the originals, due to physical errors of manual transmission, the hellish work pace of copyists, as well as other challenges – from Schubert, who would send his works to print without revising them to save on proofreaders, Beethoven, who paused the printing of his Hammerklavier Sonata, op. 106, in order to add two initial notes to the adagio (he sent them handwritten), to Ravel, who made a mistake in the meter of the first bars of 'Ondine' in *Gaspard de la Nuit* and only noticed once it was printed.

One must never be intimidated by the written text if one's musical soul senses an error. Scholarly study does not mean passive acceptance but an active transmission of the text and, as such, it is the only tool that can return to posterity literature of unimaginable richness, such as concentrationary music, inevitably affected by oversights and gaps – although a lot fewer than one might imagine. Completing incomplete works written in captivity is, thus, a mandatory scholarly, musicological, historical and moral duty.

THREE

A Testament of Talent

Prohibitions

From September 1933, the regulations of leading Nazi Joseph Goebbels' Ministry of Propaganda, as governed and controlled by the Chamber of Music, forbade Jewish musicians from practising professionally in public. This prevented them from such work as conducting orchestras, managing theatres, teaching in state institutions and being orchestral principals. Although the Jewish Cultural Association (*Jüdischer Kulturbund*) gathered Jewish musicians marginalised from German musical life and allowed performances and recitals reserved exclusively for a Jewish audience, there was no public acknowledgement of their work. A cultural federation originally of German Jews, set up in 1933 to employ Jewish people working in the arts prevented from working by the Nazis' racial laws, the *Jüdischer Kulturbund* essentially became a puppet organisation of the Reich from 1935, as it worked with the consent of the regime. The *Jüdischer Kulturbund* were all but disbanded in 1938, the day after *Kristallnacht*, (the Night of Broken Glass), many of its members either killed or deported to the camps in the pograms against Jews.

The Nazis devised the catch-all terms *Entartete Musik* ('degenerate music') and *Entartete Kunst* ('degenerate art') to cover all creative output that didn't meet with their approval. Hans Severus Ziegler, the Reich's cultural programme coordinator, infamously mounted an exhibition on the subject in Munich in 1937, which was then replicated in Weimar, Vienna and other cities. On the occasion of an exhibition in Düsseldorf, Ziegler raved about how decadence in music originated from the combination of capitalism and Judaism, and a long list of composers were blacklisted shortly thereafter.

Currents of modernist music that used innovative idioms – twelve-tone technique, jazz, musicals, Broadway – or rebelled against the Brahmsian symphonic tradition and Wagnerian opera favoured by the National Socialists, were firmly labelled *Entartete Musik* and dismissed and wiped from public consciousness. Jewish composers, such as Hanns Eisler, Ernst Křenek, Arnold Schoenberg, Franz Schreker and Kurt Weill, and non-Jews, such as Béla Bartók, Paul Hindemith, Igor Stravinsky and Anton Webern, also fell under this axe.

The Germany of thought, art and music migrated wholesale to the US, Canada, Central and South America, Oceania, Palestine (then a British mandate) and Shanghai. The Third Reich had effectively banned its most innovative artistic and musical brains, which resulted in the banished artists' new host countries, from Brazil to New Zealand, benefitting, which enriched their orchestras, concert institutions, choirs and schools.

The Third Reich hollowed itself of thought and imagination, depriving itself of brilliant innovators in musical language. Those musicians who emigrated left a Europe being devoured by the imminent war and the doctrinal barbarisation of Nazism, Fascism and inflamed militarism. The world's musical geography was simply turned upside down and radically redrawn following the rise to power of the National Socialists in 1933, the Nuremberg Laws in 1935 and the Anschluss of 1938, when Nazi Germany annexed neighbouring Austria. The musical heart of Central European Jewish talent was scattered across continents, newborn republics and overseas colonies. *Kristallnacht*, even more than the outbreak of the Second World War, provided the historical and ethical divide between the European Jewish intelligentsia and advancing Nazism in its territorial, ideological and absolutist dimensions.

Countless young Germans and Austrians found in Nazi ideology fertile ground to make up for their own personal and professional failures, and mediocrity prevailed. The mass deportations to the death camps were the culmination of an artistic climate that saw the irreversible haemorrhage of human resources and a progressive depopulation of the European music intelligentsia, both Jewish and non-Jewish. And yet, the heinous nature of the camps sometimes turned them from places of captivity to unexpected creativity for some of these men and women who, arguably, used music as a way of rising above the horrific circumstances of their daily lives, which many of them were not to survive.

Everybody's music

My Jewish faith has played a significant part in my interest in music written in captivity by other nations. *All nations*. I fundamentally believe that being Jewish does not mean singing about one's own feats, weeping over one's own tragedies or basking in one's own artistic and literary achievements: we are not a 'light unto the nations' exclusively for ourselves. To walk in other lands illuminated by the lantern fuelled by our brains and our hearts – *that* is profoundly and naturally Jewish.

In this far-from-easy research into the music of captivity and deportation, being a musician *and* a Jew is like docking the ship of my existence in two ports at once – in difficult times, one is the hawser and jetty of the other. Those of us who do this kind of research are merely shining a torch on the circumstances in which these musicians composed this music, unearthing tiny clues among papers and scores left on shelves on the planet in order to bring traces of this literature back into the light. Under these circumstances, being a Jew, a musician and a human being becomes one and the same.

Losing even one of these melodies is an irrevocable failure, a lasting injury. It's a race against time and the current: many fruits of this research will ripen later and their worth will be measured and appreciated only in years to come. And yet this is not anthological: it does not obey choices or go through filters. Musical masterpieces coexist alongside the mediocre, good and well-crafted works, their commonality that they were produced in captivity and, therefore, make concentrationary music as a whole an authentic representation of human talent.

Thousands of musicians created regardless of their human and logistical circumstances. Starvation, loss of freedom and physical distress did not present an obstacle for some but a stimulus. The expression of their talent was in inverse proportion to their physical degradation and equal to their desire to survive. Whenever the rhythms of history and humanity are turned upside down like an hourglass, the sand of music slowly starts to pour. An obscure, ancestral energy drove musicians to make music even when they faced the abyss of death. While Europe was sinking, musicians composed and played; they realised that it was their task to save civilisation.

Ghettos, concentration camps and gulags have left us incomplete, sometimes patchy works that would have required further polishing and retouching in other circumstances, made impossible by captivity or the tragic fates of their composers. Yet I like to imagine that the same hand that saved Kafka's unrevised manuscripts and did not destroy the final works left on Chopin's desk, contrary to the two creators' wishes, the hand that stopped whoever wanted to burn Virgil's *Aeneid*, left unrevised due to the poet's death, is the same hand that saved Viktor Ullmann's *Emperor of Atlantis*, Erwin Schulhoff's Symphony No. 8 and Hermann Gürtler's Sonata for violin and piano.

Just as a cathedral reveals to an architect secrets and codes invisible to most people, so a musical score written in captivity reveals historical truths that are impossible to convey through diaries and letters.

The first concentrationary music

In June 1933, in the Emsland district, between Neusustrum, Börgermoor and Esterwegen (Lower Saxony), the Nazis inaugurated a group of fifteen internment camps, known as the Emslandlager and modelled on penal colonies. The prisoners – mainly criminals, homosexuals and Jehovah's Witnesses to begin with, but increasingly including political dissidents as time went on – were tasked with digging peat for fuel from the marshes on the Dutch border. It's estimated approximately 80,000 civilians were sent to the Emslandlager, and from 1941, 180,000 Soviet prisoners of war joined them.

In Börgermoor, two Germans, the poet and trade unionist Johann Esser and actor and director Wolfgang Langhoff, wrote the protest song 'Die Moorsoldaten' ('The Moor Soldiers'), a rebellion against their oppressors. The composer of the music was political activist and member of the German Resistance Rudolf 'Rudi' Goguel, who had been arrested on 27 September 1934. 'Die Moorsoldaten' can rightly be considered the originating piece of music of the twentieth-century camps. And thanks to the tradition of oral transmission that went hand-in-hand with the transfer and liberation of the deportees, it increasingly became popular and well known outside the Emslandlager.

German actor Erich Mirek, who took refuge in Prague after a brief internment in Börgermoor, introduced 'Die Moorsoldaten' to the anti-Nazi Socialist agitprop group *Das Rote Sprachrohr*, which published and circulated it. The song was then arranged and metrically adapted by Austro-German composer Hanns Eisler – an associate of Brecht – who had taken refuge in London. 'Die Moorsoldaten' was also sung and popularised in 1937 by German singer, actor and director Ernst Friedrich Wilhelm Busch among the International Brigades who rushed to Spain to support the Republicans during the Spanish Civil War (1936–9).

In Sachsenhausen, in 1941, Aleksander Kulisiewicz created a version of the song in several languages, transforming it into a kind of hymn for those deported to Europe's concentration camps. In Ravensbrück, writer and anti-Fascist Maria 'Mara' Montuoro also wrote an Italian version of it for women's chorus, while a French version known as *'Le Chant des marais'* originated in Dachau. Between March 1940 and November 1941, 'Die Moorsoldaten' cropped up yet again at the Rieucros camp, controlled by Vichy, where Austro-German actress Steffi Spira, Czech writer Lenka Reinerová and other female deportees wrote further French and German versions.

The instruments of concentration camps

As my research continued, I increasingly found that the presence or absence of instruments would often help me map out the deported musicians, their activities and even their access to supplementary food rations. For example, the disappearance of violas, used in the previous production, from Hans Krása's short opera *Brundibár* in Theresienstadt is starkly illustrative of the issues caused to musicians by the relentless transfers to other camps or extermination sites. Yet resilience is a powerful thing and people found ways to circumvent these problems of access to instruments and to their own work.

It was thanks to imprisoned carpenters in Dachau in 1938, for example, that the Austrian Herbert Zipper was able to create musical instruments and assemble a clandestine orchestra that would perform in unused latrines in the camp. Similarly, in April 1943, the Jewish Czech violinist Pavel Kling managed to take his instrument to Theresienstadt with him, but not his scores, so he memorised his entire repertory. And then, in early 1944, the Theresienstadt musicians went from having just one piano in a very poor state to at least six, including a Steinway grand from Berlin.

In Oflag XA Nienburg/Weser, French prisoners performed

Beethoven's Ninth Symphony with an orchestra of over 150 principals; this involved the requisition of all the instruments in surrounding camps. In Stalag VIII A Görlitz (Zgorzelec in Poland), meanwhile, where 15,000 Polish, Belgian, British, Commonwealth, French, Serbian, IMI, Soviet, Slovak and American prisoners of war were interned, the French composer Olivier Messiaen wrote *Quatuor pour la fin du temps* with the cello and piano parts deliberately never playing certain notes because the appropriate keys and strings were missing from the instruments available to the musicians there. The state or absence of key instruments made performing works difficult and yet these men and women persevered, wherever they were incarcerated.

Following the introduction of new racial laws, in 1934 the Polish-Jewish musician Szymon Goldberg, leader of the Berlin Philharmonic, had to leave his position. He emigrated to the Dutch East Indies (present-day Indonesia), but was arrested by the Japanese military authorities, interned at first in Java and finally in Tjimahi (180 km southeast of Jakarta), where he assembled fourteen violins and one flute, found a piano with only nineteen working keys and a harmonium and used them to reconstruct Beethoven's Violin Concerto from memory. The harmonium substituted for the wind instruments and basses, while the piano stood in for the remaining parts of the orchestra. There were not enough bows for the violinists and some played their parts *pizzicato*. Goldberg's violin was strung with guitar strings.

I arranged a meeting in Treviso with Elisa, the daughter of the Italian prisoner-of-war Vittorio Longarato, who was interned in the British camp of Zonderwater in South Africa. It held over 100,000 Italian soldiers captured by British troops on

West African, Eritrean, Somalian, Ethiopian and Libyan fronts, between April 1941 and January 1947. In Zonderwater, there were schools, libraries, canteens, churches, cinemas, a radio station and an official newspaper. There was also high-level musical and theatrical activity, with musicians, actors, singers, a stage costume workshop and make-up, plus seventeen functioning theatres. An eight-piece symphony orchestra was formed, as well as a sixty-five-musician military band, and the music repertoire ranged from classical – some unobtainable scores were rearranged for orchestra from memory – to operettas. These were mainly Italian language adaptations of American and British plays. Elisa showed me one of the most fascinating results of concentration camp organology.

Her father had built a back-to-front banjo-mandolin – he was left-handed – with a body made from wood obtained from a camp bench (the shavings were gradually disposed of in the latrines); the top part of the soundbox was made from rabbit skin traded for cigarettes from a worker outside the camp (the skin deteriorated and was replaced when he returned to Italy) and the circular bracket, like a metal crown, was the result of melting the ferrule from an explosive.

The bridge came from the back of an aluminium-coated comb obtained from a mess tin, the keys were made with halves of mother-of-pearl buttons, four double strings were fashioned from metal threads removed from bicycle brake cables, shaped appropriately. A few holes were then drilled around the wooden body and metal crown, in order to give the soundbox the original timbre of a banjo-mandolin.

The ingenuity was remarkable. Where there's a will, there's a way.

Herbert Zipper

On 27 May 1938, the Austrian composer Herbert Zipper was picked up by Austrian police and, after spending two days in jail with other prisoners, moved to Dachau. Shortly before he boarded the train, an SS officer ordered him to sing, and so he struck up the 'Ode to Joy' from Beethoven's Ninth Symphony; he was soon joined by his fellow prisoners. The platform of Vienna railway station quivered under their feet and degradation and fear turned to celebration and a form of protest.

This act was a precursor to the European symbols we now unanimously share – and 'Ode to Joy' is now the anthem of the European Union and of the Council of Europe. Zipper and the other deportees at Vienna station were Europeans ahead of their time. In that moment, singing the most famous chorus, espousing the values of brotherhood and peace among nations, as well as arguably the emblem of the essential Germanness of the Bonn-born genius, that impromptu choir on the platform was able to stamp out – albeit only metaphorically – the Third Reich and its representatives. In that moment, perhaps nothing could be as destructive as striking up a song in German, written by a German, in the face of a German, albeit Nazi, soldier.

And yet, decades later, as the 'Ode to Joy' echoed in the

Strasbourg chamber during the new European Parliament, inaugurated in June 2014, many so-called 'Eurosceptic' members listened to the anthem with their backs turned to the President. It was meant as a political gesture, only these members were arguably ignorant of the fact that, after *Kristallnacht* and what took place that day at Vienna station with Zipper and his fellow detainees, there can be nothing more provocative than Beethoven's anthem.

FOUR

KZ Musik

The recording encyclopaedia
and the documentary

Blanka Červinková, my dear mentor in Prague, died of a terrible illness in 2002. The last time I saw her, she was undergoing chemotherapy and her hair was cropped short. Despite this, she was still busy inaugurating publishing projects for concentrationary music, and she told me she loved my recording of *Brundibár*. When we said goodbye, I held her tight and kissed her hands over and over.

During the first few years of this century, I was kept busy with the record company Musikstrasse, recording the music I had retrieved over the first fifteen years of my research. My original goal was to create a box set of forty-eight CDs, but, given the amount of production work involved, we compromised with a box set of only twenty-four. We called it *KZ Musik* and it was the physical expression of what Blanka Červinková had hoped for ten years earlier: to give a voice to the many different types of musical realities from the camps, the different professional and artistic origins and the equally varied national, social and religious contexts. The composers were Jews, Christians, Sintis, Romas and other Romani peoples, Basques, Sufis, Quakers,

Jehovah's Witnesses, Communists, disabled people, homosexuals, as well as civilian and military prisoners.

I chose works written in all types of camps: prison, transit, forced labour, concentration, extermination, military prisons and prisoner-of-war camps; stalag, oflag, opened by the Third Reich, Italy, Japan, the Republic of Salò, Vichy and other Axis Powers, Britain, France, the Soviet Union and other Allies in Europe; in north and colonial Africa, Asia and Oceania.

This is how I came across British pianist and composer Wilhelm Joseph Hildesheimer. He was born in London but lived in Berlin, his mother's birthplace, from the age of three; the political climate in Germany made him move to the Netherlands in 1935, where he taught music at the Quakerschool Eerde in Ommen. When the Germans occupied the Netherlands, he was arrested as a non-combatant from a warring nation (he was a British national) and, alongside other British civilians, transferred to Kamp Schoorl. There, he wrote a *Pot-Pourri* for piano and orchestra based on music by the Strauss family, performed on 11 August 1940 by the New Wiener Boheme Orchestra (with Hildesheimer on the piano). In September 1940 he was moved to the Ilag in Tost, then to Ilag VIII H Kreuzburg (present-day Kluczbork, Poland). There, from 1943 to 1944, he recorded some of his songs for male voice and piano for the Swedish radio network AB Radiotjänst (Sweden was neutral during the war), and these recordings were broadcast on Swedish radio in December 1944. In early 1945 he was transferred to Ilag XVIII Spittal am Drau (Austria). After the war, Hildesheimer went back to Germany, anglicised his name to William Hilsley and finally returned to the Netherlands where, in 1947, he resumed teaching at the Quakerschool Eerde in Ommen. He died in Beverweerd Castle, in the Netherlands, in January 2003.

It was a lengthy, exhausting and immeasurably costly job. But it was an equally Herculean task for many other scholars, musicians and all those who helped ensure that not a single score was lost.

At the same time as I was preparing the box set, Musikstrasse obtained financial support from the European Union for a documentary about my research. This made it possible, for the first time, for me to travel without dipping into my savings. With my friend and director–cameraman Ermanno Felli, I went around Europe not only interviewing survivors or their relatives, but also recovering music and other material. I returned from every trip with suitcases bursting with documents, scores and recordings.

Émile Goué

We decided to give this documentary a Latin title: *Musica Concentrationaria*. Filming began in France in Spring 2007. Thanks to my dear friend Nirmala Goué, Ermanno and I flew to Paris to meet her father, Bernard, the son of the great French composer Émile Goué.

I arrived at Bernard's home after two challenging days of flight cancellations, which transformed our Rome–Paris journey into a Rome–Lyon flight, a TGV to Paris and, finally, a taxi that delivered us to Rue Vincent Auriol, where Bernard was patiently waiting for us.

Émile Goué had a talent for music but also read science at university. Born in 1904 in Châteauroux, he studied composition with Charles Koechlin and Albert Roussel, and married Yvonne Burg, with whom he had three children. From 1930 to 1935, he taught Physics in Bordeaux, then, from 1935 to 1939, at the Lycée Buffon in Paris, and, in 1939, at the Lycée Louis-le-Grand, where there was a vacancy due of the war.

His main works before the war include Symphony No.1, Psaume XIII, for tenor, mixed chorus and orchestra, the two-act musical action *Wanda* (from which he subsequently drew a symphonic suite in three parts), 'Notre Père' for soprano and organ, 'L'offrande sous les nuages' for soprano and piano, 'La chanson des yeux de ma mie' and 'Chant de l'âme navrée' for tenor and piano, 'Trois chansons sur la pluie' for voice and piano, *Deux Nocturnes,* Pénombres and a sonata for piano.

When war broke out, Goué was recruited as a lieutenant in the artillery, but in June 1940 he was captured and interned in Oflag XA Nienburg/Weser. The oflag had a high standard of educational facilities, including at university level, as well as courses in music. A symphony orchestra and chamber groups were put together, as well as a jazz band and there were many stage productions.

In Nienburg/Weser, Goué composed works that showed great maturity, including: *Ambiances* (second suite), *Préhistoires*, two impromptus for piano, *Petite suite facile* for piano (lost); monumental piano scores modelled on and bearing the same name as works by César Franck: *Prélude, Choral et Fugue* and *Prélude, Aria et Final*, a violin and piano sonata; 'Nuits de velours que rehaussent les clairs de lune' for tenor and piano, *Trois poèmes de Rainer Maria Rilke* for soprano and piano, *Trois mélodies* for soprano and string quartet, Duo for violin and cello, a piano quintet, a second and third string quartet (the second completed after the war), *Trois pièces faciles* for string quartet, a string sextet and *Ballade* for soprano, vocal quartet, string quartet and piano. He also produced *Deux Mélodies* for contralto and orchestra, *Désinvolture* for jazz orchestra (incomplete), a piano concerto, Symphony No. 2 for principal violin and orchestra (performed on 6, 7 and 8 November 1943, conducted by the composer, with Jean Robin as principal violin), *Esquisse pour un paysage vu du Mont Coudreau* for orchestra, Psaume CXXIII for tenor, male chorus and chamber orchestra, the orchestral suite *Macbeth*, the incidental music for *Ubu Roi* (partially recovered) and *Volpone* (lost). *L'Apôtre*, a mimed oratorio (incomplete) for voice and orchestra, had to be staged in two days, and he created the opera-mime-oratorio *Renaissance* to a text by René Christian-Frogé, a masterful work notable for its modern orchestration and scenic language.

Goué, who had a natural talent for teaching, organised physics courses, as well as lectures, including, from 1940, a series entitled *History of Music: from its origins to today*. He also developed courses in harmony, counterpoint and fugue, twenty lessons in musical aesthetics and the history of the symphony, and took care of various productions and of the musical education of musician prisoners. He wrote a treatise on musical aesthetics and a guide to music writing. With the help of his pupil, friend and fellow prisoner of war Philippe Gordien, he set up a fifty-piece orchestra and a prisoners' choir and, with their help, performed over twenty concerts of the works of Franco-Flemish polyphonists, Beethoven, Mozart, Franck, Roussel and Honegger.

Freed in May 1945, Goué returned to Paris in a very frail state, his health compromised by his time in the camp. He devoted himself to composing and teaching and, on 1 October 1945, took up a position at the Lycée Louis-le-Grand in Paris. He completed his Theme and Variations for piano (already drafted in the oflag) and finished a monumental orchestration of *Esquisse pour une inscription sur une stèle*, which was performed in 1947, after his death, by the Bordeaux Philharmonic Orchestra.

Due to a serious lung infection – an after-effect of his imprisonment – he was admitted to the Neufmoutiers-en-Brie sanatorium, where he died in October 1946. His premature demise was a great loss to the development of post-Franck, polymodal dialectics and to Renaissance Revival idioms in the contemporary musical landscape.

I had practically devoured Émile Goué's entire piano output;

his Oflag XA Nienburg/Weser compositions are ultra-pianistic, which makes me suspect that Goué had brilliant technique and a very wide span.

My conversation with Bernard was in French and flowed non-stop as he spoke off the cuff about his father with such detail as if he had left him only a few hours before. Goué had obviously been a powerful presence in Bernard's life and for his part, Bernard, a retired engineer, had devoted his entire life to promoting his father's music.

After meeting Bernard in Paris, I performed his father's works in Rome, São Paulo and Marseilles. At our last meeting, in 2016, Bernard gave me countless scores by his father. From both a musical and human perspective, the demise of Emile Goué, one of the many brilliant concentrationary musicians who died far too early, has cost us dearly.

Robert Lannoy

After Paris, my friend Ermanno and I proceeded to Lille, where I met Jean-Cristophe, the son of the French composer Robert Lannoy. In June 1940, Lannoy was arrested and interned in an unidentified camp somewhere between the Protectorate of Bohemia and Moravia and Slovakia. He escaped but was captured in Bayreuth and transferred to Stalag 325 Rawa-Ruska. In 1942, he wrote arrangements for chorus and orchestra of 'L'amour de moy', 'Marche des soldats de Turenne', 'Roule donc, J'aimerai bien apprendre au monde', 'Dans l'cul! [Hymne de Rawa-Ruska]' and wrote and staged the mime-ballet *Pygmalion*. He also tried to escape again.

In 1943, he was moved to Stalag 328 Lemberg and subsequently to Stalag XVII B Krems-Gneixendorf in Austria, where 66,000 prisoners of war – French, Belgian, British, Polish, Serbian, Soviet and Italian – were interned. With the advance of Soviet troops, the Stalag was closed and the prisoners transferred to Waldfriedhof.

Arriving in Stalag XVII B in 1943, Lannoy took on the post of musical director, staged the *Pygmalion* he had written previously in Rawa-Ruska, wrote 'Hortense, couches-toi' for male chorus and piano, *Deux mélodies sur un poème de Francis Carco* for voice and piano, *Cantilène et danse pastorale* for orchestra, *Deux Virelais du Moyen-Age* for soprano, flute, clarinet and viola and an orchestral arrangement of 'Chant des déportés' (a version of the famous 'Die Moorsoldaten').

He was subsequently relocated to Stalag XIII B Weiden in the Oberpfalz, where he wrote the score for 'Le Berceau' (after a poem by Albert Samain) for piano and additional sax. Liberated in January 1945, he returned to France and, at the request of the US Army Signal Corps and the Office of War Information, he wrote the soundtrack for Henri Cartier-Bresson's documentary *Le Retour*, about the repatriation of prisoners of war and deportees, which was orchestrated by Roger Désormière. He came second in the 1946 Prix de Rome with the cantata *Le jeu de l'amour et du hasard*, which earned him the directorship of the Lille Conservatoire. It was during this time that he married the brilliant concert pianist Lola Delwarde. His later works include *Ballade de l'épinette amoureuse*, for female vocal quartet and wind quartet, *Lamento Ukrainien*, for orchestra, and the oratorio *Les prophéties*, for narrator, chorus and orchestra.

Lannoy's son Jean-Cristophe, who teaches cello at the Lille Conservatoire, had few yet vivid memories of his father, who died when he was very young. Jean-Cristophe's wife, Sabine Van Lerberghe, an excellent pianist, takes care of Lannoy's archive. It was Sabine who brought me here when she sent me all the musical material by Lannoy.

Maurice Thiriet

After spending the night in an expensive hotel in Bavinchove, Hauts-de-France, the French tenor Damien Top, Ermanno and I reached Puys, near Dieppe, in order to meet Elizabeth, the daughter of the composer Maurice Thiriet.

Captured and interned in IX A Ziegenhain, Thiriet wrote *Trois Motets* for chorus and the musical fresco *Œdipe Roi*, based on a text by Jean Cocteau, for narrator, male chorus and orchestra, as well as orchestral arrangements. After his release, he achieved great success in 1942 with his soundtrack to the film *Les Visiteurs du soir*, directed by Marcel Carné, in partnership with the Hungarian-Jewish composer Joseph Kosma, who was not credited, because at the time he was living in France illegally. Thiriet had a successful career as a composer of classical and film music. He died in Puys in 1972.

Elizabeth welcomed us into her home and served us almond cakes and drinks, but within minutes I knew I was in trouble, my eyes were watering so much. She had a cat and I'm allergic to them. My first half hour with Elizabeth was a disaster. I was sneezing so hard that Ermanno's headphones kept bouncing in the air and Elizabeth was stilted, probably because she felt overwhelmed. She talked about her father as though she were reading a biography. We ended up sending the cat into the garden and deciding I would start over and ask her open-ended questions to make her feel more comfortable.

And so we did.

Elizabeth told me about her father, about his internment in Ziegenhain, where the composer and conductor Jean Martinon was also detained, and about the works he wrote in captivity, and his masterpiece, *Œdipe Roi*. At one stage, the cakes vanished from the table to make room for a sea of music scores. And, as we were leaving, Elizabeth gave me a rucksack filled with a treasure trove: photocopies of her father's works.

Marius Flothuis

From Paris we went on to Amsterdam to meet the children of a few survivors of the camps. We also met with the extraordinary flautist Eleonore Pameijer, an expert on the concentrationary music written by Dutch composers. Eleonore Pameijer was also the only pupil of the famous Dutch composer, musicologist and music critic Marius Hendrikus Flothuis.

In 1937, Flothius became assistant artistic director of the Amsterdam Concertgebouw, but was sacked in 1942 after refusing to join the Nederlandsche Kultuurkamer (the Netherlands Chamber of Culture, established by the Nazi regime). His wife was Jewish. He was arrested by the Wehrmacht on 18 September 1943 for giving concerts they deemed illegal and helping clandestine Jewish artists. He was taken to Kamp Vught (Konzentrationslager Herzogenbusch), where he wrote: Sonata da camera, op. 17, for flute and piano (performed on 2 April 1944 by Everard van Royen, accompanied on the piano by the composer), Aria for trumpet and piano, op. 18, Concerto for flute and orchestra, op. 19 *Aubade*, op. 19a, for flute (dedicated to van Royen, performed and broadcast through a microphone installed at the Philips-Kommando of the camp on 14 April 1944), *Bicinia*, op. 20, for female choir,

Valses sentimentales, op. 21, for piano four hands, and *Twee stukken*, op. 22, for guitar.

On 8–9 September 1944, Flothius and three thousand other Dutch prisoners were transferred to Heinkel, a Sachsenhausen sub-camp, where he wrote *Duettino pastorale*, op. 23, No. 2 for two violins and the Sonata for solo violin op. 23, No. 3.

After the war, he had a successful career, becoming artistic director of the Concertgebouw Orchestra. From 1974, he was a lecturer in musicology at Utrecht University and, from 1980, president of the Central Institute for Mozart Research in Salzburg. He died in Amsterdam in 2001.

Eleonore Pameijer is now the director of the Leo Smit Foundation, which recovers the lost or forgotten music of Dutch Jews persecuted during the German occupation. She gave me an interesting overview of the Dutch composers who died in Auschwitz II Birkenau and Sobibór, and showed me musical material by composers Leo Smit and Armand Haagman (who died, respectively, in Sobibór and Auschwitz). In return I told Eleonore about the life and works of the Dutch-Jewish composer Daniël Belinfante, who died in the Silesian penal camp of Fürstengrube (where Gideon Klein also died). Eleonore was intrigued and, since then, with unfailing professional courtesy, has never failed to remind the press that it was an Italian pianist who introduced the Netherlands to the music of a previously unrecognized Dutch composer.

The lost music of Barcelona . . .

Once I had finished my work in Amsterdam, I took the airport shuttle and boarded an evening flight to Barcelona, to attend an international conference on music in the Third Reich, while Ermanno returned to Italy. I landed in Barcelona well past midnight. A hotel had been booked for me in the city centre, and while I could have just got a taxi, paid twenty euros and reached my destination, I didn't have much money, so decided to take the bus.

I had a huge suitcase and an equally large rucksack bursting with scores, CDs, DVDs and a computer, and I was very sleepy. I sat on the bus opposite a guy who was playing at balancing a coin on his finger. He started asking me questions and told me to put my rucksack – which I was holding tightly in my arms – up on the luggage rack, which I did, before continuing to toy with that coin. I was half asleep but at some point realised he had gone. As had my rucksack. It turned out that while the man with the coin was distracting me, an accomplice of his behind me had taken possession of the rucksack. I grabbed my suitcase and rushed off the bus, but there was no trace of them. Days and days of work in France and the Netherlands had evaporated in a moment.

The only thing left to do was report the theft to the airport police and take a taxi, paying the twenty euros I had originally wanted to save after all. I was supposed to spend three days in Barcelona, but the following morning I asked the conference organisers to spend my fee on getting me back to Italy the next day.

Back in Barletta with no rucksack, scores or computer, I realised the extent of the tragedy that had befallen me in Barcelona. I wrote to the people I had met over the previous days and reluctantly asked them to resend me the photocopies of the works, wary of trespassing further on their generosity. Not only did they all reply – more concerned about my health than about the rucksack – but they all resent the material, and some even took the opportunity to send me photocopies they had forgotten to include when I had gone to see them. The scores multiplied and I ended up recovering more material than I had collected prior to the theft on the Barcelona bus.

The miracle of research and human kindness.

Józef Kropiński

In April 2007, I went to Nuremberg. Beforehand, all Nuremberg had meant to me was colossal Nazi rallies, such as you see in Leni Riefenstahl's 1935 documentary *Triumph of the Will*, and, post-war, the epoch-defining trials of former party officials. Nowadays, however, Nuremberg is the city of my great friend Waldemar, the son of the Polish violinist and composer Józef Kropiński, whose work at Buchenwald, in particular, was important both to his fellow inmates at the time but also to concentrationary music.

Born in 1913 in Berlin, the son of Poles who then returned to Bydgoszcz after the First World War, Kropiński studied the violin and, in December 1938, joined the coal department of the Francusko-Polskie Towarzystwo Kolejowe, where he formed an orchestra and the Haslo choir.

On 7 May 1940 he was arrested by the Gestapo for sabotage and distributing anti-Fascist leaflets. In November 1941, he was sent to Auschwitz I and assigned to a sub-camp, and in April 1942 he became the leader of the camp orchestra. He wrote various pieces, including *Pange lingua* for male chorus, the song 'Złota Jesień' to his own text, and the songs 'Ach gdyby można było', 'Wieczorną godziną' and 'Zawsze i wszędzie' to texts by the Polish writer Kazimierz Wójtowicz (also sent to Auschwitz I). In March 1943, Kropiński was transferred to Buchenwald and assigned to the pathology department. There, he met the German author and screenwriter Bruno Apitz and several Polish artists, including poet Edmund Polak, writer Karl Schnog and composers Zbigniew Koczanowicz, Kazimierz Tyminski and Stanislaw Wiekowski. He wrote around four hundred and forty pieces of music, mainly during the nights he spent at the pathology department.

Kropiński wrote the opera *Buchhäuser oder Läuse-Krieg auf der Wartburg* to a libretto by Bruno Apitz (lost, but performed in Buchenwald on New Year's Eve 1944), the operetta *Król czy błazen* to a libretto by Edmund Polak (lost, and never performed because the composer stopped working on it shortly before the evacuation of the camp), *Marzenie!*, *Tęsknota*, *Zbiór pieśni gwiazdkowych* for string quartet, *Wesola trojka* and *Bez titułu* for piano, *Dlaczego?* and *Pieśń bez słów* for violin and piano, *Utwór charakterystyczny* for orchestra with piano *obbligato*, the satirical couplet *Na ja* to text by Bruno Apitz, *66 Lieder* for male voice with piano or string quartet, *Ave Maria*, *Na śniegu*, *Życzenie* and *Premières neiges*.

He also wrote a few splendid tangos, including *Kiedyś byłaś przy mnie*, *Naszą będzie ta pierwsza noc* and *Arizona* for baritone and piano, and *Żal Tango* for baritone and orchestra, about four hundred arrangements, choral pieces, and *Kopf hoch* to text by Bruno Apitz. This piece, accompanied by the camp's orchestra, was very popular in Buchenwald, partly thanks to its refrain, written in Polish, French, Czech and Russian, so as to involve the many deportees of various nationalities. When the camp was closed in 1945, Kropiński managed to take with him his works and his violin, but over the two-week march that followed, he was forced, reluctantly, to use a large number of his scores for fuel in order to boil water.

In the end, by his own tally, he managed to save only 117 manuscripts, and it was only because of his fellow prisoners stopping him that his violin survived. After the war, he abandoned composing and moved to Wrocław to work at the Agricultural Construction Directorate. He suffered a first heart attack in 1966 and died, four years later, in October 1970.

Some time after we met in Nuremberg, Waldemar and his wife, Iwona, vacationed in Metaponto, not far from where I live in Barletta. They came to visit and the baritone Angelo De Leonardis was also with me. Angelo and I have worked together for many years; he speaks German and is the singer *par excellence* of Kropiński's vocal repertoire. Waldemar assisted him in improving his pronunciation in Polish, which can be extremely difficult for a non-native speaker.

A year later, Waldemar and Iwona returned to Italy, again on holiday, and visited me. On that occasion, I was able to inform Waldemar that, in addition to the material by his father stored at the USHMM in Washington DC, there was also a large volume of material at the Academy of Arts in Berlin. Werner Grünzweig, the director of the Academy's musical archive, is one of the most important scholars on the subject.

The last time I saw Waldemar, he hugged me and thanked me for what I was doing. Buchenwald, especially the pathology department, had been a place of unspeakable horror for his father and fellow internees. And yet it was in these subhuman settings, in the middle of the night, often by candlelight, that Józef Kropiński created his masterpieces, work which I was playing my part in returning to the world.

Sara and Coco

After days of intense research in Würzburg and Nuremberg, I arrived in Berlin, where I combed through the antiquarian bookshops strewn between Charlottenburg and Humboldt University and plunged into the goldmines of concentrationary music at the Academy of Arts.

My first meeting was with singer Sara Bialas-Tenenberg (Stefania Śliwka). Sara, frequently showing emotion, told me about her deportation to Gross-Rosen and her fellow prisoners. Gross-Rosen (Rogoznica, in western Poland) was originally a sub-camp of Sachsenhausen, but, in 1941, a year after its creation, was made autonomous, becoming the administrative centre of a network of some ninety-seven concentration camps.

A Częstochowa Jew, Sara was arrested in December 1941 in Sosnowiec, where she had been hiding after her parents were killed in Treblinka. Sent to Gross-Rosen and forced to work in a sub-camp, Sara was liberated by Soviet troops on 9 May 1945 and transferred to the Displaced Persons Camp in Ainring, where she heard and memorised the song 'Treblinka' from the Biała Podlaska ghetto. She returned to Częstochowa, then moved to East Berlin in 1961. When I met her, she still sang 'Treblinka' in perfect Yiddish. Thanks to Sara, this song has not been lost.

While in Berlin, I could not miss out on the opportunity to also meet the legendary German-Jewish jazz guitarist Heinz Jakob 'Coco' Schumann. Born in Berlin in 1924, as a young man he performed in Kurfürstendamm nightclubs the new rhythms imported from the US – jazz and swing, music genres banned by the Nazi regime as 'degenerate'. At nineteen, he was deported to Theresienstadt, where he joined the Ghetto Swingers as a percussionist (the guitar parts had already been taken). From Theresienstadt, he was transferred to Birkenau. He survived the camp and returned to Berlin where he formed the Coco Schumann Quartet. He has played alongside all the greats, from Ella Fitzgerald to Marlene Dietrich and Helmut Zacharias.

Coco gave me a number of his CDs and, on his doorstep, saw me off with a very Italian *'Arrivederci!'* that sounded much like a Louis Armstrong roar. After a lifetime filled with music, Coco Schumann left us in 2018 at the age of ninety-three.

FIVE

Ghettos

Resistance in the ghettos

Under pressure to meet ageing camp survivors while I could, I had put the question of ghettos on standby, but it was the great Bret Werb who first introduced me to the 'ghetto phenomenon'.

The Third Reich's war machine and genocide and the Final Solution ran in tandem, both essential components of the Nazi high command's plans. Ghettos were arguably the tragic evidence of the Reich's confused strategy when dealing with these two contradictory objectives: obtaining an unpaid workforce to support the war effort and carrying out their plan to exterminate Europe's Jewish population. The ghettos allowed the Nazis to temporarily suspend any decisions, but, starting with the Warsaw ghetto uprising, in 1943, this strategy backfired spectacularly.

The heroism of the Warsaw ghetto inspired the Jewish communities of the Baltic states, and reinvigorated armed resistance everywhere. The stronger your enemy, the more reason to fight them: this is the important lesson imparted to posterity by the Warsaw ghetto resistance.

Polish musicians, both Jews and non-Jews, were in the frontline. Some fought with weapons; others supported the cause through the music played in the ghetto cafés, music which has come down to us almost intact.

Warsaw

In 1939, there were, by some estimates, 380,000 Jews in Warsaw, mainly of Polish and Russian extraction, most Yiddish speaking, many of whom had escaped from Tzarist Russia. In November 1940, in the Nalewki district of the old town – which included the mediaeval Jewish quarter, the industrial zone and the motorway to Berlin and Poznań, which split the area into two unequal sectors – the Nazis set up a ghetto administered by a *Judenrat* and controlled by a Jewish police corps, and corralled the Jewish population into it, walling them in.

The Warsaw ghetto soon housed a population of up to 460,000 Jews, making it the largest ghetto in Europe. Appalling unsanitary conditions led to the spread of typhus and other diseases, while starvation, physical abuse and further restrictions of living space quickly led to the population being decimated. Then, on 22 July 1942, the order was issued to begin transferring the population to the Treblinka extermination camp. Adam Czerniaków, president of the *Judenrat*, took his own life on receiving the news.

After the deportation of an estimated 265,000 people, and the dawning realisation that ghetto residents were being sent to their deaths rather than being resettled, insurgents within the ghetto began fighting back, catching the Germans by surprise – and on 19 April 1943, the eve of Passover, the Warsaw ghetto uprising began. It lasted, despite the overwhelming odds, for twenty-eight days and was the largest single revolt by Jews during the war.

SS-Brigadeführer Jürgen Stroop, personally appointed by Heinrich Himmler to deal with the problem, ordered the destruction of the ghetto in retaliation, and an estimated 13,000 Jews were killed, many of them burnt alive or suffocated. The 57,000 or so survivors were then either killed on the spot or sent to death camps.

The fall of the Warsaw ghetto marked not only the end of all hope of salvation for the city's Jews, but also the start of massive and systematic deportations; meaning to suppress any further attempt at revolt in the ghettos, Heinrich Himmler, chief of the SS, had them all closed by 11 June 1943.

The Warsaw ghetto, while it lasted, inspired a great deal of creative activity in terms of music, choreography, variety shows, concerts and plays of all kinds. It had a symphony orchestra from 1940 to 1942, conducted in turn by Marian Neuteich, Adam Furmanski, Szymon (Simon) Pullman – who took the symphony orchestra to the highest level of excellency – and Israel Hamerman. There were five theatres, with productions in Yiddish and Polish, as well as performances by chamber and choral ensembles. The cafés, oases of free thinking and the last resort for maintaining solo, chamber and symphonic concerts, were places where you could hear the greats of Polish jazz, like Artur Gold, George Scott and Bobby Fiddler.

A clandestine council of musicians was formed in Café Lira with the purpose of opposing invasive cultural pan-Germanic policies and staging clandestine recitals and concerts of contemporary classical music in private apartments, commissioning songs for the armed resistance (written by Witold Lutosławski and Andrzej Panufnik), setting up parameters for musical education appropriate for the ghetto residents, and financing musicians in need who were hiding from the German garrison. The composer Edward Bury organised a recital, performing in it as a pianist and conductor. Similarly at Café Dom, Sztuki, Bolesław Woytowicz staged solo recitals and chamber concerts of his music and that of other Polish composers who were unemployed, such as Grażyna Bacewicz, Roman Palester, Witold Lutosławski, Stefan Kisielewski and Kazimierz Wiłkomirski.

The Polish pianist and composer Władysław 'Wladek' Szpilman was born in Sosnowiec in 1911. Thanks to a scholarship, he moved to the Academy of Arts in Berlin, where he was a pupil of Arthur Schnabel, Franz Schreker and Leonid Kreutzer. When the Nazis came to power, Szpilman returned to Warsaw and embarked on a successful career as a pianist and composer. He partnered the violinists Roman Totenberg, Ida Haendel and Henryk Szeryng, wrote film scores and played the piano on Polish Radio.

After the establishment of the ghetto, he worked as a pianist in restaurants and cafés, performing with the violinist Zygmunt Lederman and in a piano duo with Andrzej Goldfeder. In 1940, he wrote a Piano Concertino, and in 1942 evaded deportation to the extermination camps. Subsequently, he wrote a Mazurka in F minor (steeped in Chopin-esque idioms) to get around the fact that Jewish musicians in the ghetto were forbidden from playing Chopin. He then remained in the ghetto as a construction worker. When the ghetto was closed in May 1943, he went into hiding in the so-called Aryan part of Warsaw with the help of friends at Polish Radio. In November 1944, Wilm Hosenfeld, a captain of the Wehrmacht, discovered him in a building in Niepodległości Avenue; recognising him, he asked Szpilman to play the piano, then gave him food and clothing.

After the war, Szpilman resumed his work at Polish Radio. In addition to his music for radio shows and films, he wrote symphonic pieces, concertos and five hundred popular and children's songs. In 1963, he founded a quintet with Bronislav Gimpel. He died in July 2000. His autobiographical book inspired the film by the same name, *The Pianist*, which was directed by Roman Polanski, himself a survivor of the Kraków ghetto, and which won three Academy Awards in 2003.

Kraków

In contrast to Warsaw's Jewish population of 380,000, a mere 68,000 Jews lived in Kraków (mainly in the Kazimierz district) and in the surrounding area before the war. With the German occupation, the city became the capital of the General Government, Synagogues were ordered to close down and a *Judenrat* and Jewish police corps were established.

In Autumn 1940, over five thousand Kraków Jews were resettled in the Lublin District, while others sought accommodation on the outskirts of the city and approximately fifteen thousand were forcibly employed in the factories built in the ghetto and adjacent areas. By 1941, an estimated 55,000 Jews had been expelled from the city. On 3 March 1941, Otto Gustav Wächter, the governor of the Galizia district, ordered the creation of a new ghetto for the transfer of the Jews who still lived in Kraków, an estimated 15,000. It was set up in the Podgorze area of the city.

From 30 May 1941, *SS-Hauptsturmführer* Wilhelm Kunde ordered the transfer of the Kraków Jews. During the first few days, four thousand Jews were transferred to Bełżec death camp, departing from Plaszów railway station, and hundreds were killed during the process. On 8 June 1942, about seven thousand Jews from Miechów, Jędrzejów, Slomniki and Wieliczka were transferred, together with those from Kraków. Many committed suicide, while the sick and the disabled were killed straight away.

In October 1942, Himmler issued an order to kill those Jews remaining in the city, apart from those needed for forced labour. In December 1942, the ghetto was divided into Ghetto A (those fit for work) and Ghetto B (unfit for work). Both sectors were closed on 13–14 March 1943, in an operation led by Amon Göth, the commander of the Plaszów camp. The last Jews left in the ghetto were moved to Plaszów and Birkenau.

Like the Warsaw ghetto, there were musicians living and working in this ghetto. An example of this is Saul Dreier, discussed later in the book, who, along with his family were interned in the ghetto, but then transferred to Plaszów. Similarly, Mordechai Gebirtig, also known as Markus Bertig, a self-taught flautist and actor, poet and Yiddish language singer–songwriter, published his first book of poems, *Folkstimlekh*, in 1920. In 1936, his friends had his poetry collection, *Mayne Lider*, printed. Politically active in the years between the two world wars, he settled outside Kraków in November 1940, but was sent to the ghetto in March. He and his wife were killed in the street in early June 1942 during a sweep and transfer operation but their daughters survived in hiding. Gebirtig's friend Julian Hoffmann's rescue operation led to the retrieval of Gebirtig's poems and songs, which live on.

SIX

Concentration Camps

Dachau: the Pfarrer-Block

Many churchmen fell from grace after making public statements against National Socialism and the Nazis, or the transformation of religious institutions into temporary SS strongholds, or because of their logistical and moral support for resistance movements and underground newspapers. Most of these men were sent to Block 17 in Dachau and, from December 1940, to Block 26, called 'Pfarrer-Block'. Many were trained musicians and brought with them music.

From 20 January 1941, the camp's authorities allowed religious worship, as well as the establishment of a small chapel for Sunday services. Despite the intervention of religious authorities and of the Holy See, demanding a more humane treatment of clergymen, the latter weren't spared forced labour or show trials for alleged acts of sabotage or espionage and were often sentenced to death. The situation deteriorated further when the clergymen who had first been deported to Sachsenhausen arrived in Dachau.

On 6 October 1943, the German Benedictine monk Gregor (Theodor) Schwake, a composer and poet who had taught liturgical music before the war, was arrested by the Gestapo, during a choral singing class in Linz, for being openly hostile to the

Nazi regime. On 2 January 1944, he was sent to Dachau, where he wrote poetry and various works, including the *Dachauer Messe* for male chorus, brass quartet and organ, known by its Latin title *Missa Dachoviensis*, which was performed in secret on 24 September 1944 in the Pfarrer-Block, probably only to the accompaniment of the harmonium there.

Schwake also wrote 'Regina pacis (Hymnus Dachoviensis)', 'In viam pacis', 'Christkönigfest Jesu Christe' and 'Rex caelorum' for male chorus, 'Ecce sacerdos magnus' for male chorus, written for the ordination of the deacon Karl Leisner (lost), Trio on *O du fröhliche, o du selige* for flute, violin and viola (lost after Schwake's death) and *Ostertrio* for violin, viola and cello (Prelude and Fugue on the melody *Christ ist erstanden*), dated March 1945. Following the liberation, he returned to his native city of Emmerich, wrote other religious pieces and organised a few performances of the *Dachauer Messe*. He died in the Benedictine monastery of Gerleve in June 1967.

The Austrian priest, pianist and organist Josef Moosbauer composed 'O esca viatorum' for male chorus and organ, and church chants (which he had presumably transcribed from memory in Dachau) for voice, male chorus and harmonium accompaniment, including 'Offertorium', 'Segenslied' and 'Marienlied nach der heiligen Kommunion'. To compensate for the absence of scores for harmonium accompaniment at Sunday services in the Pfarrer-Block, Moosbauer wrote *Prelude on 'Ihr Christ, o kommet'*, five postludes and six pieces for harmonium. After the war, he continued with his church ministry in Waldhausen. He died in Bad Mühllacken in August 1979.

On 16 June 1942, the German priest Anton Krähenheide – a pianist, organist and brilliant tenor – was sent to Dachau.

While there, he wrote the *Dachauer Singmesse* in German, for unison male chorus and organ, dated July 1944. He was liberated on 6 April 1945 and died in Hiltrup in May 1974.

During the German occupation, the Moravian priest Karl Schrammel, who had been vice-chancellor of the school of philosophy and theology in 1938 and its chancellor since 10 March 1939, opposed the cession of the Vidnava seminary to the Wehrmacht. On 7 July 1941, he was arrested by the Gestapo, accused of sabotage and jailed in Opava, before being transferred to Dachau on 16 November 1941. He wrote *Locus iste (Graduale für Kirchweih)* for male chorus, conducted the choir of priests and compiled a report on the crimes perpetrated in Dachau by the SS. He tried to get it out of the camp, but the document was intercepted and Schrammel was sentenced to death. He was moved to Buchenwald on 4 December 1944 and hanged there.

In Dachau, the Austrian Jesuit, writer and journalist Johannes Maria (Nepomuk) Lenz wrote *Priesterkameraden in Dachau* for baritone and organ. He was tortured, although eventually liberated on 29 April 1945. He stayed behind in Dachau for a few months to administer pastoral care to the last remaining prisoners. In 1954, he left the Jesuit order in order to become a lay priest. At Pope Pius XII's request, he wrote a book documenting his experience of imprisonment in Mauthausen, Gusen and Dachau. He self-published it in 1956 under the title *Christus in Dachau*; it has had many reprints since and been translated into several languages. Lenz moved to Villach in 1979 and died in July 1985.

The Franciscan Dionysius (Heinrich) Zöhren, superior and rector of the Capuchin monastery at the shrine of Maria

Einsiedel in Gernsheim, was arrested in March 1941 because, while searching the Gernsheim monastery, the Gestapo found some of his blatantly anti-Nazi papers. Transferred to Darmstadt, then, on 2 May 1941, to Dachau, he wrote *Skt. Franciscus* for baritone, male chorus and organ (lost). He died of typhoid fever, in February 1943, in Bergen-Belsen.

Auschwitz III Monowitz

On 6 February 1941, those in charge of the Third Reich's economic development and of the industrial company IG Farben set up a factory for the production of rubber, synthetic fuel and other carboniferous products at the Auschwitz complex in Monowitz (present-day Monowice, in Poland). Both Carl Krauch, the head of IG Farben, and Hermann Göring agreed with Himmler on the construction of the plants and the use of deportees for forced labour.

The industrial zone Buna-Werke (Buna IV) was then created, in which 35,000 deportees were assigned to forced labour, of which 25,000 died without Buna-Werke achieving significant productivity results. The Arbeitslager Auschwitz III Monowitz emerged in the industrial area. Between August and September 1944, the camp was bombed by the US Air Force. It was definitively shut down on 18 January 1945.

An orchestra widely called Buna, chiefly made up of Polish deportee musicians, was formed from the very opening of Monowitz. For a short time, the members of the orchestra were exempted from forced labour. The amateur Norwegian trumpeter Herman Sachnowitz, who survived, reports that, the orchestra would play as workers left for and returned from work, as well as during ceremonies and executions, which would generally take place on a Sunday afternoon or evening.

At the same time, a plethora of musical performances and traditional Jewish poetry evenings blossomed, which were open to writers, actors, journalists and teachers from various countries, as well as concerts organised and performed by Jewish deportees. A violinist called Jakob 'Zigan' would play and the Polish actor Moyshe Potashinski – a former member of the Vilner Troupe in the Vilnius ghetto – staged theatre pieces and sang Yiddish songs by Itzik Manger and Mordechai Gebirtig.

In January 1945, the Buna orchestra was disbanded and musical activity ceased as the camp was closed and various members were transferred to Bergen-Belsen. After its liberation, some surviving musicians got back together, using the few remaining instruments, and played the US, British, French and Soviet national anthems as a homage to Allied troops.

In 1913, Fritz Löhner-Beda met Franz Lehár, for whom he wrote the libretto for the operetta *Der Sterngucker* in 1916; he was one of the most sought-after librettists, lyricists, writers and musical authors in Vienna. Following the Anschluss, Löhner-Beda was arrested and sent first to Dachau, then Buchenwald; with his fellow inmate, Hermann Leopoldi, he wrote the *Buchenwalder Lagerlied*; in 1942 he was transferred from Buchenwald to Monowitz, where his wife and daughters were killed in the gas chambers.

In Monowitz, between October and November 1942, he wrote the hymn 'Bunalied' for male chorus. In December of that year, during an inspection by managers of IG Farben, Löhner-Beda, already ill, was accused of being unproductive at work and beaten to death by a *kapo*.

Buchenwald: Leo Kok

The pianist and composer Leo Kok was born in Amsterdam to a Jewish mother and studied with Willem Pijper at the Koninklijk Conservatorium in The Hague. A staunch pacifist, he was interned in Den Helder during the First World War, then worked in Berlin, playing and composing with the dancers Lili Green and Charlotte Bara. From 1925 to 1927, he wrote *Trois danses exotiques* and *Enfance* for piano and *Chanson pour les enfants qui n'ont pas de Noël* for violin and piano. When the Nazis came to power, he left for London to be trained as a spy. Following the German occupation of France, he joined the resistance. The Parisian publisher Guy Lévis helped him hide in Paris. On 24 January 1944, he was arrested, sent to Buchenwald and tortured, but he managed to conceal the fact that he was Jewish. After Buchenwald was liberated, Kok stayed behind to attend a funeral service in memory of the 56,000 prisoners who had been killed, conducting 'The Death of Åse' from Grieg's *Peer Gynt* suite. As his wrists and fingers had been permanently damaged by the torture he'd endured, he had to give up his piano playing career. In 1946, Kok settled in Ascona and opened a bookshop, the *Libreria della Rondine*, which he ran until 1979. He died on 7 August 1992.

Bergen-Belsen: Pinkhof, Heilbut, Gosschalk

The Dutch-Jewish musician Józef Zvi Pinkhof was transferred to the Sternlager of Bergen-Belsen, where he arranged the traditional chants *Shabath hamalkah* and *Parpar* for two recorders and male chorus to texts by Haim Nahman Bialik and *Scharchoret* for male chorus. He wrote down the musical score of some parts of the Shabbat ritual, with the Hebrew text transliterated according to Ashkenazi pronunciation. He died in early January 1945.

The Dutch composer Robert Emanuel Heilbut was transferred to Westerbork and, in 1943, to Bergen-Belsen. In these camps, he wrote a *Muziekboekje*, arrangements of Dutch songs, pieces for one or two guitars, *Hatikvah* for male chorus and pages of study notes for guitar. We have thirty-one pieces out of the forty listed on page two of the *Muziekboekje*. He boarded the last train from Bergen-Belsen and died on 19 April 1945 between Finsterwalde and Falkenberg/Elster.

The Dutch nurse and amateur musician Robert Marcel Gosschalk was sent to Bergen-Belsen with his parents and brother Martijn. He wrote the song 'Wir singen ein Schlager' to a popular Dutch tune and his own text in German and Dutch. Boarding the last train from Bergen-Belsen, he survived the journey but died of typhus on 26 April 1945 in Tröbitz. According to information from the Dutch Red Cross, he is buried in a mass grave, dug in a former Hansa lignite mine, south of Tröbitz.

Ravensbrück: Peškařová, Tillion and others

Ludmila Peškařová was arrested by the Gestapo in May 1943 and transferred to Brno-Cejl prison, then to Ravensbrück. She wrote over a hundred lieder, choral pieces and poems inspired by patriotism, religion or dedicated to her native Moravia, as well as carols for the Christmas of 1944.

We should particularly mention *V tom Ravensbrücku, Černe vlajky* (written as an emotional response to the failed attack on the Führer in 1944), *Wigilijna kołysanka z Ravensbrück* (in two versions, on the testimony of the Polish deportee Jadwiga Chmurkovska of Poznań), the choral pieces *Píseň 14. září 1944 – k duchu T.G.M.* (dedicated to the first president of Czechoslovakia Tomáš Masaryk on the seventh anniversary of his death) and *Largo z IX. Symfonie 'z Nového světa'* (based on the Largo from Dvořák's Symphony No. 9). Freed in April 1945, during the summer of the same year, she scored the musical material composed in captivity, adding a piano accompaniment.

Between 1934 and 1940, the ethnologist Germaine Tillion was in Algeria, studying the Chaoui people, a Berber ethnic group, but the day after the Franco-German Armistice, she returned to France and assumed the role of leader of the resistance group at the Musée de l'Homme in Paris from 1941 to 1942. On 13 August 1942, she was arrested, after being betrayed by the French collaborator priest Robert Alesch, and was transferred to Ravensbrück on 21 October 1943. There, she wrote the operetta-revue *Le Verfügbar aux Enfers*, an alternation of texts, music and arias from French opera and popular repertory. Her mother, Émilie, was gassed, but Tillion survived, devoting herself to study and research in North Africa and the Middle East.

Among the women who created original music or parodies in Ravensbrück, we should also mention the Soviet Zina, known as Zinaida – we know only her first name – who in 1942 wrote 'Ravensbrücklied' on a Russian tune, and many Polish women, among them Anna Burdówna, Jadwiga Szalan-Kopijowska, Irena Mróz Gadomska-Szabłowska (known as Zosia), and Wanda Filochowska (Orlicz-Dreszerowa).

The Italian writer and anti-Fascist fighter Mara Montuoro, who was moved from the prison of San Vittore in Milan to the Fossoli transit camp and, finally, to Ravensbrück, wrote *Compagni, per l'aspro sentiero* and the previously mentioned Italian version for female choir of the 'Canto dei deportati' based on the previously mentioned 'Die Moorsoldaten' by Rudi Goguel. After the war, she wrote short stories and poems. She died in Milan in 2000.

Towards the end of 1944, Dutch Resistance fighters Henriëtte Voûte and Gisela Söhnlein were transferred from Herzogenbusch to Ravensbrück. They were of great moral support to their fellow prisoners. They exchanged information and poetry to be set to music using the pen names Piglet and Pooh, clearly inspired by the stories of A. A. Milne. They also wrote the songs 'Wir bleiben guten Mutes', based on 'Wir lagen vor Madagaskar' by Just Scheu, 'Das Kapo-Lied', based on 'Daar bij die Molen' by Willy Derby, 'Unsere Laus hat Nissen bekommen', based on a Dutch popular tune, 'De Rode Kruis bussen', derived from the Dutch children's song 'Dorus was een Man van 80 Jaren'. After the war, they published their songs and, in 1988, Yad Vashem, Israel's official memorial to the victims of the Holocaust, conferred on them both the title of Righteous Among the Nations.

SEVEN

Heil, Sachsenhausen!

Sachsenhausen

On 12 July 1936, the Reich opened Sachsenhausen/Oranienburg concentration camp, thirty-five kilometres north of Berlin, where German civilians, Poles, Soviet prisoners of war and Jews were transferred for internment. In addition, 1,200 homosexuals were transferred there and subjected to brutal torture and systematic killings by the SS. Many deportees were the victims of brutal medical experiments. They were also forced to do hard labour: factories owned by AEG, Brabag, Daimler-Benz, DAW, DEST, Heinkel, IG Farben, Krupp and Siemens sprang up in the surrounding area. In 1941, however, a programme was launched to eliminate Soviet prisoners of war and, from December 1944, there was a sharp rise in killings of deportees evacuated due to the advance of Soviet troops. On 22 April 1945, Soviet troops liberated the camp.

In Sachsenhausen, German political prisoners with varying musical skills created a repertory of hymns and songs. In 1942, a collective notebook was compiled, containing songs written and performed in the camp, as well as song lyrics full of beautiful drawings (including some caricatures about daily life in captivity) – with or without the tune written on a stave – and images of musical events.

In the sub-camp of Demag Panzerwerke in Falkensee, the Polish Jewish musician and composer Ludwik Żuk-Skarszewski, who had come from Birkenau, set up and conducted the camp orchestra and, in April 1945, wrote 'Pieśń Obozowa', based on a text by Zbigniew Koczanowicz. In Block 39, the Polish choir master and composer Rosebery d'Arguto (born Martin Rosenberg) formed and conducted a male choir of thirty. It was not the only one: between 1942 and 1943 Jan Dunst, a Polish musician from Gdańsk, also conducted a male choir of thirty.

Homosexuals in Sachsenhausen

The Nazis considered homosexuality degenerate behaviour and thousands of lesbian and gay people were detained. Most were jailed, where they received brutal treatment, but between 10–15,000 people accused of being homosexual were deported to camps such as Sachsenhausen. In 1924, the singer, parodist and stand-up comedian Paul O'Montis (born Paul Wendel), a Hungarian Jew and homosexual who grew up in Hanover, moved to Berlin and, in 1926, took part in the revue *The Magic Lantern* by Friedrich Holländer. A specialist in *Nonsensschlager* (a song style filled with wordplay and homosexual double entendres), he performed songs like 'Was hast du für Gefühle', 'Moritz', 'Ich bin verrückt nach Hilde' and 'Ramona Zündloch', and wrote lyrics for the Jewish songs 'Ghetto' (1923) and 'Kaddisch' (1925).

When the Nazis came to power, he moved to Vienna, then to Prague. In June 1940, he was arrested by the Gestapo and transferred to Sachsenhausen, where, after being degraded and humiliated by the camp's authorities, he hanged himself in July 1940.

The German stand-up comedian, pianist, writer and composer

Robert T. Odeman (Martin Hoyer), meanwhile, was arrested in 1937 and sentenced to twenty-seven months, which he served in various Berlin prisons, including the Plötzensee prison in Charlottenburg. Arrested again in 1942 and transferred to Sachsenhausen, he managed to escape with other homosexual prisoners during a forced march to the Baltic Sea in April 1945.

The *Bibelforscher* and Eric Frost

The International Bible Students (Jehovah's Witnesses since 26 July 1931) were the followers of a Christian religious movement founded in 1870 by the US preacher Charles Taze Russell, which had its official base in the Watchtower Society in Brooklyn. The *Bibelforscher* of the Third Reich were Europe's largest community of Jehovah's Witnesses. They were discriminated against chiefly because of their avoidance of compulsory military service, reintroduced in Germany in 1935, their refusal to work in the arms industry and to recognise the authority of the Reich and adhere to Nazi symbology (such as saluting the Führer and the Reich flag or enrolling their children in the Hitler Youth). About 10,000 *Bibelforscher* were sent to concentration camps in the Reich metropolitan area and two hundred and fifty were killed. Three thousand of them, from Austria, Belgium, Czechoslovakia, Holland, Norway and Poland, were deported above all for refusing to recant. Many were tortured, and 1,650 consequently died.

In 1919, Eric Hugo Frost started studying piano and composition in his native city of Leipzig; his mother converted to the *Bibelforscher* doctrine and, in 1923, both he and his father also embraced this new faith. He suspended his music studies and, in 1924, the Watchtower Society conferred on him the role of overseer at the book depository of their Leipzig congregation. From 1928, he worked on the German and Czech distribution and exhibition of the religious film *Photo-Drama der Schöpfung*, produced by the International Bible Student Association, for which he composed the soundtrack.

Frost was also a musical accompanist to silent movies in Szczecin and proselytised with his congregation, partly in response to the discriminatory policies towards the *Bibelforscher* decreed by the Third Reich in April 1933. Arrested but released after ten days, he emigrated to Czechoslovakia. In May 1935, he returned to Germany, where he found work on the construction of the Berlin metro. On 13 June 1935, he was arrested and sent to Columbia concentration camp, in Tempelhof, for five months. On 27 March 1937, he was arrested by the Gestapo and transferred to Esterwegen and finally sent to Sachsenhausen, where he was assigned to obligatory work.

In the camp, he gave concerts for the guards and, in spring 1941, created the hymn 'Fest steht in großer, schwerer Zeit' for male chorus, which the composer and other fellow worshippers learnt by heart, one verse each, and which he wrote down on a sheet of paper he then concealed in a rabbit cage in the camp. This paper was secretly sent to some of his fellow worshippers in Switzerland, and from there on to the headquarters of the Watchtower Society in Brooklyn. In Sachsenhausen, he also wrote the hymn 'Welch ein Duften durch das Land zieht'.

In June 1940, the Wehrmacht occupied the Channel Islands. On the northern island of Alderney, the Third Reich opened four concentration and forced labour camps that were technically satellites to Neuengamme concentration camp. In late July 1941, he was transferred to Neuengamme, and, in 1943, he wrote the hymn 'Wolkengedunkel' for male chorus and organ. Frost was transferred to Alderney, in 1943, and co-opted by the *SS-Baubrigade* in the forced labour sub-camp Albany, where he wrote a *Kampflied*, or battle song, for male chorus. Liberated on 5 May 1945, he returned to Germany and became the head of the Watchtower Society in Magdeburg until 30 August 1950, when the congregation was banned by the GDR.

Moving to Wiesbaden, Frost was at the centre of a smear campaign, presumably ordered by the Stasi, concerning his alleged collaboration with the Gestapo in Sachsenhausen, though many of his hymns were still performed during this period at Watchtower Society congresses.

In 1950, the hymn 'Fest steht' was translated into English, with the title 'Forward, You Witnesses', and published with partial changes to the original text in the *Jehovah's Witness New Songbook* in the United States, as well as in many other languages in the service book used by the movement worldwide. Frost died in Lübeck in October 1987.

EIGHT

Poland

Łódź

In April 1940, in the north-western area of Łódź, the Nazis opened the largest ghetto in occupied or incorporated Polish territory, second only to Warsaw. Approximately 250,000 civilians were brought together in this ghetto, including 160,000 Jews and 5,000 Romas, who were assigned to a fenced-off sector outside the ghetto itself.

In December 1941, Jews and Romas – mainly those who were sick, the elderly and children – began being transferred to Chełmno extermination camp. By May 1942, almost a third of the ghetto's population had been eliminated. Continuing until April 1943, a thousand people a day were handed over by the *Judenrat* to the German authorities. However, in 1943, the ghetto was turned into a labour camp for 75,000 inhabitants and in the summer of 1944 *SS-Obergruppenführer* Arthur Greiser closed it; the remaining population moved to Chełmno and Auschwitz.

The cultural heart of the Łódź ghetto was the House of Culture theatre, inaugurated on 1 March 1941 by the president of the *Judenrat*, Chaim Rumkowski. Organised professionally, and equipped with lighting and four hundred seats, the House of Culture hosted over a hundred concerts and stage productions until summer 1942, when the building was turned into a blanket and pillow factory. From then on, concerts took place in private homes or in the headquarters of the ghetto newspaper, although in 1944 this was made all the more difficult when all the musical instruments were confiscated by the German authorities.

The pianist and conductor Teodor Ryder was a pillar of musical activity in the House of Culture, He moved to Łódź in 1918, having been deputy musical director at Lyon opera house and conductor of the Warsaw Philharmonc Orchestra. Ryder conducted the Łódz Philharmonic and notably met the German soprano Idę Voth, whom he married after she converted to Judaism.

They were both transferred to the ghetto in March 1940 and finally deported to Birkenau in Autumn 1944. Ryder died a few months later.

Another key player on the Łódź ghetto music scene was the Yiddish-language violinist, conductor and composer Dawid Bajgelman. Born to a family of musicians, Bajgelman had composed and staged shows in Yiddish since he was a boy. He played in the orchestra of Zandberg theatre and worked at the revue theatre Ararat in 1928. He wrote the music for the Yiddish operettas *Dos Skoytn-meydl* and *Di mume Gnendil* by Julius Adler, and *Di Sheyne Berta* by Yankev Vaksman, and did the arrangements for *Der dybbuk oder zwishn zwei weltn* by Sholem Ansky, as well as for operettas by Abraham Goldfaden. In 1940, Bajgelman was moved to the ghetto, where he wrote the songs 'Kinder yorn', 'Tsigaynerlid', 'Makh tsu di eygelekh' and 'Nisht keyn rozhinkes, nisht keyn mandlen'. He also conducted the music for a Yiddish-language theatre workshop by the choral group Hazamir.

In August 1944, he was transferred to Auschwitz; he is presumed to have taken his violin and scores with him. He was then relocated to an unidentified forced labour camp. He died in February 1945.

In 1940, Jankiel 'Jakub' Herszkowicz, a tailor by trade, a composer and troubadour by inclination, was sent to the ghetto. During the final months of 1941, Herszkowicz began performing in a duo with the Viennese amateur violinist and travelling salesman Karol Rosenzweig, who would accompany him on the guitar or the harp.

The popular tunes, parodies and satirical songs he wrote did not attack the German occupation but the *Judenrat*, which consequently often censored his shows, and finally prohibited his street performances in June 1943. In the ghetto, Herszkowicz wrote *Hungermarsh,* about the spring 1940 revolt, and the satirical songs 'Kartofl', dedicated to potatoes, and 'Rumkovski Khayim', attacking the president of the *Judenrat.* In September 1942, his parents and younger brother were deported along with 15,000 Jews to Chełmno death camp, where they were murdered. In August 1944, he was sent to Birkenau.

Born in Frankfurt in 1877, the German composer and organist Siegfried Würzburger founded a private music school with his pianist wife Gertrude Hirsch and organised the festival *Jugend musiziert,* which focused on promising young Jewish talent. Until *Kristallnacht,* he was organist at the Frankfurt Synagogue. After the Nazis came to power, Würzburger's work was drastically cut down and he could not emigrate because of his advanced state of blindness. On 19 October 1941, he, his wife and their son, Mayre Hans, were moved to the Łódź ghetto, where he died from cold and exhaustion in February

1942. His wife died in Chełmno, and all traces of their son, Hans, were lost. His work lives on. We have Würzburger's organ works *Passacaglia on Moauszur* and *Passacaglia and Fugue on Kol Nidrei*.

On 28 September 1939, the cantor Yisroel Sabiner was sent to the Łódź ghetto. He wrote *nigunim* (typically Hassidic collective religious Jewish chants) and led vocal ensemble Gerer Hasidim. He died in September 1940 when synagogues were set on fire a few days before Yom Kippur.

Oflag IID

Oflag IID Gross-Born was opened by the Reich in 1940. There, Polish prisoners of war published newspapers and organised art and music, educational and sporting events. In October 1944, Polish officers were interned who had fought in the Armia Krajowa during the Warsaw uprising.

In the oflag there were significant initial difficulties in organising musical events because of a lack of instruments and the rigid division of the camp into blocks; consequently, it was considered more appropriate to set up choirs to accompany Sunday services. Eventually, these choirs widened their repertoire to include secular music; in every block the choir masters reconstructed choral pieces from memory.

The first concerts were played mainly on the piano, since there were no other instruments; in late 1940, the Frenchman Christian Verdeau gave, in Block III, a recital of contemporary music entirely from memory, without scores.

Thanks to money and materials being sent from the home to help buy or hire musical instruments, every block was finally able to obtain scores and instruments and form small orchestras and chamber ensembles. In March 1941, permission was obtained from the German authorities to move freely between the blocks, and the French prisoners of war formed a sixty-piece orchestra that gave fifteen concerts in two years.

In both oflags, French and Polish prisoners fraternised. French musicians and actors also took part in Polish theatrical, symphonic and concerts events until mid 1942, when the German authorities separated the groups of prisoners in order to obtain more homogenous nationalities in the respective oflags.

Georges Flageollet orchestrated an *Élégie* composed before the war and wrote *Nocturne* and *Triptyque*; a certain Blanchard wrote a *Suite gasconne* and a *Messe de joie pour une fête triste*.

From 1919 to 1931, Paul Louis Challine had been an organist at Orléans Cathedral, and studied instrumentation and orchestration at the École Normale de Musique in Paris. In June 1940, he was imprisoned and interned in Oflag IIB Arnswalde. On 28 July 1940 he played the piano in a recital of Romantic music in Block II; he conducted the Francophone orchestra, wrote the musical comedy *La Reine s'ennuie*, a violin sonata, incidental music for *Fabliau*, a quartet for violin, clarinet, cello and piano, a flute quintet and a violin concerto. Subsequently interned in Oflag IID Gross-Born, he formed the Petit Ensemble Challine. After the war, he won the title 'Secretary of the Conference' at the Conférence des Avocats and embarked on a law career, although he continued composing. He died in February 1994.

Lech Karol Bursa conducted operas and operettas in Kraków, Bydgoszcz and Łódź, as well as being conductor at the regiment 19 Pułk Piechoty in Lviv. At the outbreak of the war, he was captured and interned in Oflag IIB Arnswalde and became musical director of the Teatr Symbolów. He wrote *Msza polowa*, op. 54, for male chorus and wind instruments (missing) and *Polska suita żołnierska*, op. 55, for male chorus and symphony orchestra. In 1942, Bursa was transferred to

Oflag IID Gross-Born; he wrote the *Rapsodia bałkańska*, op. 56, for baritone, male chorus and orchestra (missing), a violin concerto, op. 66, and *Taka sobie bajeczka*, op. 67, for orchestra. Transferred to Oflag IIC Woldenberg in 1944, he conducted the choir and orchestra, wrote *Misterium wielkopostne*, op. 71, *Misterium wigilijne*, op. 72 (both missing) and *Regina coeli*, op. 73, for male chorus.

On 29 January 1945, the oflag was closed and the prisoners transferred to Stalag XB Sandbostel. There were links between Stalag XB and its adjacent camp, XA. The year before, in 1944, Spartaco Lemmetti, an internee at the adjacent camp, Stalag XA, had drawn a musician playing the violin as though he were playing the cello. Certain instruments were in short supply at the camps and musicians improvised and adapted to create their music. That particular man was Giuseppe Selmi, who played at a concert holding the violin like a cello, since cellos were not available but were sometimes were lent by the French prisoners of war interned at Stalag XB.

Selmi studied cello with Ercole Brettagna, Enrico Mainardi and Pablo Casals, perfected his skills at the Accademia nazionale di Santa Cecilia in Rome and became principal cellist of the Rome radio orchestra. Imprisoned, he was interned in Stalag 328/Z Tarnopol, and, like other musicians I've focused on, began to write original works in the most horrific of conditions, including *Triste canto (Dolore e rassegnazione)* for cello and piano and the suite *Scene infantili* for cello and piano. In October 1943, he began outlining the structure of *Concerto Spirituale* for cello and orchestra, drafted in small notebooks to escape the notice of the German authorities; he finalised it at Stalag XA.

After the war, Selmi became principal cellist at the RAI Symphony Orchestra in Rome and taught at the Accademia

Santa Cecilia, embarking on an international concert career. He wrote teaching materials, chamber music and transcriptions. In 1952, *Concerto Spirituale* won the top prize in the G. B. Viotti international competition in Vercelli (composition section).

Białystok

Sent to the Białystok ghetto with her family on 1 August 1941, Rena Hass wrote, during the winter of 1942–3, the love songs 'Przed ostatnią podróżą' and 'Pesnya Belostokskikh Partizanov'.

After the ghetto was closed down, she and her family were relocated to Lublin-Majdanek. Her father, Adolf Hass, a violinist, was killed in November 1943 after being forced to play with the Lublin-Majdanek orchestra. Her mother, Ernestyna, a teacher, was transferred to Bergen-Belsen in January 1945, where she died of starvation shortly before the camp was liberated. Hass was moved to the forced labour camp of Bliżyn, then to Birkenau and, finally, to the Lippstadt women's forced labour camp, a sub-camp of Buchenwald.

In March 1945, having contracted typhus, Hass was taken by German guards, placed in a queue with other deportees and submitted to a death march to Bergen-Belsen. US troops freed her on 15 April 1945 from Kaunitz, a sub-camp of Buchenwald. After studying medicine in Heidelberg, Germany, in May 1946 she boarded the USS *Marine Perch* and emigrated to the United States. There, she got married and became a biology teacher at the Bronx High School of Science in New York. She collected her memoirs in the book *Revisiting the Shadows*.

*   *   *

After the First World War, the musicologist and journalist Pesach Kaplan founded the newspaper *Das Neie Leben* in Białystok. Following the German occupation in September 1939, he was transferred to the Białystok ghetto. Appointed head of the Education Department of the *Judenrat*, he devoted himself to championing and spreading schooling and cultural activities. An amateur musician, he translated into Yiddish a collection of lieder by Mendelssohn-Bartholdy, Schubert and Schumann, as well as songs for Jewish orphanages, and the song cycle in Hebrew, *Nevel Azor*. In addition, he wrote the music and lyrics for the chant 'Rivkele di shabesdike' about the Aktion of July 1941 in Białystok. He fell ill during the ghetto massacres of February 1943 and, emotionally devastated, died in March 1943. In an unprecedented act, the *Judenrat* held a solemn funeral in his honour.

Janowska and Lviv

Janowska was a labour, transit and concentration camp opened by the Third Reich in September 1941, in the north-western suburbs of Lviv, and entrusted to the care of the Trawniki Men (Eastern European Nazi collaborators) and volunteer Soviet prisoners of war.

In early June 1943, the Germans closed the Lviv ghetto. The Jews considered fit for work were transferred to Janowska, while others were either deported to Bełżec or thrown into the Piaski Ravine north of the camp.

Many testimonies about the musical life of Janowska concern songs that accompanied the prisoners' march to forced labour, with the *Brandmeister* walking at the head, dressed like a devil in a peculiar uniform, holding a hook, sometimes accompanied to the music of an orchestra that played in a circle around the conductor in the camp's parade ground. There were some excellent Jewish instrumentalists in Lviv before the war, including violinist, conductor and composer Leonid Stricks and cellist Leon Eber.

On the German authorities' request, the conductor and composer Jakub Mund – formerly director of the Lviv opera house – arranged *Todestango* by Eduardo Bianco for the camp orchestra – to be played during selections, mass firing squad executions and beatings. In 1943, before the camp was liberated, the guards gathered the orchestra for a final concert, shooting at them as they played.

In 1932, writer, satirist, translator, composer and singer-songwriter Emanuel Schlechter (also known as Olgierd Lech) moved from Lviv to Warsaw. A famous cabaret author, his song, 'Nie ja, nie', was translated into French and performed by Édith Piaf. Before the outbreak of the war, pieces from his theatrical repertoire satirising Nazism were well known. Following the German and Soviet invasion of Poland, he took refuge in Lviv – then under Soviet occupation – working at the Miniatura Theatre as an actor, playwright and director, but in June 1941, after the Germans occupied Ukraine, he was transferred to the Lviv ghetto and from there to Janowska, where he was a leader of the artistic life of the camp and organised literary soirées. It is believed he died in 1942, with his wife and son.

The composer and musicologist Józef Koffler, one of the avant-garde, twelve-tone composers on the Polish musical scene, studied from 1918 to 1924 with Paul Graener and Felix Weingartner, and from 1921 to 1924 in Vienna with Arnold Schoenberg. In 1923, he graduated in musicology with Guido Adler at the University of Vienna. From 1928 to 1941, he taught at the Lviv conservatoire and obtained a first-time tenure in twelve-tone composition at the Academy of Music in the town.

After the German occupation of Poland, he and his wife were taken to the Wieliczka ghetto, where he remained until its closure on 28 August 1942. He was killed in early 1944 in Ojców, following raids by the *Einsatzgruppen* (Mobile Killing Units). Many of his works were lost or destroyed, but we still have, among others, the cantata *Miłość*, op. 14, the ballet-oratorio *Alles durch M.O.W.*, op. 15, and four symphonies.

Pawiak: the 1944 uprising

In the days immediately following the German occupation of Poland, many Polish composers were imprisoned in Pawiak prison, which fell under the jurisdiction of the Warsaw concentration camp. Those internees were often suspected of engaging in political activity hostile to Nazism or else considered members of Polish resistance organisations; many underwent lengthy and exhausting interrogations and torture by the Gestapo.

In 1940, Roman Palester was arrested and imprisoned in Pawiak but released six weeks later; many of his works were destroyed during the Warsaw ghetto uprising in 1944. The composer Ludomir Marczak concealed thirteen Jews in his Warsaw apartment; he was arrested on 25 November 1943, imprisoned in Pawiak and then executed with his family and the Jews he had been harbouring.

The composer and writer Lech Miklaszewski was imprisoned in Pawiak in 1940 as well but was released eighteen months later. From 1941 to 1944, he gave clandestine performances at Cafè Dom Sztuki. The pianist and composer Bolesław Woytowicz was arrested on 22 May 1943 and jailed in Pawiak, then released after a month.

On 7 April 1944, the stage actor, director and composer

Wacław Gajdziński was arrested in Warsaw by the Gestapo. Held in Pawiak and transferred to Stutthof, he died in February 1945. The priest and composer Wacław Gieburowski, choir master at Poznań Cathedral, was arrested by the Gestapo in October 1939. Transferred to Warsaw in 1941, he died in September 1943. In 1939, the composer Jan Sztwiertnia was about to leave for Paris, thanks to a scholarship, when the war broke out; arrested by the Gestapo in June 1940, he died in Mauthausen-Gusen.

From August to October 1944, many Polish musicians fought during the Warsaw Uprising. The composer Roman Padlewski was with the Broda 53 partisan brigade. Some of his works were lost during the war, including his 1944 violin concerto. Seriously wounded in combat on 14 August 1944, he died in hospital two days later.

During the uprising, the conductor, pianist and composer Bronisław Wolfstahl was also killed. Conductor and composer Andrzej Markowski fought, too, but was captured, after which he was transferred to Oflag VII A Murnau am Staffelsee. The pianist and composer of Czech-Spanish descent Stefania Allinówna was arrested in the aftermath of the Warsaw Uprising and sent to an unidentified forced labour camp. Then sixteen-year-old composition student Tadeusz Baird, meanwhile, was captured and sent to Germany as a forced labourer; his failed attempt at escaping saw him sent to a concentration camp. Upon being liberated by the Americans, he spent a long time recovering in hospital before returning to Poland.

NINE

Italian Military Internees

Salvatore Musella and Pietro Maggioli

Following the Armistice of Cassabile, between Italy and the Allies, of 3 September 1943, Nazi forces, stationed in Italy and its colonies, arrested hundreds and thousands of Italians and transferred them to internment camps in German territories. From 20 September 1943 onwards, they downgraded these Italian prisoners of war to the category of Italian Military Internees (IMI), thus removing them from the protection and guarantees stipulated by international conventions regarding prisoners of war. From 20 July 1944, the IMI were used as labour to support the German war machine.

Among the IMI was music professor and composer Salvatore Musella who, in 1938, moved to Milan from Buenos Aires, where he was the artistic director of Buenos Aires radio. He enlisted as a captain, was imprisoned following the Armistice and sent to Stalag 307 Deblin-Irena, where he reconstructed meticulously from memory scores by Grieg and Bach on the backs of envelopes and such. In January 1944, he was transferred to Stalag 333 Benjaminow, where he held lectures on the history of music, the history of the organ and bells, conducted orchestral concerts and choral ensembles, increasing morale among his peer internees, and accompanied Sunday worship. He also wrote an opera in three acts and an epilogue, *Il Fabbricatore di Dio*, to a libretto by Alfonso Mongiardini. He died on 3 March 1944, and is buried in the Italian military cemetery of Bielany (Warsaw).

Among the other musicians interned with Musella in Stalag 333 Benjaminow after the Armistice was Pietro Maggioli. In 1935, he had taken up the position of organist at the principal church in Pesaro, then moved to Rovereto, where he won tenure. During his internment, he conducted a concert of his own arrangements of works by Grechaninov, Schumann, Rodrigo and Verdi. Transferred to Stalag XB Sandbostel, he wrote *Cantico delle creature* and *Preghiera del prigioniero*, both for soloists, male chorus and orchestra, and *Missa captivorum* for male chorus. In Wietzendorf, he wrote *Tarantella 'e notte* and *'Na stella* for tenor and piano. After the war, he returned to Rovereto, and in 1952 moved to Rome, where he died in 1963.

I was searching, in particular, for *Cantico delle creature*. A check through the telephone directory suggested the composer might be from Romagna. In actual fact, he was born in Milan in 1907. And there were not many traces left from his job as organist in Pesaro. New information then shifted the direction of my research to Rovereto, where Maggioli had written works now stored in the National Central Library of Florence. But despite my numerous attempts, I could find no trace of either his family or of the *Cantico delle creature*.

One day, however, I discovered a Diego Maggioli residing in Rome in the telephone directory. I called him and learnt that he was Pietro's son. The bad news was that during a house move, Diego had misplaced the handwritten version of the *Cantico*. In such circumstances, when your musician's soul feels despondent, your researcher's soul has to rationalise the failure of months of work: recrimination is pointless. It was no one's fault. I simply tried to see if other sources could somehow be retrieved, and Diego proved to be very helpful.

He told me that the *Cantico* had been performed in 1952 by the RAI Symphony Orchestra of Turin, while the *Preghiera del prigioniero* seems to have been played in 1956 by the RAI Symphony Orchestra of Rome.

I knew that after its symphony orchestras (except for the one in Turin) had been disbanded, all the RAI music archives had been relocated to Turin. The manager informed me, however, that the pre-1960 archives had not been computerised and that you had to search by hand, which could take weeks or months. But then he called me back ten days later to tell me that he had found the voice and piano reduction of *Cantico delle creature*. It was not the score, but it was so much better than nothing: it is a beautiful work, sacred in the most sublime sense of the word.

Giovannino Guareschi and Arturo Coppola

Following the Armistice, Arturo Coppola, a graduate of the Naples conservatoire, was captured in Dubrovnik in former Yugoslavia (today Croatia) and sent to the stalags of Tschenstochau and Benjaminow, where he became friends with Giovannino Guareschi, who later found fame as a journalist, cartoonist and humourist – in particular as the creator of *The Little World of Don Camillo*.

Guareschi and Coppola arrived in Sandbostel on 2 April 1944. Coppola would often accompany his friend's stories on an accordion lent to him by a fellow soldier. Guareschi wrote song lyrics, then passed them on to Coppola to set to music. That is how we came to have the songs 'Magri ma sani' and 'Carlotta', the humorous choral march 'Dai dai Bepin' and the masterpiece *La Favola di Natale*, for narrator, male chorus and orchestra, completed between 17 and 19 December 1944. The narrator was Guareschi, even though some sources wrongly indicate Gianrico Tedeschi.

La Favola di Natale is a successful melodic invention associated with fairy-tale characters and objects, as well as with a very Italian taste for re-creating a typical Christmas atmosphere. It was highlighted by the sound of an ocarina (a type of flute) and orchestrated for the musical instruments that were available – the ocarina, the oboe, two clarinets, an accordion and a string orchestra, with the addition of a Foley artist who used his voice to perform stage effects and eventful passages. It was performed on 24, 26 and 27 December 1944 at the stalag's little theatre, on 31 December 1944 in hut 13B and, finally, on 10 January 1945 in hut 31A. Some performances had only Coppola playing the accordion for accompaniment.

Venturing to Roncole Verdi, a district of Busseto, and birthplace of Giuseppe Verdi, means accessing the literary and fairy-tale world of Giovannino Guareschi's *Little World*, plunging into smells and colours such as only stretches of Emilian land can bestow on a pilgrim, and searching for *La Favola di Natale* became almost secondary. Paolo Candido and I went from Barletta to Busseto, getting on and off countless trains, arriving when it was almost evening on the Friday.

Our hotel was on the other side of town, and we walked down the whole length of the avenue that led to it from the station. We planned to move on to Roncole Verdi on the Sunday morning. Only there was a problem: there were no buses between Busseto and Roncole that day. I left the hotel early in the morning, while the devout Paolo was already out looking for a church to attend his Sunday Mass, and waited for him under grey skies. Calling a taxi from some town or other turned out to be unfeasible, so in the end we decided to go from Busseto to Roncole Verdi . . . on foot. We walked at the side of the road in the rain until a kind lady gave us a lift in her car. When we reached Roncole Verdi, she dropped us off outside Giovannino Guareschi's house. An almost covered-up sign saying *Restaurant* reminded us that the writer had opened one in his large house many years earlier. His son, Alberto, welcomed us at the entrance. He was, in fact, the famous Albertino from the *Favola di Natale*, written in Sandbostel.

Guareschi's work, set to music by Coppola, is a masterpiece that has been unfairly kept off the posters in major theatres, even though it is worthy of being featured alongside masterpieces like Prokofiev's *Peter and the Wolf*.

Alberto took us to the archive to meet his sister, Carlotta, the protagonist of the song named after her, which Guareschi wrote in the stalag, set to music by Arturo Coppola, and dedicated to his daughter, born while he was interned. During our exchange of letters, Carlotta had warned me: 'Don't think you'll get out of it, Francesco, you have to continue his work.'

Here we had Guareschi's entire story in one room: his papers, Albertino from *La Favola di Natale* and Carlotta from the song, the world of Don Camillo and Peppone, a huge picture of Fernandel as Don Camillo and the great Gino Cervi as Mayor Peppone. It evoked images of those films, of Bassa and the village of Brescello, where the screen adaptations were shot.

Alberto opened a few folders for us and we found everything in them, even the posters of Pietro Maggioli's *Cantico delle creature*. We discovered that the poster erroneously called it *Cantico dei Cantici*!

We retrieved the necessary material and photographed all that could be photographed. Alberto then led us to an adjoining room that looked like a small museum devoted to Guareschi. It was an enigmatic place, full of books, posters, LPs and an old record player in working order. Alberto opened this, placed a 78 on it and wound the handle, and we listened to the beautiful song 'Carlotta' while the real Carlotta was in the next room. What else could you wish for from Guareschi's world?

*   *   *

I travelled on to Treviso, while Paolo returned to Barletta.

My work on *La Favola di Natale* would never be complete if I did not explore the dark side of the moon, the musical output of Arturo Coppola, who provided the soundtrack to Guareschi's writing in Sandbostel. In the stalag, Coppola would use his accordion to create the musical skeleton of Guareschi's stories with the unforgettable atmospheres of the great Italian popular songbook.

I arrived late in the evening and discovered that my hotel was actually outside the city. Remembering Busseto, I walked there. The following morning, I met the architect Giancarlo Coppola, Arturo's son, in a central square called Isola di Mezzo. Giancarlo was waiting for me under a portico and took me to his studio and into the world of scores created by his father in Sandbostel.

In the stalag, Coppola had given the best of himself; after the war – his son told me – he got married, but, just as he was about to go on his honeymoon, Guareschi called him: *La Favola di Natale* was being staged at the Angelicum in Milan. Coppola completed the score and adapted it to the new production, replacing the ocarina with the flute and the accordion with the piano, then left for Milan. Between 1945 and Epiphany 1946, *La Favola* was performed several times in Milan and Trieste.

I spent my day in Treviso photocopying musical material by Arturo Coppola in his son's studio, then just managed to catch the last train from Treviso to Venezia-Mestre and on to Vienna.

Gino Marinuzzi, Jr and Cabiati

After the Armistice, the Italian composer Gino Marinuzzi, Jr, the son of the composer and conductor Gino Marinuzzi, was arrested and interned in Stalag XII F, then assigned to Kommando Ludwigshafen am Rhein. Using pieces of charcoal or pencils on unused sacks of cement, he jotted down a few tunes in the Russian, Ukrainian and Roma popular traditions, which he'd learnt from fellow inmates. After the liberation, he made transcriptions of these melodies for piano, four hands. That was the start of the *Lagerlieder*.

The pianist Francesco Libetta, who had studied with him, sent me a copy. I was already in contact with Marinuzzi's daughters, Giovanna and Anna Maria. Judging by the copy in my possession, the work of a copyist, I assumed there was an original score. Anna Maria vaguely remembered that it had been left with an ex-pupil of the maestro or something like that. She was wonderful: she retrieved the score and sent me a copy and it was as beautiful as the manuscript. The *Lagerlieder* are going to be published in the *Thesaurus Musicae Concentrationariae*.

In 1943, Enrico Cagna Cabiati, known as 'Enrico La Daga', wrote the score for the film *Apparizione* by Jean de Limur.

Imprisoned in the September after the Armistice, he was first interned in Biała Podlaska, then in Sandbostel. With Pietro Maggioli, he formed a symphonic and choral ensemble and organised a production of Gluck's opera *Iphigénie en Aulide*, although this was never staged. After the war, he emigrated to Mexico, where he wrote music for documentaries and TV mini-series.

Many years ago, I retrieved from a documentation centre in Berlin the songs Cabiati had written in Sandbostel. They had been noted on the blank pages of a one-sided newspaper cyclo-styled in the stalag by the IMI. I had assumed that Cabiati had written other works in Biała Podlaska, but I was unable to find out any information related to his time there, and his move to Mexico after the war only complicated my research.

Fortunately, I was contacted by Vivian Viskin, Alejandro Rubinstein, Aaron Cohen and other dear Mexican-Jewish friends at the Instrumentos de la Esperanza Foundation in Mexico City. I tried my luck and asked about Cabiati: tracking down one of his relatives would be easier for a Mexican, I felt. I was right. They immediately emailed me documents, residence certificates and other material downloadable from the internet. A few days later, I received the kind of good news that makes even a rainy day sunny as they had managed to contact Sibylle Hayem, a relative of Cabiati. *Biała Podlaska*, the rhapsody for piano and orchestra written by Cabiati in the stalag of the same name, was on its way to Italy.

TEN

The Steamroller

Paul Aron Sandfort

In Spring 2007, my friend Ermanno Felli and I travelled from Berlin to Copenhagen.

We arrived very late to discover that our reservation had gone awry and the hotel was booked up, so we had to make do with a double room in another hotel on the same side of the street. The following morning, we went to the home of Paul Aron Sandfort, the Theresienstadt boy trumpet player, who turned out to be a treasure trove of information about musical activity in Theresienstadt.

The interview lasted about two hours, and once it was over, Paul spilt the beans about Viktor Ullmann, Pavel Haas, Karel Berman, Rafael Schächter and other musicians. There were no smartphones with recording apps at the time, and I wasn't clever enough to ask Ermanno to start filming again, but I stored it all away in my memory. At one point, we had to stop because we had another engagement. Seeing us out, Paul assured me that we would meet again and that he would tell me things he hadn't told anyone else. He had time to give me a videotape of the famous short film shot in Theresienstadt in 1944 and we said goodbye at his front door, where I promised a return invitation to Italy.

Later that year, I invited him to stay. Paul accepted enthusiastically, but I had a bitter surprise at Bari airport: he was in a wheelchair, suffering from a galloping degenerative disease of the limbs.

No sooner had he left the airport with his wife and assistants than he said he had a cold, probably caught while changing flights in Amsterdam; I took him to his hotel in Barletta and called a doctor. The following day, Paul was supposed to take part in the presentation of a book I had written with my wife, Grazia Sarah Tiritiello. I was yet to hear the exclusive information he had promised to share a year earlier; however, given the state of his health, I felt it tactful not bother him that night. The following morning, Paul was still not feeling well. After keeping him company and having a bite to eat together, we drove him to Barletta's former municipal library for the book presentation.

Paul was witty, lively and remembered perfectly well all the details about Theresienstadt: his part in the short opera *Brundibár*, the trumpet player he stood in for because the latter had played a wrong note during a parade, his fear of playing the trumpet alone and being spared transfer to Birkenau. He was also worried that, because his fingers were deformed by his illness, he could no longer play. After the presentation, Paul looked exhausted, so I took him to dinner and once more did not feel it was appropriate to ask him more questions. He tried the mozzarella and burrata from Andria, something they don't have in Copenhagen.

In January 2008, after speaking to Paul two more times, I heard he had passed away.

When you do this kind of research, sometimes the big worry is having to choose between the life and health needs of a person who experienced the camps and your own obsessive desire to know. I made the best possible choice with Paul, ensuring that he was calm and content while he was in Barletta.

Thank you for what you did for me, Paul. I'll continue this journey for your sake.

Hermann Gürtler

Surprisingly, my trips to Copenhagen continued to be linguistically fortunate – just like Paul Aron Sandfort, Friedrich Gürtler also spoke fluent Italian, but with a northern inflexion. A very tall man, he had grown up in Cannobio on Lake Maggiore and now taught vocal chamber music at the Copenhagen conservatoire.

His father, the Galician tenor and composer Hermann Gürtler, had taught singing in Geneva from 1914 to 1918, and in Dresden from 1920. He had performed in Germany, Austria, Switzerland and other European countries. In 1935, he relocated to Italy, where he was arrested in 1944 for political reasons and interned in the Bolzano-Gries camp. He survived and, after the war, resumed teaching at the Geneva conservatoire.

He wrote several works in Gries, but his son was not aware of his *Rigaudon*. I had managed to obtain it in Italy, and when I handed it to Friedrich, he placed it on the piano and sight-read; the *Rigaudon* was back home.

Hermann Gürtler wrote a sonata for violin and piano with an incomplete last movement, but with a structure that enabled a plausible completion. Friedrich gave me a photocopy of the sonata and I promised to complete it.

I never lost touch with Friedrich. I heard that two Italian newspapers had interviewed him about his father. Meanwhile, the sonata for violin and piano was sleeping on my piano, waiting to be completed. It wasn't an easy enterprise because the photocopy was very dark.

In 2019 I needed permission to publish his father's sonata in my encyclopaedia, *Thesaurus Musicae Concentrationariae*. I called and a very unwell Friedrich answered the phone. He immediately recognised me but said he was bedridden.

Once again, I was caught between a witness's health and the unstoppable steamroller of research. I quickly asked permission to publish the sonata in my *Thesaurus*, and promised I would soon complete it. Friedrich granted permission straight away but then said weakly that we needed to say goodbye because his doctor was there and he couldn't keep him waiting. It was a sad phone call: I had not completed the sonata and had suddenly discovered that a dear friend was very ill.

As though that weren't enough, the infallible Donatella Altieri – co-producer of the documentary *Maestro* and manager of the ILMC Foundation I founded with other associates in 2014 – informed me that the permission Friedrich had given me over the phone was not legally binding and that he needed to sign a release form.

I realised I had only one option: to copy the sonata onto the computer and complete it. I asked Paolo Candido for help. Paolo did a superb job in a month but left many question marks in the score; many sections of the photocopy were illegible. The way things were, the sonata could not be copied onto a computer professionally, let alone completed.

I plucked up the courage to write to Friedrich's daughter, Christine, and ask her for a better copy of the score – a high-resolution PDF would be more than adequate. Christine said she would need time to go to her father's house – she does not live in Copenhagen – and retrieve the manuscript; Friedrich could be of no help to us.

Fortunately, she sent me a nice, high-resolution colour scan, which I immediately forwarded to Paolo. All the question marks were promptly deleted. What was left was the hardest part of the work: to complete the fourth movement. That was up to me.

Parallel worlds, legendary people and real musicians are with the researcher of this subject day and night; they appear in his dreams and suggest how an unfinished piece or a sonata without a finale, or the missing flute or cello parts in a score, should be completed.

I had already tested this process back in 2005, when I completed the fifty-seven missing bars in the Symphony No. 8 written in Ilag XIII Wülzburg by Erwin Schulhoff, when he was dying of tuberculosis. A hand guides you through the unfinished work, superior logic takes possession of your brain while a subtle form of energy illuminates it like a stadium floodlight, your eyes and ears turn into a radio capable of receiving signals, notes and phrases and arcs and complete patterns appear in the cloud of your imagination.

It was very hard to stop writing the *Thesaurus Musicae Concentrationariae* and devote myself entirely to the sonata, but that's what I did: I stopped everything. I studied the piano part of the entire sonata and avidly read the violin part in order to retrieve elements that would help me reach a completion that wouldn't just be the fruit of my imagination but would give the impression the ending was by the original composer. A week later, I had completed the fourth movement of Gürtler's Sonata for violin and piano.

The process turned out to be easier than I had expected:

the fourth movement – Quasi una fantasia – had clear phrases highlighted by the violin and a crystalline triplet accompaniment for the piano, which helped me recover all the logical elements for completing the sonata.

Once I had finished, I did an immediate general revision, fine-tuning everything, before sending the sonata to Friedrich's daughter, asking her to show it to her father. To my delight, Christine replied that her father had seen the sonata, and, analysing the ending as a musician, had found it perfect and totally in line with Hermann Gürtler's musical style.

At this point I tried my luck one more time. What if I asked Friedrich to donate the manuscript to my Foundation, so that it could be permanently stored in the museum of the future Citadel of Concentrationary Music in Barletta?

Completing the sonata had given me courage, so I wrote to Christine. As I waited on tenterhooks, days went by before the much-anticipated email arrived. It said the entire Gürtler family had decided to donate the manuscript to the Foundation. It arrived seven days later.

I was happy for dear Friedrich, that kind, ailing giant. I was happy for his father, Hermann, too, to whom, after seventy years, we had returned his sonata, complete.

Max Ehrlich

From Copenhagen, I went to Switzerland to meet Alan, the nephew of the Dutch stand-up comedian Max Ehrlich, who was deported to the transit camp of Westerbork.

Before the Nazis came to power, Max Ehrlich had been a prominent character in German cabaret, a true star performer in Max Reinhardt's stage revues and an actor in films like *Herkules Maier* and *Die blaue Maus*. Because of the situation in Germany, he emigrated to Vienna, then Switzerland, and finally the Netherlands. In 1943, he was arrested and sent to Westerbork. In the camp, he was allowed to form the Gruppe Bühne Lager Westerbork – chiefly made up of German, Austrian and Dutch artists – and become its artistic director.

Almost every Tuesday, they staged the *Bunter Abend* revues, complete with songs and theatre sketches, with renowned actor-singers like Jonas Blumenzweig, Camilla Spira, Jetty Cantor, Michel Gobets, Chaja Goldstein, Esther Philipse, Mara Rosen and Liesel Frank. Moreover, these revues featured dance ensembles, ten ballerinas from the Westerbork Girls ballet corps and male ballet dancers. They had a crew of fifty technicians, costume and set designers/decorators, production managers and artistic supervisors, choreographers, associate musicians and musical directors, including Alexander Lothar Ringer, the choirmaster and arranger Ludwig Belitzer, and jazz musicians such as Barnabás von Géczy, Rally Wachtel and Hans Feith.

The orchestra was conducted by Haim Heinz Neuberg and made up of excellent musicians, including Jacques Barendse, Wolf Drukker and Jean Freund, the trumpet players Jack Goudsmit and Lex van Weren (sent to the Janinagrube mines in November 1943), the percussionist Maurits van Kleef (subsequently transferred to Birkenau), the violinist Simon Hangjas, the viola player Sam Tromp, the cellist Maurice Cantor and the bass player Jack de Vries (also eventually transferred to Birkenau).

The cabaret output of Gruppe Bühne Lager Westerbork had a strong comedy streak and great precision in the choice of costumes and arrangements; political topics were deliberately avoided, but there was no shortage of controversy thanks to the sexually explicit lyrics. In any case, the artists enjoyed huge success with the audience of deportees and SS alike, so much so that *SS-Obersturmführer* Albert Konrad Gemmeker, the commandant of the camp, financed their performances by buying the required materials from specialist suppliers in Amsterdam. Transfers to other camps compelled the organisers to make frequent cast changes, in addition to having to teach the remaining acting parts to newcomers. Between October 1943 and March 1944, the cabaret shows ceased; the two final performances were staged with a cast of only ten.

In March 1944, Westerbork was remodelled into a forced labour camp. On 3 August 1944, cultural activities came to an end and almost all the Westerbork artists were relocated to extermination camps. In late September 1944, Ehrlich was transferred to Birkenau and he was killed a month later.

Alan told me this and other things as he showed me video and photographic material featuring his uncle, Max Ehrlich, as well as Willy Rosen, Erich Ziegler, Camilla Spira and others.

Zuzana Růžičková

In Geneva, I boarded a flight to Prague, where I met the harp-sichordist Zuzana Růžičková. Only fourteen when she and her family were deported to Theresienstadt in 1941, Zuzana was tutored there by the Czech-Jewish pedagogue Fredy Hirsch, who supported and took care of many Jewish children before their final transfer to Birkenau.

Zuzana welcomed me to her home with a beautiful smile and the serene face of one who by now was flying over life with large wings. Sitting opposite me, she said that she had studied music theory and harmony in Theresienstadt under the guid-ance of the great Gideon Klein.

No one had told her what was happening to European Jews in Birkenau, only that they were assigned to labour camps in Poland, but Zuzana began harbouring suspicions when Hirsch told her he had met a group of Jewish children in Białystok who had been temporarily transferred to Theresienstadt. These children would inexplicably start crying whenever they were taken to the showers.

Zuzana's father died in the ghetto and, in December 1943, she and her mother were moved to Birkenau, to an area where there were other families coming from Theresienstadt. Hirsch advised Zuzana to claim she was older – sixteen – and that saved her life.

In June 1944, a few days after the Normandy landing, the Germans selected a thousand deportees from the five thousand destined to be gassed and loaded them onto a lorry bound for Hamburg. The city had been devastated by Allied bombings and a large workforce was required. Zuzana and her mother were selected but loaded onto different lorries. As Zuzana's vehicle was leaving, her mother ran after it to hand her a small box containing the theme of the Sarabande from Bach's French Suite No. 5. On that day – Zuzana told me – she realised she would survive and become a musician.

In February 1945, she was transferred from Hamburg to Bergen-Belsen, which by then was on the brink of collapse through overcrowding and a typhus epidemic. On 15 April 1945, Canadian and British troops liberated the camp and Zuzana was found unbelievably malnourished and suffering from malaria.

Around the same time, another girl died in Bergen-Belsen from epidemic typhus. Her name was Annelies Marie Frank – we know her best as Anne Frank. She bequeathed to the world a wonderful diary and a smile full of life, just like Zuzana's.

Back in Czechoslovakia, Zuzana began studying the harpsichord under the great Franco-Polish harpsichordist Wanda Landowska. She gave her first recital in 1951. Five years later, she won the ARD International Music Competition in Munich and went on to become one of the world's greatest harpsichordists. Zuzana embarked on her final journey on 27 September 2017.

Those who research this music always see the glass completely full, even when it's empty: they know that, sooner or later, it will be refilled and, that, like wine on the Shabbat, it will overflow.

'We sang, played and clapped our hands to the rhythm of an operetta,' a survivor wrote, 'we knew the meaning of life.' Life should be handed on a silver platter at all latitudes. So much the better if it is handed to the sound of a harpsichord like Zuzana's.

'Stella del Porto'

I had great difficulty finding one particular piece, partly because it was not written down on paper but probably hidden deep in the minds of a few survivors. It was a ditty created in Regina Coeli prison, where Roman Jews were jailed after the raid on 16 October 1943. The song 'Stella del Porto', in the style of a Roman folk song, emerged out of nowhere in the corridors of the jail, a song that accused a certain Celeste Di Porto, nicknamed Stella, of being an informer. All trace of the melody has been lost, but the lyrics were published in the weekly *L'Espresso* and included in the book *Canti della Resistenza Italiana*.

The lyrics had to be reunited with the tune, but the circumstances in which the song had arisen made this reconstruction difficult. In 2006, I started an email thread that brought unexpected results, however. My email bounced to all four corners of the Earth and vague responses started coming back, until one day I received a phone call from Rome. It was from a lady who was very young during the war. She had heard the song in Regina Coeli, where she had been sent, then released, but not before she had learnt the song.

I asked her to sing it to me, but the lady was just going out to a ceremony at the Great Synagogue and asked me to call her back the next day. I was very much on edge. When I called back the following day, I found myself speaking to a totally different person, one who refused to sing me the song. Her reasoning was that she had no desire to stir up sad memories; but if that was how she felt, why had she contacted me? When a survivor does not wish to talk, however, you cannot go any further. I guessed this lady had spoken to someone about my research and that they had advised her to desist. I had reached a dead end and did not think I would ever find a second witness. A few days later, though, Cesare, a friend who now lives in Ra'anana in Israel called me: his mother, Ester, had been in Regina Coeli too, remembered the tune well and was willing to sing it to me that very evening. I was at the Rodi Garganico conservatoire at the time, so I asked Cesare to make sure that would really happen.

He confirmed that his mother was expecting my call at 8 p.m.; that's when the conservatoire closed, so I asked the staff to wait ten more minutes and they agreed. I used the conservatoire's landline and the lady sang me the Regina Coeli song. Since I was writing very quickly on a stave, I asked her to sing it five times, just to make sure, and she did. As she sang, I checked that the lyrics I had were correct, and everything matched. This is how, in such an unusual way, I managed to reconstruct 'Stella del Porto'.

When Ester was arrested and sent to Regina Coeli, she was pregnant. A nun helped her give birth in prison. Her husband was later deported to Birkenau. Yet, despite this, Ester sang so well that evening on the phone, the same melody I requested five times, unfailingly effective.

We owe her a standing ovation.

ELEVEN

With Chains on their Feet

Greta Klingsberg

In 2004 and 2005, in Jerusalem, I met Greta Klingsberg, who had played Aninka in the short opera *Brundibár* in Theresienstadt, where she had been deported at the age of thirteen with her twin sister, Trude. Greta was also there when International Red Cross officials visited the camp in June 1944. A few days before that, the German authorities 'solved' the problems of overcrowding by shifting excess deportees elsewhere. Subsequently, Greta and the other children in Theresienstadt were transferred to Birkenau, where she was assigned to forced labour while her sister, Trude, was led to the gas chamber.

The first time I asked Greta to remember previously unpublished songs or nursery rhymes created in Theresienstadt, I came up against her frequent refrain: 'I can't remember.' The following year, I changed my approach. All it took was to sit at the large wooden table in her garden, in the Arnona quarter, at dusk, eat fruit and drink orange juice. Her memory returned, crisp and rich in music. Until 2008, it was always I who visited Greta, but in 2009, she came to see me in Barletta.

Edith Kraus and others

In Jerusalem, I twice went to the German Colony to meet the Austrian pianist Edith Steiner Kraus. Born in Vienna in 1913, Edith made her debut at the age of nine, playing a Mozart piano concerto. We spoke for a long time about the great Viktor Ullmann, whose Piano Sonata No. 6, she had premiered in Theresienstadt and then performed again eleven more times. After the war, she moved to Israel and recorded Ullmann's seven sonatas. I met Edith for the first time in 2004 with the brilliant writer of Azeri origin Elena Makarova, a researcher into the paintings produced in Theresienstadt. Three years later, I met her again, but she had lost her sight, and an Eritrean carer was helping her. She died, aged one hundred, in September 2013.

Still in Jerusalem, I met Noemi Cohn, the daughter of the German-Jewish pianist, flautist and composer Leo Cohn, and wife of David Cassuto, an architect and pioneer of the Italian-Jewish community in the Israeli capital. In 1933, her father's parents and siblings had emigrated to British Palestine, as it was then called. Cassuto stayed in Paris and subsequently moved to Strasbourg with his wife, Rachel, and formed the Kriyatenu scouts group. Hoping to acquire French citizenship, Cohn enrolled in the Foreign Legion and also joined its choir.

As director of the Jewish scout group Éclaireurs Israélites de France and the author of songs and hymns, in 1942 he organised a rescue network for children in the clandestine group La Sixième. On 17 May, he was arrested by the Gestapo while taking some children to Toulouse train station. Sent to the transit camp of Drancy, then to the camp of Natzweiler-Struthof (or Birkenau, according to other sources), Cohn died on 28 December 1944.

In Modi'in I met Chaim Refael. He was from Thessaloniki and spoke excellent Italian, with a characteristic Greek inflexion. He survived Birkenau with his partner Ester, whom he then married. Chaim gave me the Birkenau song 'Con le catene ai piedi' ('With Chains on their Feet'). In Birkenau, the SS beat him ruthlessly, snatching from his hands the accordion he had brought with him from Thessaloniki. 'I wept like when they took my sisters away,' Chaim says. 'A person who doesn't make music can't be happy in this world.'

Uri Spitzer

In a luxury care home in the Israeli city of Rishon Le-Tzion, I met the Czech musician Uri Spitzer; he had a very interesting story, which he told me one hot summer afternoon.

In December 1939, about 4,000 Austrian and Czech Jews who were living in the Gdańsk corridor somehow managed to obtain from the German authorities an expatriation permit, and went to Bratislava, hoping to reach British Palestine via the Danube, the Black Sea and the Mediterranean. They were lodged in the hostels of Patronka and Slobodarna, under the control of the Slovak Fascist paramilitary corps, *Hlinkova garda*. In the Slobodarna Hostel, they originated the hymn 'Slobodarna Hostel'. Uri Spitzer was among the guests. In August 1940, they were boarded onto four cargo ships bound for Tulcea (in the delta of the Black Sea) and redistributed aboard the ships *Pacific*, *Milos* and *Atlantic*, which sailed and reached Haifa on 24 November 1940.

The first time I met Uri, he struggled to remember the first two verses of the hymn. He would freeze up and there seemed no way of restoring them to his memory. The second time I interviewed him with Ermanno, complete with TV camera, I initially led him to believe the camera was off, but Ermanno had left it on. Finally, Uri relaxed and we started joking. I uncorked the good bottle of wine from Golan I had brought him and after we had drunk just the right amount, I pounced. I asked him point-blank about 'Slobodarna Hostel' and Uri sang it to me straight through, without a moment's hesitation, including all the verses and the chorus.

Gabriele Mandel

Born in Bologna in 1924 to the Afghan writer Yusuf Roberto Mandel and the Jewish writer Carlotta Rimini, Gabriele Mandel was a world-famous writer and artist, and the godson of Gabriele d'Annunzio. From a young age, he'd embraced Sufism through his uncle, Keki Efendi khan-i Hetimandel rûd. After gaining a diploma in violin, under the guidance of Arrigo Pedrollo, in 1939 he started to publish Sufi short stories in the *Corriere dei Piccoli*, but in 1940 he was expelled from the journalists' register because his mother was Jewish.

Towards the end of the Second World War, Mandel and his father were imprisoned and he was tortured by the Germans in San Vittore. In cell 108 of area 5, he wrote *Canto* for tenor and piano, a beautifully written and bewitching gently Eastern piece.

Surviving the war, he graduated in Languages and Classics, Psychology and Medicine, and taught Islamic Art at the Brera Academy in Milan. His publications include Italian translations of the Quran (with commentary) and a mystical 50,000-line poem by Rumi in six volumes.

When I contacted Mandel about his *Canto*, he had been ill for some time, but with his well-known amiability and helpfulness, he offered to locate it and send me a copy of the manuscript. I returned the favour by making a nicely printed copy of his *Canto* and Mandel replied, 'How can I repay you? I'm going to Niguarda hospital tomorrow and we'll be in touch when I get back.'

Shortly afterwards, when I sent him a package with the CD of *Canto*, Mandel wrote back, 'Thank you for your interpretation: it's like a balm. The stage I'm at, I think the only thing that counts is the nearness and affection of friends.'

On 9 January 2010, just before being hospitalised for the umpteenth time and foreseeing his demise, Mandel sent all his closest friends – including me – a letter. It's an intense document, a testament that contains the treasures of this great man's spirit. Here are a few extracts: '*I thank God for giving me the possibility to keep believing in Him and adoring Him with the necessary intensity [. . .]. All the time we spend on material matters will be foiled in the Beyond; all the time we sincerely devote to God in the phenomenal world will be for us a favourable testimonial in the Beyond. What a wonderful evolution, God, what wonderful strength, what a wonderful gift you gave me! Thank you.*'

Gabriele Mandel died in Milan on 1 July 2010 from a lung tumour, His *Canto* is now the property of the Institute of Concentrationary Music Literature in Barletta and will be published in the *Thesaurus Musicae Concentrationariae*.

However old-fashioned it might be, it is beauty that we will feed on in the centuries to come. People like Mandel never move far away from us; they precede us in creating ideas, projects and life cycles, and prepare us for long-awaited golden ages.

A better life cycle will return, and we will know how to welcome it in time with the final movement of Viktor Ullmann's last sonata, written in Theresienstadt: 'Allegro giocoso, energico e sempre martellato'.

In the San Vittore prison, as in Regina Coeli, music was an anchor in the harbour of the spirit, a mental buoy. In catapulting the prisoner's imagination towards the future, it made it possible to build bridges between past and present, but music alone would not have had that innate universal calling if it hadn't been for people with superhuman powers to make it into a true Esperanto in the world of camps, people like Gabriele Mandel.

Remain in Light, *khalyfa*! Because the last among those who knew you, admired you and loved your greatness will not die.

Christof Kulisiewicz

From the moment we met, in Kraków in 2015, a strong bond was formed between Christof Kulisiewicz – son of Aleksander Kulisiewicz, a pioneer in this research – and myself. Christof knew about my work. I was preaching to the converted when I told him I was not only looking to learn more about the 150 songs written by his father in Sachsenhausen, but also, and above all, about the great and unique contribution of Aleksander Kulisiewicz to the research on concentrationary music in terms of criteria, classifications and cataloguing, as well as subdivision by genre, camp and author.

Friendly and talkative, Christof promptly showed me the material his father had crammed into a summer cottage in a forest not far from Kraków, and which he had looked after with total diligence, sorting it into folders, sheets, cassettes and photographs.

His father had spoken four languages and went on to speak six in Sachsenhausen – eight, according to some sources – including Italian. A perfect German speaker, he wrote documents in both Polish and German.

One day, in Sachsenhausen, the Jewish choirmaster Rosebery d'Arguto told him, 'Alex, you're young, you're Polish and you speak German: you'll survive', and gave him instructions for what he predicted would be his destiny, to become the mental archive of the Sachsenhausen musicians, a forerunner of the immeasurable paper and sound archive constituted after the war.

Rosebery d'Arguto sang him 'Jüdischer Todessang', the Jewish chant of death; Alex learnt it by heart. The reputation of Kulisiewicz's prodigious memory spread through the camp and other prisoners went to see him, saying, 'Alex, we've heard you're able to learn a song by heart.'

Christof told me: 'My father memorised dozens of secret songs his fellow prisoners entrusted to his brain. After the war, he left the camp in a terrible state and contracted tuberculosis.' Christof believes he would have lost his mind if a nurse had not supported him during his convalescence after the war, and *emptied* his memory, writing down the music and lyrics for him.

'The nurse typed up these songs, transcribing 716 of them. He continued to search for others until his death in 1982.'

Christof immediately photocopied his father's copious material for me. One day, six gigantic parcels arrived at my home: Aleksander Kulisiewicz's archive, bequeathed to Christof. A larger proportion – as well as Aleksander's guitar – is in the A. Kulisiewicz Collection at the USHMM in Washington, DC, ceded by Christof many years ago. I hope one day he'll be able to join together the two branches of this huge collection.

After the war, Aleksander could not persuade a single publisher to produce a small anthology of thirty Polish songs written in captivity. His 2,200-page essay was left in a drawer. Things have now, undoubtedly, changed. Although we are not yet in the golden age of concentrationary music, Aleksander would not meet with quite so much resistance today. We are fortunate that he bequeathed us such a wealth of knowledge on this subject, and a high-level lesson in research.

TWELVE

Deep Connections

Sand in the desert

Concentrationary music, some claim, was born in Sachsen-hausen, because that was where the criteria for the classification of genres, authors and sites of captivity was developed, as well as the aesthetic classification criteria for musical and literary material, as perceived by the pioneer of concentrationary music, Aleksander Kulisiewicz. Such information is held in this music. In 1943, he disclosed the lethal use of Zyklon B in the lyrics to 'Jüdischer Todessang', which Rosebery d'Arguto had dictated to him before being transferred to Birkenau.

A book is a door to higher dimensions, a music score is a passkey to that door. Music written in captivity is both the door and the passkey, which can let us into more recent and tragic history, so that we can reach landscapes of unequalled beauty.

This music resembles a tornado that does not destroy but rather preserves; a tsunami, which, instead of sucking in the soil, restores it to the coast; the images and sounds of art as we have always studied and imagined them are irreversibly altered.

In the Japanese internment camp of Palembang, on the island of Sumatra, Norah Chambers, conductor of the vocal orchestra that was formed there during captivity, told the women singers to perform the final chords of the Largo from Dvořák's Symphony No. 9 as a kind of triumphal hymn in defiance of the Japanese authorities. The 1997 film *Paradise Road*, directed by Bruce Beresford, was inspired by their experiences.

Again and again, the deportee and interned musicians would express their human nobility of spirit by blending – carefully and in a timely fashion – honour and sarcasm, dignity and irreverence. It is hard to imagine anything more humbling than what the deportees in the Börgermoor camp did in 1933: after seeing an inmate beaten to death, they sang 'Die Moorsoldaten' in chorus, dressed as clowns and trapeze artists in the Zirkus Konzentrazani, for an audience of guards and SS officers, who enjoyed the show and even paid for their tickets. Equally astonishing is the thought of conducting Verdi's Requiem, with a choir decimated by transfers to Birkenau and only a piano instead of an orchestra, without even as much as acknowledging with a nod the cheering SS commandant, as Rafael Schächter did with Adolf Eichmann in Theresienstadt. Or applying stage make-up after an eighteen-hour work shift and casting a seemingly benevolent look at the Japanese guards, as Fergus Anckorn, Tom Boardman, Norman Smith and dozens of British and Australian prisoners did while building the Siam-Burma Railway, also known as the Death Railway. (It is estimated 90,000 civilians died building it, along with 12,000 Allied soldiers.)

Raised by the winds, the nourishing sand of the Sahara Desert crosses the Atlantic and travels 3,000 kilometres to then land in the rainforests of Latin America, fertilising their soil; termites, migratory birds and dolphins communicate between continents through quasi-imperceptible sounds and basic forms of telepathy. Similarly, while in Ravensbrück, the Moravian musician Ludmila Peškařová was arranging the Largo from

Dvořák's Symphony No. 9 for female chorus just as, across the globe, in the Japanese civilian internment camp of Palembang, British conductor Norah Chambers was arranging the same melody for her vocal orchestra.

The Durmashkin family

The Belarusian composer, conductor and cantor Akiva Durmashkin lived in the Polish city of Radom and in Vilnius. Before the German occupation, the Jewish population of Vilnius amounted to 60,000 people. On 6–7 September 1941, about 20,000 Jews were assembled in the zone assigned to the ghetto, divided in two separate quarters by the Deutsche Gasse/ Vokiečių gatvė, under the control of the *Judenrat*. From July 1941 to August 1944, in Ponary forest (Vilnius), units from the *Einsatzgruppen* and the Lithuanian police killed between 60,000 and 100,000 people, mainly Jews who were Polish nationals and living in Vilnius, Polish army soldiers, prisoners of war, Soviet civilians, Romani and Lithuanian Communists. Transferred to the ghetto, Akiva and his wife, Sheina, died in 1943 during the Ponary Massacre.

Akiva's son, the pianist, conductor and composer Wolf Durmashkin, was a music teacher and the conductor of the Vilnius Philharmonic. After the German occupation, he was sent to the ghetto in 1941, but, following a petition on the part of the orchestra principals, the German authorities allowed him to periodically leave the ghetto and carry on conducting. In the ghetto, the president of the *Judenrat* invited Durmashkin to form a symphony orchestra, inaugurated on 15 March 1942 with a performance of Chopin's Piano Concerto No.1, conducted by Durmashkin, with his sister, Fania, at the piano. Not only did he write the music for David Pinski's play *Der ewige Jude*, as well as a few songs for his sister, Henia, he also helped set up a music school with over a hundred students, and founded and conducted a choir.

The ghetto orchestra held its last concert on 29 August 1943, a few weeks before being closed down altogether. In January 1943, during a rehearsal, Durmashkin was arrested with Lyube Levitski, and transferred to the Estonian camp of Klooga. He was killed in September 1944, the day before the camp was liberated by Soviet troops.

Wolf's sisters, Henia and Fania, were moved to different forced labour camps and finally to the Landsberg sub-camp. They survived a death march and were freed in early May 1945. Relocated to the Displaced Persons Camp in St Ottilien, they joined the St Ottilien Orchestra, made up of musicians who had survived the camps. It is there that Fania met her future husband, Lithuanian viola player Max Beker. He had fought in the Polish regular army, been captured in September 1939 and was taken to Stalag VIII A Görlitz.

In 1946, the orchestra moved to Fürstenfeldbruck and, in 1948, performed at the Opernhaus in Nuremberg in an operatic and symphonic concert conducted by Leonard Bernstein in honour of the burgeoning State of Israel. In 1948, Fania, Max and Henia emigrated to the US. Fania embarked on a singing career, the three of them occasionally performing together.

Shmerke Kaczerginski

Captured and sent to the Vilnius ghetto in early 1942, the poet Shmerke Kaczerginski made his skills available to the resistance, writing songs and lyrics to lift the morale of the ghetto's inhabitants, and staging theatre productions, literary soirées and educational programmes. He also wrote what became the anthem of the ghetto youth, 'Yugnt Himn'. A member of the FPO Resistance group, he formed the Paper Brigade – along with the Yiddish-language poet Abraham Sutzkever and others – to oppose German plans to destroy rare books and Jewish material. Intending this repertoire of songs about heroes and martyrs to serve one day as a historical document of the events, he meticulously collected the ghetto's Yiddish vocal repertoire. After the failed partisan uprising in September 1943, Kaczerginski escaped from the ghetto and, in August 1944, took part in the liberation of Vilnius by Soviet troops.

Having moved to Paris in 1946, Kaczerginski collected further material by doing research in the Displaced Persons Camps in Germany. In 1947, he published his collection of Vilnius songs and poems in Yiddish, *Dos gezang fun Vilner Geto*. A year later, his major work, *Lider fun di getos un lagern*, was published in New York: it consisted of 435 pages, containing

233 songs and poems, and was a milestone in traditional and popular Jewish music from the war years. In 1950, he settled in Buenos Aires, wrote for newspapers and launched a campaign for the promotion of Jewish culture. He died in a plane crash over the Andes in April 1954.

Alexander Wolkovsky becomes Alex Tamir

In 1943, the song 'Shtiler, shtiler' by the eleven-year-old Alexander Wolkovsky won a musical contest organised by the *Judenrat*. The Polish lyrics were written by his father, Noach, and subsequently replaced with a Yiddish text by Shmerke Kaczerginski. For the same contest, Wolkovsky wrote *Theme and Variations* for piano and the music for the Yiddish poem 'A nem ton dem ayzn' by Abraham Sutzkever. In September 1943, Wolkovsky and his mother were moved to Stutthof and Dirmingen, while his father died during the closing of the ghetto. After the war, Wolkovsky emigrated to Israel, changed his surname to Tamir, and resumed his piano studies at the Rubin Academy in Jerusalem, with Alexander Schroeder. He met and married the pianist Bracha Eden and together they formed a piano duo. Tamir became Head of Piano and Head of Piano Duo at the Jerusalem Academy of Music and Dance.

In 2016, I was driving to Ein Kerem, a district in the Jerusalem hills where Christians say John the Baptist was born. As I walked into his villa, Alex Tamir came towards me and offered me a coffee. I was struck by the passion Alex channelled into boiling that coffee, and we began talking about music.

At one point, he stood up and took me to a large room where the Eden-Tamir Music Center is now based (named after his wife), dominated by a wonderful Steinway. He sat down at the piano and I immediately asked him to play 'Shtiler shtiler'.

Even though Alex had retired, he still played with confidence, and you could tell he had been an excellent pianist. As he played, he talked and looked at me, while I tried to make him talk as little as possible because I wanted him to play his song without interference. But I couldn't get him to keep quiet, so all I could do was sing while he played.

After he had finished, it was my turn, so I played 'Shtiler shtiler' again, my way. Alex asked me to play something else, and I chose the first movement of Viktor Ullmann's Piano Sonata No. 6 and Rudolf Karel's *Pankrác Valzer*, op. 42c – my meeting with Alex was turning into a private concert.

I knew that he had entered the piano section of the 1943 *Judenrat* contest, and he vaguely remembered the piece, *Theme and Variations*, but said that he had unfortunately lost it. I asked him if he had liked his original name, Alexander Wolkovsky. Alex evaded the question, instead telling me how dreadful the ghetto years had been, with people dying of hunger in the streets and the danger of being killed at any moment. Making music had saved the life of his spirit, his intellect, and that was more important than physical life.

I attempted to call him after that, but he seldom answered the phone. He died on 15 August 2019.

Arno Nadel

Born in Vilnius – then under Russian control – in 1878 to a family of Hassidic Jews, Arno Nadel studied synagogue singing in Königsberg, then moved to Berlin in 1895 and graduated from the Jewish teacher-training college after studying composition with Max Julius Loewengard and Ludwig Mendelssohn. A number works by Nadel in handwritten form, composed after 1933, have survived, but not *Zemirot shabat: Die häuslichen Sabbatgesänge*, the prelude to the 1935 film *Hebräische Melodie*, the Organ Prelude on Hebrew Themes (performed in March 1936 by the organist Herman Schwarz in the Friedenstempel synagogue in Berlin-Halensee) or *Der Herr segne und behüte dich* for male chorus and soloists. A conductor, arranger, musicologist, painter, playwright – Nadel wrote seven plays and over 2,000 poems and theatre texts – as well as a poet deeply inspired by Expressionism and steeped in Jewish thinking, but equally close to Daoist philosophies and spirituality, his poetry was well known and popular. It was compared to the works of great German lyrical poets such as Alfred Mombert, Theodor Däubler and Oskar Loerke.

An acknowledged authority in matters of Jewish music and a renowned collector of ancient Jewish music manuscripts, from 1903 Nadel was in charge of the music supplement of the Zionist paper *Ost und West*, taking on the same post from 1916 to 1918 for Martin Buber's magazine, *Der Jude*, and working as a music critic for other publications, too. In 1923, the Jewish community in Berlin gave Nadel the task of putting together an anthology of synagogue music and producing new music for the Jewish liturgy. When the Nazis came to power, all further publication of his poetry was forbidden, however.

Nadel had produced a vast compendium of synagogue music for cantor, choir and organ in seven handwritten volumes and was ultimately hoping to publish the complete work under the title of *Hallelujah*, but in November 1938 he was arrested and imprisoned in Sachsenhausen for a few weeks. In 1940, he failed to emigrate to the US and refused to emigrate to Great Britain instead, despite obtaining a visa. Two years later, he was assigned to forced labour at the library of the Reich Security Main Office in Berlin. On 12 March 1943, he and his wife were transferred to Birkenau, where they are assumed to have been killed shortly afterwards.

THIRTEEN

Music Lives in the Air

History becomes legend . . .

In honour of the recently arrived Polish-Jewish musician Artur Gold, the commandant of Treblinka, Franz Stangl, put together a top-level orchestra, ordered the purchase of musical instruments and concert uniforms, guaranteed Gold and the orchestra extra food rations and brought a dancer, singers and artists from Warsaw for what arguably became the most prestigious Polish music group of that time. And one located in an extermination camp. Despite their prestige, and Stangl's esteem, the members of the orchestra and Artur Gold were nevertheless eventually killed.

It is difficult not to make comparisons with the animals we first fatten, then slaughter – it is the only way to describe the actions of some camp commandants, who first granted the musicians' wishes by providing musical instruments, benefits and preferential treatment, only then to eliminate them, as though that were natural, logical and par for the course.

The world of concentration camps is an anomaly in the history of thinking and art. And this chapter is not yet complete as we are waiting to discover its final pages. While the history of music has developed new idioms and tested new paths, we are still in the limbo of an unfathomable present, waiting to write the final chapter of the past and the first chapter of the future.

The past cannot be changed but it can be healed and music is both therapy and recovery, doctor and medicine, language and text.

In the front line

Who led the 1943 uprising in the Sobibór extermination camp, ordering the barbed-wire fencing to be torn down, allowing the deportees to escape past the minefield surrounding the camp? The Ukrainian Jewish musician Alexander Pechersky, known as Sasha, a Red Army officer who took almost 300 fugitives to safety, humiliating the SS, who ended up by closing Sobibór later that year.

Who became the head of the ex-deportees trapped in Theresienstadt awaiting repatriation and led them to the Prague town hall, in June 1945, so that someone would take responsibility for them? The Czech pianist and musicologist Václav Holzknecht, who taught at the Prague conservatoire and, post-war, in 1957, became president of the renowned Prague Spring Festival.

Who sent messages out of Sachsenhausen on postcards, on which some syllables were deliberately written in incorrect German, thereby disclosing, with the war in full swing, the smallpox medical experiments carried out on the prisoners, as well as the fate reserved for Jews and Soviet soldiers? The Polish singer and composer Aleksander Kulisiewicz.

After an execution by firing squad during the roll call, the choir members of Mauthausen sang a heart-breaking 'Hymn an das Leben' in the face of their executioners, annihilating them ideologically in the face of their brutality.

The pianist Ignacy Paderewski, president of the Polish Parliament in exile in London, following the German occupation in 1939, gave numerous concerts around the world to raise funds for the Polish cause.

What did all these people share? They were all musicians.

In Janinagrube, the Dutch trumpeter Lex van Weren played 'Stille Nacht, heilige Nacht'. Because of this, he was 'humiliated' by the German authorities and sent to play in the women's orchestra. Transferred to Dachau, when he saw US vehicles, Lex ran towards them playing 'Yankee Doodle' as a thank you for liberating the camp. The soldiers were moved; some even cried.

From 1936 to 1939, Pablo Casals tirelessly travelled across a Spain ripped apart by civil war, playing his legendary cello: to those who asked why he was playing, he replied that it was precisely at that moment that the people needed music.

During the 1948 Israeli–Arab war, the twenty-nine-year-old pianist and conductor Leonard Bernstein conducted the Israel Philharmonic Orchestra – the Israeli musician Heinrich Haftel recalls that there was not enough bread and water in Jerusalem then, but the concerts were sold out.

Music – not the musician – lives in the air; wherever the musician may be, they breathe that air in and then breathe it out into the arteries of the fruit of their genius.

Those who make music have their hands and feet tied to the soil, are forever experiencing its vicissitudes, injustices and desires until they synthesise them and raise them all into form, sound, art and literature. Musicians were, are and always will be in the front line of history's most tragic events, eternally defending the most fundamental moral and social values.

It could be said that Modern Europe was born in 1943, in Sachsenhausen, where the hymns were written in at least eight languages so that all the prisoners in the camps could sing them. Or perhaps it was born in 1944, near the Ventotene border, in the mind of Manlio Rossi-Doria, who wrote anti-Fascist songs and musical parodies? The camps' musical output turns every consideration of musical poetics and aesthetics upside down. This music has no past, but a huge, unfathomable future.

Class and satire

Places of captivity reproduced on a reduced scale the social models that inevitably tended towards strata, from the working classes to lower and middle classes, to the privileged classes. In the oflag and stalag, too, there were group models typical of Central European life. Most officers were not career soldiers but professionals inserted and enrolled in the armed forces when the war broke out. Theatre, cabaret, music and opera – from the point of view of the quality of the actors, singers, musicians and staff, as well as the quality of the instruments, costumes and logistics – generally mirrored society while in captivity.

A masterpiece of satire and parody in concentrationary music consisted in the more or less concealed insertion of patriotic hymns or national anthems into the texture of the score: either those of one's own country, to celebrate it, or those of the enemy, to exorcise it. From the 'Hymn of St Wenceslas' in the *Čtyři písně na čínskou poezii* by Pavel Haas, to the 'Kaiserhymne' in minor mode in Viktor Ullmann's *Emperor of Atlantis*; from 'Bandiera Rossa', ridiculed in *Dai dai Bepin* by Arturo Coppola, to the lyrics by Giovannino Guareschi, to the

'Marseillaise' and 'Inno di Garibaldi' in *Diario di prigionia* for piano by Berto Boccosi.

Social differences persist in music but remain barely perceptible, and creativity and the sense of solidarity prevail.

Jazz in Theresienstadt

In January 1944, Martin Roman and Kurt Gerron arrived in Theresienstadt from Westerbork; the commandant, Karl Rahm, put them in charge of musical entertainment for the officers and their guests, as well as for the deportees who enjoyed 'prominent' status. The Roman–Gerron partnership led to the creation of the ironic and irreverent cabaret *Karussell*, with music by Roman, design by František Zelenka and a cast of top-level singers, including Annie Frey, Gisa Wurzel, Fiedel Schönemann, Machiel Gobets, Ernst Raden, Ernst Österreicher and Kurt Gerron himself.

The texts for *Karussell* were created by the German writer and cabaret librettist Manfred Greiffenhagen – transferred to Birkenau in 1944, then to Dachau, where he died in January 1945 – and by the Austrian librettist, composer and *Karussell* star performer Leopold 'Leo' Strauss, the son of the operetta composer Oscar Straus, who had taken refuge in the US.

There was a crucial breakthrough in the development of jazz and musical styles typical of the American big band in Theresienstadt with the arrival of the Czech jazz trumpeter and arranger Eric T. Vogel, an engineer from Brno, who became unemployed following the 1939 German occupation of Czechoslovakia, and who was moved to Theresienstadt in March 1942. On 8 January 1943, Vogel asked for, and obtained from the German authorities, permission to create a jazz orchestra, assembling a good-quality group of individuals with the help of the Czech double-bass player Pavel Lipensky. This orchestra was called the Ghetto Swingers. Some of the best jazz arrangers and musicians from the Central European jazz circuit joined this band, among them Czech clarinettist Bedřich 'Fritz' Weiss and German jazz guitarist 'Coco' Schumann.

When Martin Roman arrived in Theresienstadt, in January 1944, he was asked to become band leader, until then Peter Deutsch, as well as to write arrangements for the ensemble, notably an arrangement of *Avant de mourir* by Georges Boulanger. The Ghetto Swingers performed in *Karussell*, giving as many as fifty shows between June and July 1944, and, in August of the same year, were co-opted for the documentary film *Theresienstadt* (1944), performing in the gazebo already set up for Karel Ančerl's string orchestra. The band was subsequently moved to Birkenau, where it was assigned to welcoming deportees arriving at the camp, to provide the evening entertainment of SS officers, or at times to play during the transfer of people to the gas chambers. Gerron, Goldschmidt and Weiss were eventually gassed, while Schumann returned to Berlin; Roman emigrated to the US, and Vogel escaped while being transferred from Birkenau to Dachau; he also emigrated to the US.

Cabaret in Theresienstadt

One of the most versatile cabaret authors and stage innovators, capable of involving both professional artists and amateurs, was the Czech-Jewish poet, actor, composer and playwright Karel Švenk, an artist engaged in the Communist-inspired youth movement Mladá Kultura. From 1926 to 1938, he conducted Prague's *Divadlo ztracených talentu*, which also involved the actors Cajlais (Jiří Süssland) and Loris Sushicky.

Arrested and sent to Theresienstadt on 24 November 1941, Švenk staged his works in the attic of the Magdeburg pavilion, including *At žije život*, *Poslední cyklista* (prohibited by the *Judenrat* during rehearsals), and wrote songs performed in his revues, including 'Balada o hladovém břichu', 'Hola hou', 'Ukolébavka', 'Rozloučení' and 'Vsechno jde!' The latter was very popular in the camp and generally sung with the audience at the end of the show. On 28 September 1944, Švenk was transferred to Birkenau and then to Meuselwitz.

Vilém Süssland (Jiří's brother) wrote in a letter dated June 1945 that a month earlier he had hidden from the German guards an already very ill Švenk in a barn during the march from Graslitz to Žatec: it was the last time he saw him.

*   *   *

The Czech cabaret artist and actor Hans Hofer (born Hanuš Schulhof), arrested with his wife, Elisabeth 'Lisl' Steinitz, an actress and singer, and transferred to Theresienstadt in late July 1942, devoted himself to developing cabaret theatre in the camp. He created the *Hofer-Kabarett* and worked with director Irena Dodalová on the filming of *Theresienstadt 1942*.

He staged revues and serious plays, including *Spiel im Schloss* by Franz Molnar and *Souper zum Abschied* by Arthur Schnitzler, as well as the Johann Strauss operetta *Die Fledermaus*. He was transferred to Birkenau in late September 1944, Dachau two weeks later and, finally, on to Kaufering, where he was liberated in 1945. He returned to Prague and, in 1960, settled in Rostock.

Czech writer and producer Felix Porges (also known as Prokeš) penned, in collaboration with Vítězslav 'Pidla' Horpatzky, Pavel Weisskopf and Pavel Stránsky, the music for the cabaret *Smějte se s námi*, inspired by the theatrical model of Prague's Osvobozené Divadlo and staged in 1944 with Karel Berman. Czech Otto Skuteczky, born in Brno and at that time living in Vienna, was arrested and sent to Theresienstadt, where he wrote the song 'Drunt'im Prater ist ein Platzerl' to text by Leo Strauss, which is dated 3 April 1944. He died in Theresienstadt the same year.

Czech Adolf Strauss, born in Žatec, was also a resident of Prague, and was arrested and sent to Theresienstadt too, where he wrote the song 'Heimweh' and the tango *Ich weiss bestimmt, ich werd Dich wiedersehn!* On 28 September, he was moved to Birkenau, where he is presumed to have died a few days later. Similarly, Czech Evald Weiss, who lived in Prague as well, was arrested and transferred to Theresienstadt. There, he wrote the song 'Eine Kleinigkeit' from the German revue *Die Welt von oben*, dated August 1944. On 28 September, he was transferred to Birkenau, where he is believed to have died a few days later.

On 1 April 1943, the Austrian-Jewish journalist Walter Lindenbaum, founder of Vienna's socialist writers' union, was send to Theresienstadt with his wife, Rachel, and daughter, Ruth. He staged cabaret shows and wrote *In einem kleinen Café in Terezín*, based on *In einem kleinen Café in Hernals* by Peter Herz and Hermann Leopoldi – who also cowrote the *Buchenwalder Lagerlied* with Fritz Löhner-Beda – and *Und die Musik spielt dazu*, based on *Und die Musik spielt dazu* by Fred Raymond. He was relocated to Birkenau, where his wife and daughter died, on 28 September 1944, then to Buchenwald and finally on to the sub-camp of Ohrdruf, where he died in February 1945.

FOURTEEN

A History that Needs Rewriting

Kurt Widmann and degenerate music

Between 1938 and 1942, the German jazz musician and conductor Kurt 'Kutte' Widmann was repeatedly 'reprimanded' by the Nazi higher ranks for what they considered to be the overtly 'Jewish' and 'degenerate' style of his music, as he continued to ostentatiously play swing, jazz and other unseemly music in German nightclubs.

Between 1944 and 1945, however, even though the Third Reich was engaged in an exhausting full-scale war and Berlin was a city on the frontline, its theatres and concert halls were still giving top-quality concerts to large audiences of civilians and soldiers not directly involved in combat. So much so that, in 1944, Widmann exclaimed: *'Die entartete Musik hat doch gesiegt!'* ('Degenerate music has won anyway!').

Some would even argue that more important than victories on the war front are such victories of talent as these; the former redrawing national boundaries, the latter rebuilding entire civilisations. Over the centuries, musical language has perfected mechanisms of indestructibility and transmutation from one medium to another; where paper cannot reach, other media come in to aid direct and reconstructed memory.

Music is a universal language, the only immaterial reality

capable of making everybody human, even if it's only for a few seconds. We have a duty to believe that. In the camps, when everybody was playing music, the skies opened. Singing about the camp helped exorcise some of the horror. Those who made music glued together the pieces of a shattered world.

Tango

Tango is pain remodulated into music, eros in pure form with a man and a woman in a tight embrace and unequivocal body language, and some claim it originates in Jewish ancestral rhythm used in synagogue chanting. 'Lechà Dodì', 'Kedushà' from the 'Amidà' and 'Adon Olam' are marked with the rhythm of the tango, for example. It is said cantors and musicians in the Second Temple created the rhythm and *melos* we know as tango, which should in all respects be attributed to Jewish heritage, as is the primordial Gregorian chant, a translation of the Temple chant into the Christian liturgical repertoire. Tango has survived the diaspora, transcontinental migrations and many attempts at imitation, and is still here, today, passionate, intense, brimming with energy and indescribable urges. Tango is music, singing, dancing, poetry and the metric scenario of a vast traditional and street repertoire. It was exported to Argentina two centuries ago by Galician Jews.

You can die from tango, some feel. Singers and musicians have been dazzled by it, bewitched by it and even the concentration camps could not remain immune to it, since they were absurd, small-scale metropoles which, when the Nazi regime was in full swing, became a kaleidoscope of rhythms and musical traditions constantly on the verge of meeting and influencing one another.

In Auschwitz I and Buchenwald, the Pole Józef Kropiński wrote monumental tangos. In Auschwitz I and Płaszów, unknown hands drafted a Polish text to the melody of *Niewolnicze tango*. Polish texts were brought back by Elżbietą Bogacką (an Auschwitz I survivor) and Józefa Janeczek; that was how the heart-wrenching 'Tango fun Oshwientschim', mentioned by the survivor Irke Yanowski, came about. In 1948 in New York, the Lithuanian writer and partisan Shmerke Kaczerginski published the 'Tango fun Oshwientschim' in his volume *Lider fun di getos un lagern*, replacing the original Polish text with its translation into Yiddish.

It is known that Adolf Hitler adored music by the Argentinian Eduardo Vicente Bianco, but nobody could ever have imagined that Bianco's famous tango, 'Plegaria', would become an earworm in many concentration camps, loved by both German officers and deportees. There is also the 'Yiddishe Tango' written in Lithuanian ghettos, and the tango 'Moyshe halt zikh', performed on the day the Vilnius ghetto was closed. It is also worth listening to the tangos from Dachau, Sachsenhausen, Gusen I and II, Kraków-Płaszów, Stutthof and Stalag II C Greifswald, where the French prisoner of war Sylvain Raiter wrote the melancholy 'Un jour tu me reviendras'.

An ocean of pathos flowed through the ranks of those sentenced to death, who – making sure the guards heard them – would sing new lyrics to famous tangos. 'Todestangos' (Tangos of death) were created in Sachsenhausen as well as in Janowska; the final wishes of convicts who jeered at death and drank a toast to life. They would have preferred freedom and life; they found suffering and death instead and gave us back music.

The most beautiful tango in the world, to my mind, was

written in Birkenau and was composed by an anonymous Pole. Aleksander Kulisiewicz and Jan Tacina wrote it down in notation and in two different versions in terms of tonality, metre and rhythm. When, on beat 37, the tenor sings to an inhuman melody the name of this notorious concentration camp, it takes your breath away and you can't catch it again.

While Europe was sinking, musicians played the last tango not in a splendid Viennese café, but in Block 5 of Auschwitz–Birkenau (the so-called *Notenschreiberblock*), red-hot from the heat. It fell to deported musicians to hold the torch of human dignity high; and they did so finely.

To the beat of the tango.

Memory as the true muscle of the spirit

Music is the *fil rouge* that connects Auschwitz to the Siam-Burma Railway – the tragedy of war is universal, deaths in camps are equivalent in their tragedy, and the works of music written by anybody who has suffered coexist like the animals in Noah's Ark. There may be differences in life but not in death. A name must be attributed to every musician who spent even a single day of suffering in captivity and deportation, and the sounds and designs they created must be returned to them. That is the importance of concentrationary music studies.

Memory is not an option for the intellect; memory is the true muscle of the spirit, and it finds its broadest creative expression in music. The notes, signs and structure visible on every sheet are but the tip of the iceberg. In captivity, music writing becomes sculpture; the music sign is etched on paper and contains physical effort aggravated by the environment; it is etched on paper so that the testimonial of the talent produced in the most devastating human discomfort may long remain.

Humans are the planet's geniuses at preserving the mechanisms of time. In the eye of the storm of the war's deportation catastrophe, people belonging to all social and religious spheres laid the foundations of a new world and remodelled the

Metropolitan Museum, the Sorbonne and the Library of Congress. This is the secret of the music written in captivity: it has codified on thousands of scores as many responses of the intellect and the heart to the tragedy.

In Hebrew, you say, '*Bemotàm zivu lanu et hachaim*' or 'with their deaths they commanded us life'. To bring thinking, art, and music written in the camps back to the forefront is not a free choice but a mission; it is what the German Jewish (naturalised Israeli) philosopher and educator Emil Ludwig Fackenheim called 'the six-hundred and fourteenth mitzvah' – in other words, 'Do not grant Hitler posthumous victory.'

To liberate this music – all of it – from the camps for ever is a political and democratic objective.

Coats and jute sacks

Scores sewn into the lining of coats, musical instruments taken apart and hidden in suitcases, an abundance of sheet music rolled up tightly and concealed in dirty laundry in the prison infirmaries, chords for guitar pieces slipped in as codes when writing postcards sent from the camp to one's personal address. Piano concertos written on the clean side of wrapping paper for food, musical sketches on jute sacks used for shovelling coal or concrete, piano or choral pieces written on scrap paper. Prison walls turned into music albums, works for soloist and orchestra written in many little music notebooks and stashed among the internees' clothes to evade the dormitory guards. Sheets of music slipped into books in the camp's small library so that they could be picked up and tucked away by the librarian. Religious hymns marked on the topsoil of potato fields during forced labour, so that they could be reconstructed from memory that evening in the dormitory and jotted down on toilet paper. Songs passed on from memory on board trains that arrived at the camps filled with deportees, mess tins for rations covered in melodies scratched out with a little knife concealed in a piece of clothing or in the latrines. Songs in strophic form sung from one prison block to another in the evening, after the roll call, which have reached posterity intact, like a giant, momentous tom-tom. I could go on for hours, listing the ways in which concentrationary music was created, as well as the stratagems used to safeguard it, hand it down and define it.

A large portion of the musical output born in captivity could be seen as a giant trick musicians played on the camp authorities. Musicians not only metaphorically rebuilt Darmstadt but also the Greek theatre of Syracuse and the Opéra Garnier. From the triumph of Spanish flamenco in Mauthausen to the great symphonic masterpieces of Theresienstadt, they dug deep into the foundations of the musical language of Europe, handing down to posterity a new notion of music and theatre.

The first music groups in Buchenwald (1938) and Mauthausen (1942), however, were not assembled by musicians who were political deportees or Soviet prisoners of war, but by Sinti and Roma. Those who, like Jews and Roma, breathe music as though it were oxygen, could not do otherwise and would certainly not have been stopped by barbed wire and fortified walls.

As the author and playwright Miguel de Unamuno says, if an exhausted man in the desert sees a puddle of water on the horizon, runs towards it and has a life-saving drink from it, nobody can tell him one day that it was a mirage and that there has never been a puddle of water in that part of the desert. The man in the desert really did drink that water.

Beauty as resistance

Concentrationary music could be described as an evolved form of electromagnetism of the spirit, capable of transforming the negativity of the physical location into positivity in a mental and spiritual location: in other words, deep and total regeneration. The totalitarianisms of the past century produced wars, massacres, starvation, tragedies and humanitarian disasters. Wars provoked by clashes between totalitarian regimes are not errors of calculation but planned acts of territorial, economic, social and human destruction.

Literary, artistic and musical output in captivity is a constant of human talent in the total inequality of the collapse of civilisation caused by the Second World War.

Music, painting, theatre, dressmaking, sculpture, football and chess tournaments. Libraries and crafts, farming rabbits, building places of worship. A magazine printed with gelatine retrieved from an X-ray, constructing cameras with lenses obtained from the bottom of drinking glasses. Radio equipment, surgical tools, clocks made with metal and wood. Topographical instruments to measure the altitude of mountains, telescopes and threshing machines. Blood transfusion devices, turbines with a boiler, carpentry utensils. Violins and guitars with square soundboxes, given how hard it is to make string instruments (the strings were original but the wires from Jeep brakes were good enough too). In the camps, you gradually fell prey to despair if you didn't have an occupation; it was essential to have a purpose, a goal, to keep your muscles and brain in good shape.

Music from another world

In contrast, a controversial voice free from any post-war sentimentality, and an opponent of the widespread belief that music infused the deportees with hope and mental endurance, Szymon Laks writes in his book *Mélodies d'Auschwitz* – forty years after his *Musiques d'un autre monde* – that in Auschwitz, music was a tool in the hands of the oppressor and not the victims, that it exacerbated the psychological state of the prisoners by encouraging them to work without thinking and caused them distress. At Christmas 1943 in Birkenau, for example, Laks and his orchestra were instructed to play for the sick women in the infirmary. In an atmosphere made oppressive by the unbearable stench of the dying, the musicians performed Christmas carols, while the women cried and screamed to be allowed to die in peace. Laks was deeply disturbed by this.

I have known André Laks, Szymon's son, since he was a university lecturer in Lille, then at the Paris Sorbonne. I asked him for material by his father and the formidable orchestral arrangement of the Birkenau *Trois polonaises Varsoviennes* which Laks wrote down after the war. André sent everything to me within a few days.

With regard to his father, André wrote: 'Auschwitz had little to do with music, real music. [. . .] My father was a composer before and after Auschwitz'; not during it. These statements are the opposite of what Aleksander Kulisiewicz thought, and in direct contract to what my own research has led me to believe. No wonder our meeting in Paris in 1974 was disappointing, a total failure; two irreconcilable visions of the artistic phenomenon of concentration camps – Kulisiewicz and Laks – both the result of deep suffering and bitter existential reflection, but, to me, Kulisiewicz's argument is the stronger. And yet.

'I go back to Birkenau every night,' wrote the Trieste-Jewish author Ida Marcheria, a survivor. The challenge for those who gather music where there is death is to try to relieve the distress of an unbearable night journey to Birkenau, say, thanks to the ancestral sound of the *Amen* and the coolness of spring water that only music can rekindle in the senses of a human being.

This music is not from another world – as Laks might think at first glance – but the song of the Earth. Our music. One day, when we remember Auschwitz, we will talk of music; only then, I believe, will we have freed and redeemed both Auschwitz and music.

I completed my arrangement of *Trois polonaises Varsoviennes* for a small orchestra – it comes as near as possible to the numbers Szymon Laks presumably used for these pieces in Birkenau. They belong to another world, as Laks correctly asserts. They smell of the prison block; they're full of false cheer and have nothing of Lak's, apart from the fact that he found them jotted on a sheet of paper that stank of urine, and arranged them to liven up an evening at the officers' club in Birkenau.

FIFTEEN

Maestro

One film, a hundred journeys

Although the film *Musica Concentrationaria* came about on the back of *KZ Musik*, which I was recording for Musikstrasse in those years, the genesis of *Maestro* was very different. The process began with the book of the same title by the Frenchman Thomas Saintourens, which happened to fall into the hands of the Argentinian director Alexandre Valenti. He read it in one sitting and decided he absolutely had to meet me and the writer to see if it could be turned into a documentary. With film producers Loïc Bouchet, Marco Visalberghi and Donatella Altieri – who would later become the manager of my foundation – we established a basis from which to develop an Italo–French partnership.

Fortunately, joining forces increased the budget and the number of journeys, as well as the opportunities to travel reasonably comfortably, and added a few more colleagues than for *Musica Concentrationaria*, which Ermanno Felli and I had made totally on our own. As a result of two years of travels and meetings, we took home over 150 interviews that would be used in two versions of the film: a shorter one, of 54 minutes, and a longer one, of 72.

Harry Berry

One of our first destinations was the UK, and we reached Dover by sea. The day before we sailed, I received sad news: for serious health reasons, my sweet friend Linda Berry – Harry Berry's daughter, as well as one of the first people to have contributed to my research – would be unable to meet me in London.

Henry William (Harry) Berry was born in Islington, north London, in 1916; he was editorial assistant at the London evening paper *The Star* and played the piano in a dance band. On 18 February 1942, he was captured by Japanese troops and sent to Changi prison, then to Taiwan, along with 1,100 other prisoners of war. When the Japanese discovered that he was a journalist, they transferred him to Camp 1 Ōmori, in Tokyo, in order to try to persuade him to help with Japanese propaganda. Even though they failed, he was spared forced labour and was able to stage shows in the camp, as well as writing songs and theatre pieces for the entertainment of soldiers, with the help of Sergeant Derek Clarke. Decades later, in 1987, he sent his godson Christopher a cassette called *Songs from FEPOW Shows 1942–1945*, on which he had recorded – singing and playing the electric organ – the songs written in the Japanese camps. He died in 2004.

Linda sent me the songs recorded by her father and various books, too. I quickly recovered the arrangements and recorded them for *KZ Musik*. Although Linda found the singers' English very Italian, she likes these recordings. So, I was upset not to be able to meet her.

Hans Gál and Tom Boardman

In the absence of meeting Linda Berry, we skipped the London stop and headed north to York. The driver set the satnav to the shortest route, which, however, turned out to be the one with the most traffic. Consequently, we arrived in the city, late in the evening, after all the restaurants were shut. Our meeting with Eva Fox-Gál, the daughter of the Austrian-Jewish composer and musicologist Hans Gál, was scheduled for the following morning.

Born in Vienna in 1890, Gál had studied then taught at the Vienna conservatoire, then been the director of the Mainz conservatoire. In 1938, following the Anschluss, he took refuge in Edinburgh. In 1940, because he was a foreigner with an Austrian passport, he was interned at the Huyton camp, near Liverpool. During this internment, Gál wrote the *Huyton Suite*, op. 92, for flute and two violins, the only musical instruments available in the camp.

Eva told us her father was reasonably calm during that period, having already suffered exile and emigration. After Huyton, her father was transferred to the Isle of Man, where he wrote the short opera *What a life!* and even stayed on there for an extra day in order to stage it.

Eva had huge, wonderful portraits of her father in her home, and invited us to stay for lunch after our meeting, but we just had a quick bite because we were on a very tight schedule with other people to interview.

The next morning we met Tom Boardman, who had been detained in the Wang Po Japanese prisoner-of-war camp, along the Siam-Burma Railway. During his imprisonment, Boardman – a keen guitarist – had built himself a ukulele and become a virtuoso on it; he would play and sing nostalgic songs to his fellow inmates.

When we arrived, Boardman's son told us his father was very elderly and would not be able to grant us more than half an hour. In actual fact, Tom Boardman was extremely polite and turned out to be like an overflowing river. He was still telling me about his adventures in the Japanese camps when I realised we had been there for over three hours.

He sang me his prison songs and I took pictures of his music notebooks and the ukulele tablatures. When I asked him to play, he told me he had donated his ukulele to a museum in Manchester. Time flew by, and after taking all the equipment down, we left Boardman's house, all the richer.

The Death Railway

As part of Japan's strategy, the Siam-Burma Railway – the so-called 'Death Railway' – was supposed to link Bangkok and Rangoon with 415 km of tracks. It was built not only to ensure logistic and military supplies to the Japanese troops but also as a breach through British lines in preparation for an invasion of the Indian peninsula, which did not happen. Some 250,000 people, including prisoners of war and *Rōmusha* – the Japanese word for the civilian population roped into forced labour – were used on its construction, with over 100,000 people dying.

The Death Railway was the largest concentration and prisoner-of-war camp in the Second World War, and technically the largest forced labour camp. If we did not know what it cost in terms of human lives, the Death Railway might simply be considered a masterpiece of narrow-gauge railway engineering, with the majestic bridge over the River Mae Klong and Kwai Yai, the suspended railway link of Wang Po and the stretch of Hellfire Pass.

Nowadays, the Death Railway is almost totally derelict or abandoned on both the Thailand and Myanmar sides. Just a few short stretches of rail track are used in Thailand and on the bridge over the River Kwai Yai in Kanchanaburi.

IWM and Fergus Anckorn

There was no time to have something to eat after our visit to Tom Boardman. We returned to London as quickly as we could, because the next day a full immersion was awaiting me at the Imperial War Museum (IWM).

I was going to penetrate this mausoleum of war history, in particular that relating to the Second World War. Of particular interest were the upper floors, where the offices and archives were situated and the technicians made available to us dozens and dozens of folders literally brimming with music.

Here, at the IWM, I once again came up against the fundamental conundrum of my research: if music remains shut away in archives and box files, it might as well be dead. No one will perform it, publish it or restore it to life. We can use box files to store war reports, chronological papers, photographs and everything you need in order to document history, but not music. That must be performed and played.

I decided to take advantage of the two hours I had been granted as best I could to photograph the material and take note of every single piece of music, so that one day I could work out which piece belonged to which composer. After two hours of photographing, covering barely one-fifth of the material, I knew without a doubt that another trip to the museum had to be organised.

In the afternoon we went to Brighton, where the magician of Wang Po, Fergus Anckorn, was expecting us. He was the man who had won over the Japanese soldiers by entertaining them with magic tricks, singing songs and improvising comedy sketches. Fergus owed everything to magic, even his life. He had fought in Southeast Asia between 1941 and 1943, evading death more than once, then was transferred from Changi to the Death Railway.

When we arrived at his place, I immediately asked him to perform a couple of magic tricks for me and the crew. Fergus, to our delight, would take little balls and thimbles that would vanish and reappear, springing from his arms and legs. I found myself watching him in amazement, the way the Japanese soldiers must have done.

Fergus then put the tricks aside and went on to tell me about the realities of the camps, the most tragic sides of the deportation. About how the prisoners were so hungry they ate dogs, large rats and anything they could lay their hands on, since food rations in the Japanese POW camps were insufficient for tackling a daily eighteen-hour work shift.

'And yet in the evening, we, the prisoners, found a way to play music, do some theatre and create art and music all the same,' he added good naturedly.

Once the daily process of building the Death Railway was finished, he would put aside his exhaustion, apply make-up, take up the guitar or the violin and make music or theatre. Among the most popular songs was the famous 'Colonel Bogey March', a piece written in 1914 by Lieutenant Frederick Joseph Ricketts, a British army band master. It was an ironic, salacious song, and the Japanese soldiers, not speaking English, paid no heed to the banal words and rude adjectives in the concentration camp version the prisoners of war created.

Before we left, I asked Fergus for another magic trick, and he took a thimble out of my ear.

Bangkok and the River Kwai

At Bangkok airport, the first thing I noticed was a sign warning visitors that it was a crime to offend the name of Buddha. We dropped off our suitcases at the hotel reception, and then headed off with a driver and an interpreter to a village with an unpronounceable name a hundred kilometres outside the city. Once we arrived, I felt as though I were walking through the living rooms of other homes before reaching that of our witness, a lady who had been an interpreter for the occupying Japanese authorities and who remembered many songs.

The woman explained that the Japanese occupation had been very harsh towards the prisoners of war building the Death Railway, but had been relatively peaceful in Thailand, Japan's valuable ally in its plans for continental expansion.

The interview went on for a long time and my jet lag was beginning to make itself felt. We finished in time to walk back to the car and there my jet lag gained the upper hand, and we fell asleep for the whole drive back to Bangkok.

The following day, with the same driver and a guide, we headed to the bridge over the River Kwai Yai at Kanchanaburi, which lives in the imagination of anyone who has seen David Lean's

242

1957 film. In Lean's version, you see a wooden bridge being blown up: the bridge today is made of solid iron, but during the war there was a timber one next to our bridge, and that one was subsequently demolished.

After changing to a minibus during the journey and a stop for lunch, consisting of rice at a street food place where the restaurateur was chopping raw chickens in the street, we finally reached Kanchanaburi. Our hotel was right opposite the bridge. When the train is not passing through, you can walk along the bridge on foot; there is a temple nearby with a Buddha sitting up straight. The guide explained that the Buddha's posture suggested this was a Chinese temple (in Thai temples the Buddha reclines).

We had to go on to Chungkai next, where there is a military cemetery. The Chungkai camp was opened in November 1942 and closed in June 1945. It stood on Thai territory and had 11,000 prisoners of war engaged in forced labour on both the northern line of the railroad bound for Wun Lun and the construction of the two bridges over the River Kwai Yai. Those interned at Chungkai included the British lieutenant Norman Smith – trumpeter, conductor and arranger of the prisoners' orchestra in Kanchanaburi – who wrote a bolero for two violins, clarinet, two trumpets and guitar called *The Exiles*; in 1944 the bolero was performed in Chungkai in an arrangement by the jazz musician, stand-up comedian, clown, bandleader and music producer Han (Henri Jacques) Samethini, a colonial Dutchman born in 1916 in Bondowoso (Java Timur).

It started to rain, and since the quickest way there was by river, we took a boat, and the guide told us we were lucky, because the monsoon season would be starting shortly. But thankfully I obtained so much information and material that I was able to reconstruct the entire history of concentrationary music during the Japanese occupation in Thailand.

The following day, the driver and the guide were waiting for us at dawn because we had a very long way to go; en route we restocked on water in a kind of park where hapless elephants were carrying visitors on excursions and were throwing balls at each other with their trunks.

We reached the Hellfire Pass, one of the most tragic chapters in the building of the Death Railway, which involved the gutting of the mountain in order to allow the train through.

We were met by Rod Beattie, one of the greatest experts in the history of Japanese occupation in Thailand. An Australian by birth, he was a soldier and an engineer and knew practically everything there was to know about the history of the Hellfire Pass and the Death Railway. We went to his office, where Beattie opened a huge Excel sheet and scrolled down the names of all the prisoners of war who had died or survived.

Hellfire Pass

We had to get organised to reach the Hellfire Pass, which was deep in the forest, but before that we had a stop at the museum, which showed a documentary in a loop about the history of the Death Railway. At the museum, Australian soldiers were distributing bottles of chilled water; that day the humidity was at 100%, so you practically couldn't breathe and you couldn't reach the ill-reputed Hellfire Pass except by walking through the forest.

The Hellfire Pass was a concentration and forced labour camp for Australian and New Zealand prisoners of war and *Rōmusha* (civilian). The silence that hung over this place, as well as the humid air, left us speechless: there was nothing for me to do except observe, take notes and reflect, just as in the concentration camps of Europe. Rod Beattie told me that during the days when the Hellfire Pass was being dug out, the prisoners got so used to death that they sometimes saw their inmates fall off the mountain or crushed under the stones without expressing any reaction.

We had two more days available and Alexandre, our director, needed good light to film the documentary, so we decided to wake up at 6 a.m. one day and rush to the bridge over the River

Kwai Yai. There was hardly anyone there when we arrived. We crossed it on foot, slowly. A few hours later, in Kanchanaburi, we met a Thai couple who had been co-opted into work on the railway – two elderly people with gaunt faces and small, glistening eyes. Sitting on two rickety chairs, they took it in turns to speak and, once they had finished their stories, sang the forced labour songs.

It was just two songs. I could not understand the language, but the tunes were enchanting; a phrasing far removed from Western tradition, in which the verse is not clearly distinguishable from the refrain, and at times the song turns into a trill like that of a bird. I recorded it.

We skirted the railroad, where it is still possible to see stretches of dead or disused track, and where the new railway uses segments of the old tracks laid down by the POWs. In Wang Po, we came across another tragic monument to the Death Railway, just as it was built by the POWs: a railway junction that skirts around the mountain on the River Kwai Yai, all made of timber, stretching along the flank of the mountain and still intact.

The plan was to walk along the railroad as far as possible and film it, but Alexandre was carrying a large heavy camera. It suddenly occurred to me that if a train suddenly arrived, our only way out would be to dive into the River Kwai Yai with all our equipment.

On the last day of our trip, our guide took us to a district a long way from Kanchanaburi. In a village, there was a hut and, in the hut, just like in a fairy tale, there was a very old man, who had also been co-opted by the Japanese to build the Death Railway. The old man seemed to have been there foever – you would have thought he was a thousand years old. We sat listening to him while our guide translated his story: the man had worked on the Hellfire Pass and, every day, had been taken to the site. Whenever they stopped work, the *Rōmusha* would create songs and our elderly friend sang me at least half a dozen of them, leaving me astounded. We were interrupted by the arrival of an officer of the Thai army. Our expedition had been authorised by the government and he was checking all was well. He stayed with us a long time, then waved goodbye and left.

When it was time to go back to Kanchanaburi and from there to Bangkok, we decided to take an ancient little train. We had to film the landscape and Marc, Alexandre's son and our photographer, climbed on the top of the train like a squirrel and placed the GoPro cameras so they would record the journey. As we travelled, he took pictures of us all and, in order to see him, we leant out of the window and he'd yell at us to keep our heads in when we were approaching tunnels.

We reached Kanchanaburi via the legendary bridge, and the 'Colonel Bogey March' started in my ears in a loop. I imagined it whistled and its trivial lyrics sung by the heroic builders of the bridge. We collected our suitcases from the hotel and the driver took us back to Bangkok, where we arrived almost at midnight.

The next day, we made a stop a world away in Paris and I was back in Barletta in time for Yom Kippur.

SIXTEEN

New Encounters

Wally Karveno

No doubt one of my most thrilling encounters during my research was in Paris with the French pianist and composer Wally Karveno. I had a lot of information about a Concertino, op. 28, for piano and chamber orchestra, which she had written in the French internment camp of Gurs, at the foot of the Pyrenees. We reached her on a rainy day in 2015; the meeting had been meticulously prepared so that it would be one of the highlights of the documentary, *Maestro*. The director, Alexandre Valenti, and his son, our photographer Marc, were with me.

Wally was a woman from another era; she was a hundred years old but looked seventy at most. Much admired and courted, she was still very beautiful.

'I was born in Berlin; my father was German. My maiden name was Loewenthal, a Jewish name. My mother told me Jews were hated in Germany and that I had to have another name. "What name?" I asked. She replied that she'd tell me the following day. The next morning, while I was still in bed, I heard my mother approaching. She woke me up and put a piece of paper in my hand. It had *Wally Karveno* written on it. My mother had decided that would be my new name.'

With the witty, sprightly manner of a lady used to having

the world at her feet, Wally occasionally said something in French which I did not understand, but, judging by the way Alexandre's sparse hair would stand on end behind the camera, I gathered it had something to do with her life as an attractive young woman. Then, she sat down at the piano.

She played an extract from the Concertino. At one point she stopped and looked at me as I stood staring at her hands. 'Ah, that's right – the score,' she said.

We went to the archive that extended along her corridor, I opened all the box files and finally found the one called *Piano*: the Concertino was there, as I'd hoped. Wally gave me the manuscript so that Marc could photograph it that same evening and return it to her the following day.

'Take good care of my Concertino, I only have one copy.'

I promised I would study and perform it within a year. Paolo Candido wrote the score on the computer and adapted it for two pianos so that I could study it, but my work on the documentary took up a lot of time. When I went to see Wally again the following year to complete the filming, she was a hundred and one years old and I looked as sheepish as a schoolboy sitting an exam unprepared.

I played a few passages and Wally scolded me fiercely. I will never know how she could tell that I was not playing her Concertino well, since that morning – so she said – she had misplaced her hearing aids, but she did. I promised her again that I would play it on my next trip to Paris. This time I kept my promise, and, in September 2015, we recorded it for the documentary.

On the day of the dress rehearsal, the first viola asked me, 'Is this Karveno's name Carla Loewenthal, by any chance?'

'Yes – why?'

'Because she died two months ago.'

My heart sank.

Still we made a marvellous recording of the concerto for the documentary, with me at the piano and Paolo conducting, a dedication to the talent and verve of a marvellous woman.

Two days after *Maestro* was broadcast on France 2, I received a phone call from Orlane Letourneur and an email from Renaud Paquin, Wally's two children. The French company that produced the documentary had given them my details.

Renaud and I promised to meet in Paris as soon as we could and I asked him if I could possibly have the manuscript of the Concertino someday for the Foundation. Renaud promised to discuss it with his sister.

When we did meet, he shared a detail about his mother's death. 'Almost every Sunday I would pick her up and take her to lunch in a restaurant. One Sunday, my mother looked at the other guests and, when dessert came, told them that would be the last time they would see her. "Tomorrow I'm going to bed and not getting up again."'

Renaud did not take this very seriously; he knew his mother well and that she was a wit and a prankster. But that was exactly how things turned out: Wally went to bed and did not get up again. She let herself go. At the age of a hundred and one, she felt she had given everything.

Renaud and I parted, agreeing to be in touch about the manuscript in another two months, but time flew, as well as all our good intentions. I wrote to him on WhatsApp but he did not reply and I noticed that he had not used the app for months. I wrote to Orlane, who lives in Saint-Tropez, and she replied that her brother had passed away only recently.

I asked her about the manuscript, and for permission to publish the Concertino in the *Thesaurus Musicae Concentrationariae*, and she generously agreed.

Palmyra and Mosul

Music begins while history beats its tempo and dictates its cadenza. Then, as now, a fundamental mission of this musical literature is to rattle history, save the human brain and heart and, like an elixir of long life, produce the best possible future. Humans, animals and plants are born; however, only humans are given the opportunity to retrace their steps and recreate what has been destroyed by other humans or chance and natural causes, through art.

We will rebuild Palmyra and Mosul, razed to the ground by ISIS, the Bamiyan Buddhas blown up by the Taliban and Notre-Dame burnt down by a short-circuit: heritage the contemporary human has seen. But we can equally rebuild the huge library of Alexandria, burnt to ashes by the Arab army of Amr ibn al-ʾĀṣ, and the alluring city of Shangri-La, hurled into the abyss of collective imagination: a heritage no contemporary human has seen.

In May 1972, when the Australian geologist László Tóth took a hammer to Michelangelo's *Pietà*, some people suggested the work should be kept damaged, as a testimonial to the state of abomination we had reached, but the Vatican authorities decided to restore it exactly as it was before being vandalised.

It was the right decision and not just because it returned the work to its original splendour – an American tourist who had picked up pieces of marble in the throng and taken them home sent them back to the Holy See anonymously; this made it possible for the restorers to glue back together the original pieces instead of copies. The processes of artistic regeneration do not work intermittently but must be followed meticulously step by step and letter by letter, from the first stone to the last capital. You do not start from where the author finished but from where they began.

Every work has its creator and co-creator, from the restorer to the archeologist to the musician; regardless of whether the creator leaves the work complete or unfinished, they nevertheless insert numbers, codes, indicator lights, brain materials with which to reconstruct it – in case of damage – or else to complete or perfect it.

Giuseppe Capostagno

During the period we were working on the documentary, I received an email from a certain Roberto Stringa, from Bassano del Grappa, saying he was the nephew of one of the Italian prisoners of war interned in Yol, at the foot of the Himalayas. About 10,000 Italian officers captured by British troops in Africa were transferred through Axum to India (then still under British control) and subsequently interned in various camps, including Yol, in the province of Himachal Pradesh. Stringa had seen me on TV and wrote to say he had materials and information about the musical activities of Italians in this huge British camp.

We did not meet straight away; my mother had been ill, so I kept postponing my trip to Bassano del Grappa. I then decided to combine Bassano with a trip to Poland. Once I was there, looking through the documents, the name Capostagno jumped out of a Yol music programme at me – the composer of a *Himalajana Suite*, spelt with a 'j'.

The programme did not list Capostagno's first name, and having only his surname was not much help, but it was still the only original piece in a programme that also included Beethoven, Geminiani, Bellini, Liszt and Verdi. All listed strictly by surname only.

I left for Poland, but when I returned I started looking for this Capostagno. It's a common surname throughout Italy, but after some specific online research I found a certain Giuseppe Capostagno, a musician and general stationed in Spoleto but born in Palazzo Adriano, the Sicilian town featured in Giuseppe Tornatore's 1988 film, *Nuovo Cinema Paradiso*.

As so often before, I resorted to a tried and tested technique: I contacted the town library. Capostagno was very well known in Palazzo Adriano. The librarian promised to have one of his relatives call me. A few hours later, I received a phone call from Lilly Capostagno, Giuseppe's niece. She told me about her uncle and, most importantly, put me in touch with his son, who lived in Catania.

I called Claudio Capostagno, who immediately understood what I was talking about: he was aware of *Himalajana* but did not have the score. He thought it might still be in his father's house in Spoleto – his last residence as a general: Claudio would have to go and find it. I told him to take all the time he needed, but in truth I was terrified it had been lost.

One day, while flying back from Pisa, where my father and I had taken my mother to a private hospital in a final, desperate attempt to get her well, I received a call from Claudio Capostagno. He informed me that he had found the manuscript in Spoleto and we promised to meet in Rome, where he was going for work the following month.

Shortly afterwards, I lost my mother.

Himalajana

During a very sad phase in my life, tracking down *Himalajana* from a surname read in a photocopy of a music programme from Yol restored my confidence. And I was further rewarded in the lobby of the Hotel Mediterraneo in Rome, where I met Claudio Capostagno. He had made a photocopy of the symphonic poem. I discovered that in Yol, his father had also written 'Rose a Firenze', a delightful song for tenor and piano. Not only had my search been fruitful, but it was enriched by this find as well.

We parted, promising to meet again, and I intended to record and publish the work in the *Thesaurus* and, above all, perform it. As soon as I had left the hotel, I started dancing all alone in Via Cavour in celebration. I probably was not quite alone, though, because a traffic warden gave me a nasty look.

Months later, Alexandre, the team and I went to Palazzo Adriano to film *Maestro*. I wanted to delve deep into Capostagno's birthplace, a town I had until then only seen artfully transfigured in Tornatore's film. The local residents gave us a warm welcome and Claudio was there with his brother, Eros, who had come specially from The Hague, where he lived. The mayor welcomed us to the town hall, the cathedral priest took us up to the bell tower, from which there is a breathtaking view. I almost took a tour of the town on Alfredo's bicycle – Alfredo was the character played by Philippe Noiret in the film and it is in the small museum dedicated to all things *Cinema Paradiso*.

While interned in Yol, Capostagno had been a lieutenant, but he ended his career as a general. He wrote a few other songs and short pieces, including a popular song a young female singer sang for us with a trio of guitar and mandolins. It must have been written by a very young Capostagno, but it has stayed in the historical memory of the town.

On 27 January 2018, at the Teatro Massimo Bellini in Catania, the first modern performance of *Himalajana* was given. Paolo Candido, having rewritten the score on the computer, was there that evening, holding the baton, ready to conduct, with both Claudio and Eros Capostagno in the audience. All this thanks to chance, a surname on a photocopy, I thought.

Berto Boccosi

I found information on Berto Boccosi thanks to a diary published by Nazareno Gabrielli, which suggested he was from Ancona; it was then relatively easy to locate a 'Boccosi' in Ancona through the telephone directory.

After the defeat of the Axis powers in the African campaign, thousands of Italian soldiers were interned in military prisoner-of-war camps established by the French in their North African colonies. Going against the Geneva Convention, the Anglo-American authorities had handed German and Italian soldiers over to the jurisdiction of the Free French Government, which, in collaboration with colonial troops, transferred them to prison camps in Tunisia and Algeria.

The composer and infantry captain Berto Boccosi, born in Ancona in 1910, was captured by the Allies during the African campaign and interned in the French camps No. XVIII Gabès (Tunisia) and No. VI Saïda (Algeria). In Gabès, he wrote *Rapsodia*, op. 16, for piano; in Saïda, the trilogy *Nell'Uadi Saida* for cello and piano (called *Prima Suite*), the songs 'La mia compagna' and 'Mia stella appari anche tu' for tenor and piano, and *Seconda Suite* for chorus and orchestra (lost).

Back home, Boccosi made deletions in his works and, with a

colour pencil eraser, eliminated from the score of *Rapsodia*, op. 16, all references to Gabès. He continued to compose, developing late-tonal idioms and twelve-tone technique in an original manner. He wrote piano concertos, as well as symphonic, piano and chamber works, and invented a keyboard tuned to third-tones. This man, who died years later in Falconara, in 1985, must surely be included among the best Italian contemporary composers?

Italy's musical landscape is, even now, bereft of great composers like Boccosi. So many musicians tried to restart their work and get back into the circuit once they were back from the war. Some had been interned when they were too young and there were other life demands once they were back in Italy, necessities that probably made it preferable to practise music as entertainment or a pastime after work, rather than as a profession. In other cases, deportation and imprisonment left such a mark that, although they carried on their musical work, reality probably did not come close to the great career promised before the war; that was not what happened in Berto Boccosi's case, thankfully.

His *Concerto di Mezzanotte a Venezia* is epic, as is his *Diary of Anne Frank* and other works written after the war, but his opera, *The Scarlet Letter*, which he drafted in Saïda, is a masterpiece.

Paolo Candido and I went to see Riccardo Boccosi, Berto's son, in Falconara. We had a mammoth job before us: the material was lying in a loft abandoned for years and, within ten minutes, we realised that the powerful itching of our arms and legs was caused by an infestation of parasites. The best thing to do was close everything and ask Riccardo if we could come back with the necessary disinfectants. Two weeks later, Paolo and I turned up in the loft dressed like astronauts, complete with white overalls that covered everything down to our shoes, plus latex gloves.

The music material was collected and moved to Riccardo's basement in central Ancona. From that moment on, it was up to Paolo and me to wait three days for the chemicals to take effect and then tackle preliminary filing. At this Paolo was a genius – he has the mind of a librarian and all I did was hand him the scores and check my watch periodically so we could go to lunch.

Once the first stage of filing was complete, we left everything in this basement. A few years later, Paolo and I decided it was time to resume where we had left off. We asked Riccardo if we could transport the material to Barletta, where we would prepare an archive for his father's works. He had no objection.

Without further delay, Paolo dived into the scores of *Concerto di Mezzanotte a Venezia*, and the *Diary of Anne Frank*, and I avidly studied his piano masterpieces written in captivity: *Diario di prigionia* and the *Rapsodia* – huge, complicated, extraordinary pages.

On 27 January 2018, at the Teatro Massimo Bellini in Catania, in addition to Giuseppe Capostagno's *Himalajana*, Paolo conducted the modern premiere of *Diario di prigionia*, which Boccosi had subsequently transcribed for orchestra.

We decided to dedicate to Berto Boccosi a section of the Biblioteca della Cittadella della Musica Concentrazionaria di Barletta, the one devoted to the output of soldiers in camps. I would have liked to share this news with Riccardo, but, after the umpteenth unanswered call, I found out that he, too, had passed away. Another person to whom I was sorry not to have been able to say goodbye.

Costabile Ambrosano and Cesare Savino

One day I received an email from Carlo Ambrosano, in which he wrote about his musician father, Costabile. I rang the number below the signature before I had even finished reading the message, and the following Sunday, I was driving with my wife to Carlo's house in Campania.

Following the Allies' landing in Sicily in July 1943, Costabile Ambrosano, from Castellabate (near Salerno), was captured by Moroccan troops serving in the British army. Transferred first to Tunisia, then to the French prison camp No. 127 in Chanzy, south of Oran in Algeria, he was given instructions to set up a music ensemble. He filled a whole notebook with songs, which Carlo gave me the time to look through. I have seen so many photocopies of manuscripts that I sometimes have trouble getting used to an original, handwritten document.

Another email came, this time from Leo Marinelli from Sammichele di Bari. He wrote about his musician grandfather, Cesare Savino, and, once again, I was on the phone to Leo before I had even finished reading it, and the following Sunday was back in the car with Grazia, heading to Sammichele.

After the fall of Gondar, on 27 November 1941, and British

troops entering Italian East Africa, Savino – a soldier stationed in Ethiopia – was captured and interned in a prisoner-of-war camp in Britain (presumably Huyton). A talented string instrument player, he took his violin with him and wrote a fifty-nine-page music notebook while there. He survived and died in his birthplace in 1989.

Leo's mother, Savino's daughter, is a good pianist and promptly played a lovely waltz composed by her father in captivity on an upright piano in her home: a true generational transmission. Leo's relatives further gave me a copy of Savino's notebook and showed me his violin, which was in good condition, albeit without strings.

SEVENTEEN

Globe-trotting

Jack Garfein

There are 613 mitzvot, or Jewish laws. This number saved Jack Garfein, a Ruthenian, who was deported to Birkenau with his mother, father and sister. Thirteen years old, he told Dr Josef Mengele he was sixteen to avoid being sent to the gas chamber. Instead, he was transferred to the Riese forced labour camp in Märzbachtal. In 2013, Garfein was in Italy for a film they were shooting in Trani and one of his colleagues called me; I was in Israel at the time, but she said Garfein would wait for me. The day after I returned, I invited Jack to the gardens of Castello Svevo in Barletta.

We were sitting outside the castle, me armed with pen and music manuscript paper. A tune by a prison inmate – a Pole whose name he cannot remember – gushed out of Jack's soul with all the lyrics in their right place in traditional Yiddish. There were a few intonation problems at first, but then he grew more confident until we sang it together several times. The fourth time, history took the upper hand and his singing turned into weeping, but we had made it. From that moment on, the melody was finally freed from the camp.

He told me about 613 children who were apparently going to be transferred to Britain as part of a prisoner exchange, but these Jewish children were able to count how many they were and it seems had an inkling of what would really happen. Besides, why would the British authorities want exactly 613 Jews – the number of mitzvot – for a prisoner exchange? The Germans left out one boy and limited the number to 612.

While loading the children on the lorries, however, they turned out to be 615 instead of 612, so the guards commanded three 'volunteers' to get off. Garfein hesitated at first, then raised his hand and got off with two inmates, while a Polish boy his age started singing his Yiddish song, 'Zi is mein herz', the song I had just learnt.

The 612 children (including the author of the song) were taken to Birkenau and gassed; the prisoner exchange had been a farce to prevent unrest. Garfein was saved because he was number 613.

When he told me that, I said, 'Jack, you're the 613th mitzvah!' Jack was the last law; he had to live and one day tell the story of the last Yiddish song of Europe's Jews, which had now travelled from New York to the Apulian coast.

In the afternoon I invited Jack to visit a Trani synagogue that Rav Shalom Bahbout and I had reopened for Jewish worship after five hundred years. He made a small donation and asked for two plaques to be put on the synagogue benches: one for his family, lost in Birkenau, the other for the children who could not be saved because, unlike him, they were nobody's 613th.

I met him again in Paris for the filming of *Maestro* and asked him to sing me 'Zi is mein herz' once more, but this time he could not get to the end of the filming – the floodgates of his memory burst open.

Jack left us in late 2019 and I like to think that in his final moments his Polish friend took him by the hand and led him to the wonderful worlds of the Light.

Würzburg

Würzburg is the city of Guido Fackler, and of Martin Hummel, a teacher at the Hochschule für Musik, as well as the son of Berthold Hummel, a German composer–musician who escaped from multiple prisoner-of-war camps to go home across Belgium and Luxembourg, on foot.

Captured in Emerkingen (near Ulm) by the Free French forces on 25 April 1945 because he was a soldier of the Wehrmacht, on 1 May Berthold Hummel was transferred to the internment camp Dépôt 132 Saint-Bonnet-Tronçais (in Allier, France) and put to work on railroads and in coal mines.

A cellist with the Dépôt orchestra, he wrote a number of works, including 'O Herr, dir will ich freudig danken' for male chorus, *Tagebuchblatt (Gedanken über Baudelaire)* for string quartet, *Motette im alten Stil* for mixed chorus, *Adoramus te* for trumpet, clarinet, string quartet, piano and male chorus, *Humoreske* for piano, *Romanze* for cello and piano, 'Wanderlied' and 'Schönster Herr Jesus' for mixed chorus and *Tantum ergo* for mixed chorus and organ. On 15 June 1947, he escaped again and managed to return to Germany. His other works include Sinfonietta, op. 39, for a large orchestra of wind instruments and the oratorio *Der Schrei der Märtyrer*, op. 90, for solos, mixed chorus, treble chorus, narrator, three organs and large orchestra. Hummel died in Würzburg in 2002.

Martin met me on a Würzburg bridge, arriving by bicycle. In a nearby café, he gave me many of his father's works, including the *Humoreske*, which Hummel wrote and performed on the piano in the Dépôt.

I was also in Würzburg for the music of Hans Martin. An organist at the Kilianeum in Miltenberg and, from 1935, at the Hofkirche in Würzburg, he wrote many works while at the Russian front, including 'Das zerbrochene Ringlein' and 'Da sang eine graue Nachtigall' for soprano and piano, 'Et incarnatus est' and *Tantum ergo* for mixed chorus and organ, a piano sonata and a string quartet. In 1944 Martin was interned in Atkarsk (near Saratov); he wrote dozens of pieces while there, including *Atkarsker Weihnachtskantate* for tenor, bass, male chorus and harmonium obbligato, a monumental score performed during Christmas 1944 by the choir of prisoners conducted by the composer. Released in 1945, he died in Würzburg in 2007.

Thanks to his sons, Hugo and Johannes, I was able to access the Nachlass Hans Martin at the Archiv und Bibliothek des Bistums. The manager, Thomas Wehner, arranged for me to access *Atkarsker Weihnachtskantate* in the archive, and I spent three days photographing Martin's materials.

The music composed in the Dépôt by Hummel and in Atkarsk by Martin were worth a hundred trips to Würzburg.

I left Würzburg at 5 a.m. the following day to travel, this time to South America.

Brazil

The heart-wrenching singing of a female Polish-Jewish survivor who emigrated to Brazil involved this great nation in this research of mine, and that was just the tip of the iceberg. The Brazilian scholar Silvia Lerner had sent me the recording of a song created by young deportees to the female forced labour camp of Parschnitz, a sub-camp of Gross-Rosen, patrolled by female guards who were members of the SS. Of the three authors of this song, Bela, Lena and Radassa, only Bela Bogaty Lustman has been identified so far. I listened to the song, 'Pieśń rozpaczy' ('A song of despair'); the sound was not brilliant, but the song so beautiful it deserved a trip to Rio de Janeiro, where Dona Bela (that's what everyone calls her) lived. We included this trip in the film *Maestro*.

In the musical landscape of concentrationary music, Brazil and, by extension, South America represents the new frontier of my research. A serious historical reconstruction of this subject must be done in order to include musical discoveries in Rio, São Paulo, Manaus, Buenos Aires, Paramaribo and Willemstad.

It was impossible to delve into the vast amount of Jewish material in the museums and libraries of a metropolis like Rio de Janeiro in just four days, but I had to try. The first stop, however, was Dona Bela. So alluring, with her soft Rio accent, Dona Bela was the human portal through which you could glimpse an abyss of suffering and wounds not yet healed. Her husband, Josef Lustman, an Auschwitz and Mauthausen survivor, listened in silence to his wife's story.

I wanted to give Dona Bela the opportunity to sing her 'Pieśń rozpaczy' to a grand piano accompaniment, something that had been denied to her and her unknown inmates, the co-authoresses of the song. The film production company contacted the Sala Cecília Meireles in Rio, a breath-taking auditorium with a Steinway grand. Bela took a little time to warm up, but in the end sang wonderfully. After seventy years, 'Pieśń rozpaczy' came back to life.

This was the first of several trips to Brazil with friends and colleagues eager to hear music that first saw the light during the darkness of the war, in ghettos, camps and gulags.

Thanks to Eduardo and Cristina Kobbi, and Ana Rosa Rojtenberg – my friends in São Paulo – I visited the city's Jewish museum and met many survivors who sang me the songs they had heard in the camps.

A gentleman from Rio read about me in a Brazilian newspaper, looked me up in the telephone directory, called Barletta and found my dear dad, who managed to give him my number. This gentleman introduced himself and told me about Alexander Laks, a Polish musician transferred to the Łódź ghetto. I arranged to meet him, but, alas, Laks died two weeks before I arrived in Brazil.

I returned to São Paulo in 2019 to conduct a concert organised by Keren Kayemet Leisrael; on this occasion, the gentleman from Rio came to give me Laks's scores.

Washington, DC, and onwards

Back in Europe just long enough to change suitcases, we then headed to Washington, DC, with the director and crew of *Maestro*. There, I met my lifelong friend Bret Werb at the USHMM: it was his turn to be interviewed that day. From the summit of his vast knowledge of the subject, Bret provided an ample view of the musical literature in ghettos and camps. We spent three days in Washington and I turned the USHMM and Library of Congress inside out, like a sock, and retrieved endless important documents.

After four days in Washington, we had to cross America, so we went to Baltimore and got on a plane to Minnesota. In Minneapolis, we hired a car and drove to its twin city, Saint Paul, across the Mississippi river. I was going to meet the most authoritative researcher in Japanese concentrationary music, Sears Eldredge. His fame preceded him and I had devoured his book about the musical phenomenon in Japanese prisoner-of-war camps in the Far East.

Sears received us at Macalester College, where he was emeritus professor. After a long conversation, he led us to his archive, a basement bursting with university theses, books and records. Sears had never stopped his research. It was invigorating.

We left Saint Paul bound for Los Angeles, the last stop on our American journey. We arrived in the late afternoon and chose a hotel near the airport.

Mukden

The Japanese set up prisoner-of-war camps in Taiwan, some in Taipei, others in Chinguashi/Kinkaseki, Chiayi/ Shirakawa, Taichung/Taichu, Ping-Tung/Heito, Hualien/Karenko, Touliu/ Toroku, Kaohsiung/Takao and Yuanlin/Inrin. In November 1944, about a thousand prisoners of war – mainly American and British, from the camps of Takao and Keelung – were transferred to Taiwan. Other prisoners were moved to the Japanese metropolitan territory, to Tokyo, Osaka and Sendai.

Two years earlier, in 1942, in the camp of Chinguashi/ Kinkaseki, Arthur Smith (nicknamed the Robbie Burns of Kinkaseki), a British trumpeter from the 155th Field Regiment of the Royal Artillery, wrote two songs, 'Laughing Boy' and 'Songs Down the Mine'.

Mukden (now known as Shenyang) in Manchuria had a concentration camp complex set up by the Japanese. Called Hoten Camp, it had prisoners of war from the US, Britain and, to a lesser extent, Australia and New Zealand.

On 11 November 1942, the first group of 1,500 prisoners arrived at the camp north of Mukden. On 1 September 1943, they were transferred to a second camp west of Mukden, a scene of horrific abuse and unspeakable torture and experimentation. British Major Robert Peaty, a prisoner of war there, recorded in his diary that US prisoners were being injected with viruses to study their effects and test vaccines. Mukden was liberated by joint US and Soviet troops on 19 August 1945.

In April 1942, Edmund Jones Lilly, Jr, commanding colonel of the 57th Infantry Philippine Regiment, had to capitulate to the Japanese troops. After surviving the Bataan Death March and a number of transfers, in May 1945 he was moved to Mukden, where he remained until August. After the war he served in France and, in 1950, returned to the US, where he was assigned to the General Inspectorate of Fort Sam Houston, in Texas. He died in Fayetteville in November 1978.

Having joined the US Navy in 1938 as a sailor second class, in May 1942 Dallas Eligah Hogue was captured by the Japanese. He too survived the Bataan Death March and was transferred to Karenko and Shirakawa (Taiwan), and finally to Mukden. Liberated in August 1945, he was dismissed in 1946, and died in October 1999 in Winnsboro, South Carolina, after a long illness.

Edmund Jones Lilly, Jr filled a few notebooks for himself and his comrades in arms, Dallas Eligah Hogue, William Albert Lowry and Charles Gurdon Sage. They contain pieces written by Lilly, as well as arrangements of pre-war American light music and hit songs.

There were guitars, two violins and two mandolins available in Mukden. The vocal ensemble Double Quartet was set up soon after its members were interned in Shirakawa, while the American Octette performed in Mukden. Lilly, Jr's notebook includes: 'Ev'ry waking moment' (written in the C.G. Saja Shirakawa in Taiwan), 'My obsession' and 'Golden Gate Serenade' (written in the Hoten prisoner-of-war camp in Mukden), and 'Moon above the Gobi', 'Banner in the sky' and 'Lovely Lady' (written in the Hoten prisoner-of-war camp in Cheng-Chiatun). Some pieces date from late August 1945. Following Hiroshima and Nagasaki, it was several weeks before the Japanese camps were reached and liberated, despite the Japanese surrender.

EIGHTEEN

Internment

Factory of dreams

In the stillness of time in captivity, camps became a factory of dreams, a kind of *Sagrada Familia* of Barcelona in constant and obsessive construction, an industry of art and musical science.

In the stalags and oflags, soldiers demonstrated solid acting training and stagecraft, and the cross-dressing – since there were men only – was of a very high level. There was the danger of becoming, unwittingly and paradoxically, accomplices of the deportation and extermination machine: it was an alternative way of being victims in the camps. Musicians were aware of this and were fully accountable in their actions and thoughts.

That is not necessarily our case, and we will take up the challenge of the most fascinating battle – about the past as well as the future – that of preserving beauty and truth.

The little bird of Manzanar

War Relocation Centers (WRCs) were instituted by US president Franklin D. Roosevelt after Pearl Harbor, and 120,000 Japanese and US nationals of Japanese origin living on the West Coast and in California and Washington State were sent to them. The WRC authorities encouraged the internees to engage in recreational activities: music departments, contests and courses were set up in every WRC, and jazz bands and dance orchestras were formed. In some WRCs, orchestra members were paid a monthly salary in addition to the department subsidy, and they were sometimes allowed to leave the WRC to perform in neighbouring cities. Light music ensembles and bands for musical entertainment and dancing were formed in Gila River, Granada, Heart Mountain, Jerome, Manzanar and other locations.

The large presence of first and second generation Japanese in WRCs encouraged the development of many musical, narrative and theatrical genres in the Japanese tradition, like *kabuki*, *gidayk* and *rōkyoku* (also called *naniwa-bushi*). In the Poston WRC, the internees built an open-air stage modelled on a traditional Japanese theatre. On 1 February 1943, in the Lordsburg WRC, an *engei-kai* was staged: a traditional Japanese show, punctuated with American popular songs and Hawaiian dancing, with the accompaniment of a piano and a harmonica, called *Cherry Blossom Theater*, in traditional Japanese costumes and hairstyles.

The day after we arrived in Los Angeles, we met Mary Kageyama Nomura, nicknamed 'the little bird of Manzanar'. She was of an advanced age but had retained her beauty. I wanted her to sing and she handed me the score of 'The Song of Manzanar', which Lou Frizzell had written for her; since there was no piano in the house, we sang it together unaccompanied. Her voice was faint, but she still sang wonderfully.

We travelled across much of California to Manzanar, and stayed in a motel in Independence. We even managed to unearth, in the middle of the desert, a French restaurant; it had a piano and, after two days of inactivity, I got my fingers back into shape by playing before dinner.

At the WRC Museum in Manzanar, I was gratified that everything had already been arranged so that the filming and research could be done as quickly as possible. The ranger who escorted us to the camp told us in detail about the typical timetable of a Japanese internee. Afterwards, we packed all our stuff and returned to Los Angeles.

When we arrived at the airport the next day, Alexandre was horrified to discover that he had misplaced all the footage of the American legs of our journey: days and days of filming in Washington, DC, Saint Paul, Los Angeles and Manzanar. A disaster. Alexandre flagged down a taxi and rushed back to the hotel. He found the bag with the film in his room. It was white, so had been confused with the bedding. He came back smiling and everybody sighed with relief.

Giuseppe Moschetti

Born in Florence in 1905, the organist and composer Giuseppe Moschetti was arrested while playing the organ in Walmer Road Baptist Church in Toronto and interned in Camp 33, Petawawa, charged with being a Fascist spy. In Camp 33, he wrote religious pieces for organ and chorus. Released on 4 December 1940, he moved to the US with his wife and son in 1948 and accepted the post of composer, choir master and organist at St John's Lutheran Church in Allentown, Pennsylvania, where he died in 1963.

I discovered him in Canada, in 2013, while at a conference organised by the cultural centre Casa d'Italia in Montreal. I had just finished giving an interview with a local radio station when the manager of Casa d'Italia, who was escorting me, informed me with quiet irony that she had in her office a score written in Petawawa by a certain Moschetti. I immediately forgot about the conference a few hours later and badgered her until she gave it to me: 'Preghiera dei prigionieri di Petawawa' ('Prayer of the Prisoners of Petawawa') for chorus and organ.

I know, happiness lasts but a moment, but I encapsulated it as I held Moschetti's work in my hand in Montreal.

Paris again: Losay, de Foucaud, Herbin

For this latest trip to Paris, I went to the home of Dominique, the son of the French composer André Losay, who was interned in Stalag III B Fürstenberg an der Oder, and who was the author of a beautiful, illustrated notebook full of songs written during his internment. Born in Normandy to a very poor family in 1913, Losay was marked by the tragic events of the last century. His father had gone to war in 1914, was captured by the Germans and only returned home in 1919, when Losay was six. Twenty years later, André, too, went to war and, like his father, was a prisoner of war.

Before we met in Paris, Dominique had sent me two volumes of *Semper laus ejus*, which contained the collection of his father's works. Then, while I was with him, he showed me his father's charming handwritten notebook from the stalag: a carousel of colours suffused one of the most beautiful collections of songs written in imprisonment, easily equal to the Sachsenhausen notebooks. Dominique kindly allowed me to photograph it, but he also had something else in store for me.

I soon learnt I had found a new partner for my research. Dominique demonstrated his ability to obtain useful data and addresses, so much so that, in the years to come, it would be only thanks to him that I would find the names and contact details of the heirs of many French prisoner-of-war musicians.

In the afternoon, in the hotel lobby, I met Frédéric, the son of Max de Foucaud, who, in 1997, had released the CD *Quo Vadis?* in France. It was entirely dedicated to the works his father had composed while a prisoner of war in Stalag I A Stablack, in east Prussia. It was a stalag where winter temperatures dropped down to -20°C. While there, his father wrote beautiful works like *Symphonie Mystérieuse* for orchestra and the piano suite *Solitudes*, with the second movement for two pianos.

Frédéric and I are very good friends: I performed his father's Nocturne in New York and had his *Élévation de l'esprit* for violin, cello and organ played in Dachau.

The day after that encounter with Max, there was a national religious holiday and the Bibliothèque Nationale de France-Richelieu was closed. Instead, I went to Gentilly, in the suburbs of Paris, and met Elizabeth, a pianist and the daughter of René Herbin.

A keyboard virtuoso with giant hands, Herbin embarked on a dual career as a musician and composer, accompanying the cellist Maurice Maréchal on many tours. In 1940, he was arrested and interned in Oflag IXA/H Spangenberg and in other oflags. He wrote many works in small notepads, including *Album d'images* for piano (drafted in 1940 on the train to the oflag), *Préludes baroques* for piano, *Préambule pour le 'Châpeau chinois' de Franc Nohain* for piano, string quintet, flute and clarinet, a piano sonata, and *Deïrdre des douleurs* for chamber orchestra. He resumed his piano career after the war. Along with French violinist Jacques Thibaud, Herbin died on

1 September 1953, when their flight from Paris-Orly to Saigon crashed on Mount Cimet.

I had already met Elizabeth on other occasions and that day she was with her brother . . . and a cat. I spent the afternoon sneezing, thanks to my allergies, and in the evening returned to Paris with a swollen nose but with many of René's works in hand, including his mammoth piano sonata.

Maurice Soret

My French journey continued. The time had come for me to tackle the most elusive and mysterious work of this research: the symphonic poem *Rêve de France*, written in Stalag III A Luckenwalde by the French composer Maurice Soret, who had been the conductor of the Radio PTT- Nord orchestra.

Tracking his relatives was a complex, laborious enterprise but, years later, thanks to Dominique Losay's help, I located his only daughter, Frédérique Andrée Soret, in a town in the Pyrenees. I met Frédérique at her home, where bad news awaited me: Soret's score was missing.

When all seemed lost, Fréderique remembered having preserved two Pyral discs similar to old 78s. We discovered that the four sides of these records still had a recording of *Rêve de France* that her father had made after the war for French radio. True, the original score had been lost, but after a patient remastering job, cleaning the noises and incrustations, and some sound engineering, we would be able to reconstruct the paper score based on the audio. Difficult, but not impossible.

I could not leave France before diving into the music department of the Bibliothèque Nationale de France in Rue de

Richelieu. In over thirty years of research, I have visited and frequented dozens of libraries, but the Paris Richelieu and the Prague Klementinum are at the top of my list of favourites. And if I were to chisel a physical image of this research, it would be in the likeness of these two cathedrals of knowledge.

NINETEEN

Secular Rite

Stalag Luft I Barth-Vogelsang

In 1941 the Reich opened Stalag Luft I Barth-Vogelsang Prussia 54 on the Baltic Sea, for the internment of British, US and Canadian airmen. The stalag was later evacuated from 13 to 15 May 1945, thanks to Operation Revival, carried out by US planes.

The YMCA had supplied musical instruments and stage tools to the prisoners of war; Lieutenant Clair William Cline – an ebony carpenter in civilian life – built a violin with timber obtained from chairs and glue taken from tables and bunk beds. Every sector had a block assigned to music and theatre, with its own orchestra and theatre company; the US prisoners formed a big band conducted by the saxophonist and singer airman Dorman Fred 'Shady' Lane.

German authorities were initially hostile to the setting up of orchestras and jazz bands (jazz was contemptuously called 'Cow Music'), but eventually allowed them after the widely disregarded promise on the part of US musicians that they would play only classical music.

The first show staged at the stalag was the 1939 George S. Kaufman and Moss Hart comedy *The Man Who Came to*

Dinner, which had many performances at various prisoner-of-war sites. While extra music and songs were written for the production, unfortunately this material appears not to have survived.

Korger, Lashly, Bliss

On 19 September 1943, during a US air raid on oil deposits in Ploieşti, in Romania, the bomber flown by Lieutenant Harry (Harold) Francis Korger – musical director of Eagle River Schools – was hit by German anti-aircraft artillery and had to make a forced landing. Captured and interned in Stalag Luft I Barth, he formed a Glee Club made up of thirty-six members and performed a repertoire that ranged from spirituals and popular American dance music to 'The US Air Force' song by Robert MacArthur Crawford, as well as various medleys of military songs. Korger's Glee Club included a Catholic choir that accompanied Sunday Mass, for which Korger wrote and arranged hymns; with the help of Lieutenant Marshall E. Tyler, he reconstructed arrangements and medleys from memory, and wrote the music and lyrics for the ballad 'All Through the Night', as well as the march *Kriegies on Parade*.

The American lieutenant pilot, musician and arranger John Henderson Lashly, on the other hand, wrote the song 'Low is the Sun' in Stalag Luft I Barth. This song featured in the three-act musical comedy *Hit the Bottle*, by Nelson Roosevelt Gidding (who also directed it) and Nathaniel L. Bliss, which was staged in the stalag on 3 July 1944 at what the inmates referred to as the Little Theatre of Times Square. While imprisoned, Gidding drafted his first book, *End over End*. He escaped from the stalag in 1945. After the war, he became a famous screenwriter and, in 1958, received an Academy Award nomination for the screenplay of Robert Wise's film *I Want to Live!* He also taught screenwriting at the University of Southern California in Los Angeles.

Stalag Luft III Sagan

In Stalag Luft III Sagan, American prisoners of war formed the Luft Bansters Band. There were several break-out attempts in the stalag, including the most famous, led by RAF Squadron Leader Roger Bushell, on the night of 24–25 March 1944, through a tunnel network. Seventy-six pilots managed to escape. This escape was immortalised in Jack Lee's 1950 British film *The Wooden Horse* and John Sturges's 1963 American film *The Great Escape*. During the war, the US musician Leland Forsblad was interned here, too; he performed as an accordionist and was once put into a punishment cell for playing the American national anthem. He concealed a radio in his accordion so that he could secretly listen to the BBC.

Forsblad wrote music for the Luft Bansters Band in the style of Benny Goodman, Count Basie and Artie Shaw, and arranged pieces for chorus and orchestra. After the war, he obtained a degree in composition at the University of Southern California in Los Angeles, and worked as a film music composer in Hollywood.

Jean Martinon

In June 1940, the violinist and composer Jean Martinon was captured and interned in Stalag IX A Ziegenhain, where he wrote Sonatine no. 3, op. 22, for piano, Sonatine no. 4 for reed instrument trio, *Stalag IX (Musique d'exil)* for orchestra, 'Absolve Domine (en mémoire des français morts à la guerre)' for male chorus and orchestra without violins (performed in the stalag on 2 November 1940), *Appel de parfums* for narrator, male or mixed chorus and orchestra, Divertissement for orchestra, and Psaume 136 *(Chant des captifs)*, op. 33, for narrator, soloists and orchestra, to a French translation of Psalm 136, produced in the stalag by the French army chaplain Abbé Robert Petit, also a prisoner of war. Martinon partly altered Abbé Petit's text in order to circumvent German military censorship and restored the original after his return home. Liberated in 1942, he became conductor of the Paris Conservatoire Orchestre and, in 1946, of the Bordeaux Aquitaine National Orchestra. He died in Paris in March 1976.

In Paris, I turned Éditions Billaudot inside out to track down all the scores Jean Martinon had written in Stalag IX A, but there was much missing. In a vast, beautiful, workshop-like apartment in a large building in Neuilly, however, I met Daniel

Dominique, one of Jean Martinon's sons (the other, Jean-Paul, lives in London). Daniel was very generous: he gave me *Chant des captifs*, *Absolve Domine*, *Appel de parfums* and other scores written by his father shortly before the liberation.

Dautremer, Thimonnier, Chenevier

After several postponements, I finally managed to meet the tenor Damien Top in Paris and, together, we went to see Marcel Dautremer's widow, Anne-Marie. Damien had told this immensely refined lady about me and my project and so she showed me the works her husband had written in captivity: 'Lorsque je rentrerai' for singer and piano and *Page d'exil* for clarinet and orchestra, both composed in Stalag II A Neubrandenburg.

It is a secular rite I have witnessed hundreds of times, and yet it preserves intact the emotions age has never toned down, like a constant series of first occasions repeating themselves. In these moments, a strong desire conquers all the others: a desire to share these treasures with the human race. To restore even the tiniest of these pieces of music back to life is man's first step not on the Moon but on Earth, the least explored of planets.

In Oflag IIB Arnswalde (present-day Choszczno, Poland), René Marie Hilaire Thimonnier conducted concerts and wrote *Missa brevis*, the cantata *Hommage à Jeanne d'Arc*, *Héroïde funèbre* and *Sonate d'été* for violin and piano. I had already obtained *Missa brevis* at the Paris Richelieu library, and the excellent German researcher Andreas Linsenmann had provided an abundance of material about Thimonnier; but it was the great Dominique Losay, the Sherlock Holmes of French musicians, who put me in touch with Michèle Thimonnier, René's niece.

Michèle lives in a village outside Poitiers. I went to see her because she owned an old published copy of *Sonate d'été* – just one, so it needed to be photocopied, which was easier said than done. Finally, we located a colour photocopier that was still coin-operated in a superstore and were able to make a copy. I said goodbye to dear Michèle just in time to catch the TGV back to Paris.

The composer Paul Chenevier joined the 4th Engineers' Regiment in Grenoble as a volunteer and was promoted to corporal; in June 1940, he was captured and interned. From 29 January to 14 October 1941, he was assigned to Schwarzenborn Kommando 405. Freed on 30 March 1945, he died in 2015.

I had made up my mind to see Nelly Quercia, the daughter of this composer of *Marche du Kommando 405* and *Marche du Kommando 1350*, *Conseils à l'Enfant blond*, *Retour au Kommando* and the lighthearted song 'Dans l'cul!', which he composed while at Stalag IX A. I realised too late, however, that Pontcharra (Isère), the city where Nelly lived, was over 500km from Paris. It would have been quicker for me to see her in Milan, but my flight from Beauvois to Bari was scheduled for the following day. I wrote to Nelly instead and she was glad to send me all her father's works. I was elated when the large package from Pontcharra was delivered and immediately understood the joy children feel when Santa Claus arrives.

TWENTY

Romani

Five families

The Romani people can essentially be subdivided into five social families or groupings: *Roma* in Central-Eastern Europe and the Balkans, *Sinti* in Germany and German-speaking countries, France and Northern Italy, *Manouches* in France and Italy, *Kalè* in Finland, Wales, Brazil, Algeria, Iraq and the Iberian peninsula and *Romanichals* in the UK, Australia and North America, but their generic name is Romani, no matter what their social family, and they are Christians.

For pseudo-racial motives, the Third Reich enforced on the Romani people a ruthless policy of discrimination and extermination, ordering forced sterilisation, mass deportations and physical elimination, It is believed some 500,000 Romani died in extermination camps, In the Romani language, this genocide is called *Samudaripen* (literally 'all dead' or 'mass killing') or *Porrajmos* (also *Porajmos*), which can be translated as 'great decimation' or 'devastation'.

Thanks to the meticulous phonographic, documentary and ethnographic reconstruction of the Romani music phenomenon, carried out by ethnologists, researchers and linguists, including Jana Belišová, Ursula Hemetek and Mozes Heinschink, we have obtained a body of music created by Romanis in Birkenau and in many other camps of the Nazi regime, which includes many songs of excellent vocal and instrumental quality.

Musicians such as singer Růžena Danielová, a Czech Romani, must be included in this. She and her family were transferred to the Familienzigeunerlager in Birkenau, where she lost her husband and five children, and underwent medical experiments. In 1944 she wrote the lyrics for 'Auschvitsate hi kher baro', one of the best-known songs of the post-war Romani tradition. Similarly, the Austrian Lovara Romani writer, painter and musician Ceija Stojka was sent to the Birkenau Familienzigeunerlager in 1943, to Ravensbrück in 1944, and finally to Bergen-Belsen. Post-war, she moved to Vienna and began a cultural battle to spread the culture of Romani people and bear witness to the *Porrajmos* tragedy. Stojka brought back Burgenland-Lovara songs created in Birkenau, including '*Mamo, mamo, mamo*' and its variation 'Maj avla o cajto', 'Jaj de či na pilem, či na chalem' and 'Čaj kamau tu' which she recorded in 1990. She died in Vienna in January 2013.

It is worth mentioning the Slovakian Romani songs 'E mašina maj piskinel', 'Merav, dale, merav', 'Imar aven o "telune"', or 'Imar aven, joj, o burume', 'Merav pal e parochňa', about the haircut the camps imposed on the deportees, 'Andr'oda taboris' (basedon 'Čhajóri romaňí'), the Serbian Romani song 'Phabol lamba, merel lamba ando štraflageri', about the lamp that burns in the camp huts, and the Burgenland Romani song, 'But fačunge, but maro pekal'.

Jana Belišová

A researcher such as I am cannot go to the Czech Republic just for Prague, Terezín and Brno; there are also Czech Romani, custodians of musical memories transmitted by mothers and fathers to their children. The performer Andrea Bartošová, of the International School in Prague, was contacted by the producers of our documentary *Maestro*. Andrea took Alexandre, the crew and me to the outskirts of Prague to hear their singing; an ensemble of splendid male voices and guitars, conducted by a Romani who bore a striking resemblance to my maternal grandfather, delighted us with wonderful songs created by Czech Romanis in various transit and concentration camps. I recognised one of the songs and joined in with a counter melody.

The next day we went to the Brno Museum of Romani Culture, which literally overflowed with musical material concerning my area of research – books, CDs and DVDs. The exchange rate with the Czech koruna was very advantageous and I was able to buy everything that interested me.

We then went on to Slovakia, where Jana Belišová, the greatest expert in Romani musicology and musical literature, was expecting us. She is a very sweet woman and gladly told me about her research into Slovakian Romani music. After a couple of hours, we remembered that we were both musicians – Jana is an excellent pianist – so we sat at the upright piano and played, four hands, half a dozen Romani songs.

Two days later, Jana was travelling with some of her students and colleagues to a Romani village on the border with Ukraine. There would be no better opportunity for me to stock up on Romani songs created in the camps; it would have been difficult to do this anywhere else.

The night before we were meant to meet up, we reached a town not far from the village after grappling with a phenomenal hailstorm and almost taking the wrong road on several occasions; the vegetable broth in the restaurant that evening was a balm for the soul. On the following morning, we joined Jana and her friends and went to the village. There were women with faces that almost seemed chiselled from marble, and deep-set eyes of a type of beauty we are not accustomed to, missing teeth and dazzling smiles: they were all waiting for us, drowning in an endless sea of children, stepping out of huts supported by prayer instead of lime and plaster.

We glimpsed the occasional dour, silent man. Although we were not familiar with their social rules, I got the impression that, in this village, and presumably in similar settlements, the authority was held by women. Six or seven village matriarchs gathered around and Jana explained what she was looking for.

After exchanging a few words, they started to sing.

A parallel world unfolded immediately in my ears and I could practically see through them, rather than my eyes. It was a song that gushed out of the entrails of the earth and took shape in their voices. The hoarseness of heavy smokers vanished and sounds and words drifted from bygone days, unfamiliar places where you could glimpse streetlights and dry walls.

Their parents had created these songs in captivity but what I grasped in that moment was the sense of ancient legends about sounds that opened doors carved in the rock. Marco Polo had surely heard similar songs as he crossed the continents to reach Kublai Khan. I understood the meaning of Gog and Magog. Alexandre was recording and I could not bring myself to take notes, I was so absorbed. I could see all this with my ears, while my eyes were half-shut.

Three of the women were very young when they were taken to the camps. They said German soldiers often raped them and I gradually realised what I was hearing, that there was nothing connected with entertainment or joy in these songs: it was weeping frozen into sounds.

When the singing finished, I came back to Earth. They asked for money for their performance and we paid them. Outside the hut, the children were by now a stirring tide. It was time to say goodbye.

The journey back

After leaving the Romani village on the Ukrainian border, we were supposed to head to Heidelberg; for reasons unfathomable to me, the satnav took us to Budapest as though it were compulsory. We ended up in the thick of the capital's traffic, but it was not all bad news. Through the car windows I was revisiting places dear to me, the happy time of the Franz Liszt Academy, when I was studying piano all day long, the Keleti pályaudvar railway station, from where I would head to Vienna, and my digs in Buda.

During the long journey, the books I had bought or been given had grown in number and I only had one suitcase. We arrived at the Documentation and Cultural Centre of German Sinti and Roma in Heidelberg, one of the best institutions on the art and literature of Romani people. After hours of pleasant research, as though I didn't have enough books, I bought some more.

Back in Paris and before returning to Italy, I realised that there were too many books to fit into my suitcase and rucksack. I took out all my dirty laundry and put it into a large bag. With a gigantic suitcase, an obese rucksack and a bag filled with dirty washing, I turned up at Orly airport. I explained that my suitcase was full of books of inestimable historical value and that it should travel with me in the cabin; the check-in clerk did not shed even one tear at my story, however, and sent the suitcase and all the books into the hold.

At Fiumicino airport, in Rome, I rushed to luggage claim to grab my precious volumes. The conveyor belt spewed out all the luggage in the world except mine; I was petrified. Sweating and upset, still remembering the rucksack stolen from me years earlier at Barcelona airport, I ran to the luggage claim office. The female official checked my ticket stub carefully and said, 'But your luggage isn't on that conveyor belt!' Before my flight there had been another one, with a different company, also from Orly to Fiumicino. I had checked the flight but not the schedule; my luggage was riding all alone on the conveyor belt. I learnt so many things from that episode – which fortunately had a happy outcome. You must be alert, prudent and keep calm on all occasions.

And, above all, you must check the flight, the airline and the schedule.

European passports

When analysing concentrationary music it is natural to encounter the ethnic-musical background of the vocal, choral and instrumental traditions of both Continental and Eurasian Jews – including those on the Mediterranean – and the Sinti, the Roma and the entire Romani population rooted in the Old Continent.

We cannot ignore the phenomenon of persecution and socio-cultural devastation, as well as the disastrous extermination, that was unleashed during the war on more pan-European peoples – Jews and Romani – in a Europe of art and music, the forerunner of its political and sovereign institutions. Madrid and Budapest – now both under the EU flag – had nothing in common, but both possessed Romani musicians playing in the streets and many Romani families earnt their living performing in music, dance and entertainment ensembles and companies.

Slav- and German-speaking nations had nothing in common and their borders were the cause of epoch-making wars, as well as territorial, language and culture disputes. However, from the Baltic to the Black Sea, people could speak and sing in a single great language: Yiddish, a kind of Jewish Continental Europe Esperanto.

The most pan-European peoples were those who ended up in concentration camps. Their music, created in the camps, reactivated the right geopolitical and geo-humanitarian coordinates by returning their European passports, confiscated by the hecatomb of deportation.

TWENTY-ONE

Gulags

Parallax errors

Generations of intellectuals, artists and musicians went through lagers and gulags for the most varied discriminatory reasons and left us a bequest that is hard to manage. The rise of Nazism and the beginning of de-Stalinization in the USSR are the extremities of a wide historical pattern in which the common denominator of the human variable is artistic creativity.

The reasons a researcher is urged to extract the historical and geopolitical coordinates of the concentrationary music phenomenon from 1933 – six years before the Second World War broke out in 1939 – are the same ones that make it necessary, I feel, to widen the range as late as 1953. In the continuum of the war and post-war periods, there are clear interconnections and deep similarities between historical events and the phenomenology of deportation, which – in the deportation, confinement, exile, internment, concentration and psycho-physical annihilation of humans in sites of captivity – have social discrimination in common.

A parallax error leads us to consider the lagers to be the forerunners of the gulags, and the coercive, punitive and exterminating system to have borrowed from one and been applied to the other. In reality, the first gulag was opened in 1917 on the Solovetsky Islands in the White Sea in a monastery seized by the Bolshevik government.

The Soviet deportation phenomenon, which reached its dramatic humanitarian finale in the gulags, is the longest-living camp reality. It started in 1919 and lasted, technically, until 1956, with a period of standstill explained by the USSR entering the war and a significant drop in deportations. It was the most monstrous concentration camp system in history and caused the deaths of approximately 40 million people. The extermination plans devised by Stalin were interrupted only by his death in 1953, which was followed by the proclamation of a general amnesty.

Since criminals were interned with intellectuals and political prisoners, gulags swallowed up generations of philosophers, teachers, thinkers, artists, musicians and exceptional minds; the USSR's true cerebral lung was radically expelled from the cultural movement of Soviet social reality.

Another dimension and eradication

An extreme prison system – in which the scarcity of food was inversely proportionate to the amount of work – was in force in the gulags. Calculated strictly on the number of calories, food rations there were smaller than those given out in the civilian camps of the Third Reich.

In addition to the superhuman pace of the work and appalling living circumstances in the huts, as well as the diseases caused by unsustainable sanitary conditions, there were the rapes and physical abuse perpetrated by guards and team leaders – who were generally picked from among the criminals and delinquents, just like the *kapos* in the lagers.

The Soviet authorities adopted extremely harsh deportation and imprisonment methods, causing the deaths of hundreds of thousands of prisoners from strain, hunger, dysentery, poisoning, murder and exposure. In Komarivka, Krinowaja, Oranki, Suzdal and Tambov, the death toll among prisoners of war was very high and significantly added to the stress of the exhausting transfers in dreadfully overcrowded train carriages with no food or water for days, and the death marches to the camps.

An estimated 20 million civilian and military victims is the high cost the USSR paid because of the aggression by the

Third Reich and for which the Nazis faced judgement at the Nuremberg Trials. No Nuremberg has ever been instituted for the 40 million victims of the gulags, however. The dissolution of the USSR supplied the alibi for not rectifying this historical debt towards the human race.

After his Symphony No. 9, op. 70, was slated by Stalin in 1945, following the mainly negative reviews of his Symphonies No. 7, 8 and 9, the Soviet composer Dmitri Shostakovich resigned from his teaching post at the Leningrad conservatoire. In Tallin, the Estonian conductor Roman Matsov recorded his symphonies with the Estonian national radio orchestra straight after the avant-premières in Leningrad and Moscow and prudently hid the tapes under his clothes to keep them safe in his home.

During the Stalinist regime, the output of Jewish music by Joseph Achron, Joel Engel, Michail Gnesin, Moses Milner, Solomon Rosowsky, Lasare Saminsky, Ephraïm Skliar and Aleksandr Krejn – founders of the Society for Jewish Folk Music in Moscow – was deleted from dictionaries and almost entirely annihilated. This attempt at eradicating Jewish culture, literature, art and music preceded the one carried out by the National Socialists, yet was no less systematic or devastating. Sympathisers were also punished.

Aleksandr Lokshin was expelled from the Moscow conservatoire for promoting the music of Berg, Mahler, Stravinsky and Shostakovich among his students. The pianist Maria Yudina was thrown out of the Moscow conservatoire for dedicating some of her recitals to the victims of the regime. In February 1948, the Spanish singer Carolina Codina, Sergei Prokofiev's wife (from whom he was separated), was arrested for alleged espionage and sentenced to incarceration in a gulag for twenty years. She was released in 1955.

Alexander Moisejevich Veprik also taught at the Moscow conservatoire, from 1923 to 1941, and was an expert of the Jewish musical tradition in the USSR. His works became internationally renowned in the 1920s, and in March 1933 Arturo Toscanini conducted his *Plyaski i pesni getto*, op. 12, at New York's Carnegie Hall. In 1950, he was arrested and charged with Jewish nationalism and sentenced to eight years. In prison, he was tortured and physically abused; he was subsequently transferred to a gulag in the Urals. Exempted from heavy work, he was given the task of forming a balalaika orchestra and composed the opera *Toktogul* and the cantata *Narod-geroy*. Released in 1954, he returned to Moscow, where he died in October 1958.

For some composers fallen into disgrace and considered 'dangerous' by the Soviet Communist Party – just like intellectuals and artists – there was a repeat of the events of 10 May 1933 in the Königsplatz in Munich when more than 25,000 books were burnt in an effort to purge and cleanse anything deemed 'un-German' and promote Aryanism. Here, their musical scores were set on fire and they had to admit responsibility for their 'crimes', rather like the heretics who confessed to crimes they were unaware of under the Spanish Inquisition, centuries before.

Performances in the gulags

Every gulag had a cultural education department, or *Kulturno-vospitatelnaya chast* (KVCh), for the social and cultural re-education of the prisoners. The KVCh made it possible to stage theatrical productions, perform in concerts, read and publish newspapers, listen to the radio, watch films, hold discussions and conferences, post propaganda posters, promote table games and sports activities, set up libraries and carry out artistic-musical activities. Gradually, the KVCh would allow writers, journalists, theatre artists and musicians to sometimes be given non-gruelling duties and get better lodgings, clothes and special footwear.

The KVCh tended to privilege criminal prisoners as being more malleable to re-education – a more difficult procedure when it came to political prisoners. These prisoners were generally prohibited from theatrical activities, giving talks and singing: they were only allowed to compose music and play musical instruments.

From dance to drama, to opera and operettas, theatre reached top-quality performance levels in Magadan and Vorkuta. To ensure high standards on stage, a professional was even brought specially from Moscow to direct a few shows.

Besides Soviet propaganda and pro-Communist plays encouraged by the gulag authorities to pander to directives from the top, most theatres staged Russian classics and popular shows, from Chekhov to Gogol, Gorky and Pushkin. There were also popular songs, comedies and vaudeville: preference was usually given to works that were jolly rather than sad or nostalgic.

Just as in the Third Reich's lagers, music would accompany prisoners when they left for and returned from forced labour in the gulags. Professional and amateur bands, as well as the occasional solo musician, would play marches and military-style music at the gates.

The story of a German trumpeter

The German Jewish trumpeter Eddie Rosner was born in Berlin in 1910 and studied classical music in a private school. A great fan of jazz, Rosner left the conservatoire and began performing with the Weintraubs Syncopators, playing two trumpets at once. The Syncopators was formed by saxophone and clarinet player Horst Graff and German jazz pianist and percussionist Stefan Weintraub, and included Ansco Bruinier (trumpet, tuba, sax, sousaphone, singing and whistling), briefly brother Franz S. Bruinier (Bertolt Brecht's first composer), Paul Aronovici (trumpet), John Kaiser (trombone), Freddy Wise (tenor sax, bass sax and clarinet) and Cyril 'Baby' Schulvater (banjo and guitar). They played in clubs and aboard steamships on the Hamburg–New York route and were highly successful, even appearing in the 1930 film *The Blue Angel* with Marlene Dietrich.

With the rise of Nazism, the Syncopators, who were all Jews, had to leave Germany: the other band members took refuge in Australia, where they were arrested as Enemy Aliens, but Rosner fled to Poland and opened a club in Łódź. When the Germans occupied Poland, Rosner relocated to Białystok, which was then in Belorussia, where he formed a jazz band. The Belorussian secretary of the Communist Party turned the band into a state orchestra and Rosner played for the Soviet troops at the front. After the war, his New York sound was frowned on by Moscow. He tried fleeing but was arrested, convicted of treason and espionage, sentenced to ten years and deported to Siberia, first to the gulag of Chabarowsk, then, in 1949, to the gulag of Magadan, where he formed at least two orchestras. Granted amnesty after Stalin's death, he finally returned to Berlin in 1974.

Leibu Levin

In 2007, I met Ruth Levin in Israel. For years Ruth had been singing Yiddish songs written by her father, Leibu, a Romanian-Jewish musician who, in 1941, was arrested by Soviet troops and deported to Ukhta (Komi Republic), west of the Urals.

Leibu Levin was born in May 1914 in Kimpolung (Câmpulung Moldovenesc), in the Duchy of Bukovina, part of the Austro-Hungarian Empire. From 1919, he lived in Czernowitz (Chernivtsi), in Ukraine. He had studied Yiddish language and literature at the Yiddisher Shul-Farayn, given prose and poetry recitals in Yiddish and performed his own songs in Romania.

Following Operation Barbarossa, when Hitler invaded the Soviet Union, in June 1941, he was recalled and transferred to a labour camp in the Urals (Romania was backing the Third Reich). Arrested in 1942, he was sentenced without trial to fifteen years in the gulag of Ukhta (Northern Urals) and then in Tayshet (north-western Siberia). During his imprisonment, he wrote the Yiddish songs 'Iber fremde vegn', 'In sumne kazematn', 'Marsh lid' and 'Vos eynzamer, eyner'.

Released in 1956, Levin went back to performing for another six years, but had to retire because of the severe health problems caused by his lengthy imprisonment. In 1972, he emigrated to Israel, where he set many Yiddish poems to music, translated from German to Yiddish the poetical works of Selma Meerbaum-Eisinger and set six of her poems to music. He died in February 1983 in Herzliya.

His daughter, Ruth, is one of the most prominent performers of Yiddish music. I met her on several occasions: the first time in Jerusalem for the documentary *Musica Concentrationaria* in 2006. Ermanno Felli and I got lost taking taxis and buses and arrived terribly late at her home, so she was very put out. Ermanno saved the day because he spoke Russian, Ruth's native language. That way, we regained her trust.

Ruth incarnated her father Leibu's Yiddish soul entirely. The *melos* of distant countries, East European Judaism is rich in largely unexplored musical treasures. Ruth switched easily between English, Russian and Hebrew. She gave me the works her father had written during and after his imprisonment.

I also met her on the occasion of the film *Maestro*: we went to see her in Haifa, where she was giving a concert. We arrived late again but managed to catch most of the concert, after which she granted me an intense interview.

Almukhamedov, Valdgardt, Kenel

Gaziz Salih uli Almukhametov, a Tartar Bashkir, was born in October 1895 in the village of Muraptal (Bashkortostan). He moved to Tashkent in 1908. In 1914, he embarked on a long journey to the Volga region, Siberia and Kazakhstan, to collect the songs of ethnic Tartars and Bashkirs. He also joined the counter-espionage section of the Orenburg military department, and studied first at the People's Conservatoire of Tashkent, then in Moscow.

After moving to Ufa in 1929, he began creating a Soviet Bashkir musical literature. From 1932 onwards, he worked at the Ufa school of music. Contracting typhus twice in Ufa, he lost both his daughters to the disease. A victim of Stalin's purges, he was arrested on 11 December 1937 and was shot in 10 July 1938. In 1957, he was rehabilitated by the USSR Supreme Court.

The composer, pianist and conductor Pavel Valdgardt, born in Tambov in January 1903, was arrested in Leningrad on 10 January 1929, accused of being a member of the religious and philosophical group *Voskresenie*, whose focus was akin to anthroposophy. He was sentenced to three years in the gulag on the Solovetsky Islands and released in late 1930. He composed songs and pieces for folk instrument orchestras and wrote the children's musical *Koshkin Dom*. He died in September 1978 in Tambov.

The pianist, folklore expert and composer of French origin Aleksandr Kenel was born in November 1898 in St Petersburg; arrested on 14 June 1927 and charged with being a member of the Order of the Knights of the Holy Grail (illegal in the USSR), he was sentenced to three years in the gulag on the Solovetsky Islands. He wrote incidental music for the gulag theatre, including 'Solovetskomu gimnu', and staged part of his opera *Kozbar*. He was released in 1930 and, from 1933, worked as a piano accompanist in Tashkent and Sverdlovsk. He died in July 1970 in Abakan.

Protopopov and Nosyrev

Sergei Protopopov, a member of the Association for Contemporary Music (ACM) – an organisation abolished by the Communist Party in 1932 – was arrested on 4 March 1934 and charged with the crime of homosexuality. He was the author of a treatise on the technique of musical language founded on a scale of seventy-two microtones. He was sentenced to three years in the Siblag of Mariinsk. There, he wrote various works, including five Preludes, op. 32, for piano. He performed his own works as a piano accompanist to a baritone (the piano being the only musical instrument available in the camp) and conducted a small orchestra for which he did special arrangements. On 12 November 1935, he was transferred to the Dmitrov Dmitlag in Moscow, where he wrote the *Marsh betonschikov* for a music competition. After his release, he taught at the conservatoire. He died in Moscow on 14 December 1954.

On 30 September 1943, during the Leningrad siege, Mikhail Nosyrev was arrested while playing the violin for an operetta. Charged with counter-revolutionary agitation and treason towards the Motherland, he was sentenced to be shot, but the sentence was commuted to ten years in the Vorkuta gulag in the

Komi Republic. There he wrote, among other works an Andante and Sonatina for piano and the symphonic poem *Skazka* and took part in theatre-related activities.

Released in 1953 and exiled to Syktyvkar, from 1955 to 1958 he was a conductor and arranger in the local theatre. In 1958, he moved to Voronezh. In 1967 – on Shostakovich's recommendation – the Union of Soviet Composers accepted his application to join. He died in Voronezh in March 1981 and was definitively rehabilitated in 1988.

Zaderatsky and Mosolov

The composer and pianist Vsevolod Zaderatsky was born on 21 December 1891 in Rivne, Ukraine, into the family of a Russian Imperial Railway official. He taught piano to Tsesarevich Alexei, the only son of Tsar Nicholas II, in Saint Petersburg. From 1918 to 1920, he fought in the civil war, then graduated in piano in 1923. Three years later, he was arrested in Ryazan and attempted suicide while in prison. His works were destroyed. Released in mid-1928, he was deprived of his civil rights. He was allowed to live in Moscow, in 1929, where he worked as a composer for the All-Union Radio. With Dmitri Shostakovich and Alexander Mosolov, he joined the ACM.

He was arrested once again in March 1937 for playing Strauss and Wagner at his concerts – composers considered Fascists by the Communist Party. Charged with being a public enemy and sentenced to ten years, he was sent to Magadan gulag in the Kolyma region. He wrote twenty-four Preludes and Fugues for piano, using telegram forms which the guards would give him, as well as on a few squared sheets, without having access to a piano. Released in July 1939, when the Second World War broke out, he was evacuated with his family, first to Merki, Kazakhstan, then to Krasnodar. From 1949, he lived in Lviv, where he taught at the local conservatoire. He died on 1 February 1953.

The pianist Alexander Mosolov was born in Kiev in August in 1900. At the beginning of the Bolshevik Revolution, he enlisted as a volunteer and fought on the Polish and Ukrainian front. In 1925 he graduated and joined the ACM. After the success of his first string quartet at the International Society for Contemporary Music in Frankfurt, he devoted himself to composition. His opera, *Zavod*, inspired by Arthur Honegger's *Pacific 231*, brought him international fame. Expelled from the Union of Soviet Composers in 1936 for allegedly being drunk in a public place and brawling, in 1937 he was arrested for alleged counter-revolutionary activities and sentenced to eight years in a gulag. Released on 25 August 1938 thanks to the intervention of his teachers, Glière and Myaskovsky, his sentence was commuted to five years in exile. Mosolov also took an interest in Turkmen, Tajik, Armenian and Kyrgyz music and made sure his musical idiom, from that point onwards, conformed to the aesthetics dictated by the Soviet authorities. He died in Moscow in July 1973.

Weinberg and Haubenstock-Ramati

Born in Warsaw in December 1919 to Jewish parents, Mieczysław Weinberg (born Mojsze Wajnberg) interrupted his music studies in Warsaw in September 1939 due to the German invasion of Poland and fled to Minsk. His family died in the Trawniki concentration camp. Weinberg then studied composition in Minsk but, when Operation Barbarossa was triggered in 1941, he took refuge in Tashkent, in Uzbekistan. In 1943, he submitted his Symphony No. 1, op. 10, to Shostakovich, who became his friend and mentor. He moved permanently to Moscow. On 13 February 1948, his father-in-law was killed in Minsk on Stalin's orders. In February 1953, when Weinberg was arrested and charged with Jewish bourgeois nationalism, for allegedly supporting a Jewish republic in Crimea, Shostakovich wrote to influential secret police chief Lavrentiy Beria a letter in his defence and he was released shortly after Stalin's death that same year.

His works include twenty-two symphonies (the last one incomplete), a violin concerto, a trumpet concerto, four solo cello sonatas and six piano sonatas. His opera, *The Passenger* – completed in 1968 – was given a concert performance in Moscow. He died in February 1996 in Moscow.

* * *

When the Germans occupied Poland, Roman Haubenstock-Ramati, a Jew from Kraków, fled to Lviv (part of Ukraine after the Molotov–Ribbentrop Pact). Arrested by Soviet troops and accused of spying, he was sent to Tomsk and enlisted in the II Korpus Polski under Władysław Anders, a unit that depended on the Polish government in exile. He was then incorporated into the British Army, and relocated to British Palestine. Back in Kraków in 1947, he became the head of the Radio Kraków music department and then, in 1950, he emigrated to Israel. Eventually, he and his family moved to Vienna, where he became editor and music consultant for Universal Edition.

He taught composition at the Academy of Music and Performing Arts in Vienna and created new forms of notation and music writing. He died in Vienna in March 1994.

Mikosho and Pavlov-Azancheev

Born in 1897, Vladimir Mikosho taught at the Worker's Faculty and the Military Faculty of Moscow conservatoire and was the conductor of the ensemble Persimfans. He was enlisted in the people's militia during the war and was captured. He escaped and returned to the front, where he was employed as a band master. In 1943, he was arrested in Kursk, charged with treason towards the Motherland and sentenced to ten years in the Vorkuta gulag.

In the gulag, he became a theatre composer, directed shows, gave concerts, taught and organised conferences. After being released, he was deprived of his civil rights for five years. Rehabilitated in 1958, he moved to Moscow with his family. He died in 1991.

Matvei Pavlov-Azancheev (known as Pavlov-Azancheev) was born in the Kursk Region, Russia, in March 1888. At a young age, he and his family, apart from his father who was working in Moscow, moved to Batumi, Georgia. In Sochi in 1941, while on a tour, he was accused of anti-Soviet propaganda and sentenced to ten years in a penal colony in Southern Russia. He wrote works for seven-string guitar, including *Danse acrobatique* and Sonata No. 2 *'Velikaya Otechestvennaya voyna'* ('the great patriotic war', as the Soviets called the Second World War). After he was released in 1951, the Soviet authorities turned down his application for a pension and he died in Armavir in January 1963.

Walden and Rusakov

The German Jewish writer, publisher, gallery owner, musician and composer Georg Lewin, also known as Herwarth Walden, was one of the promoters of the German avant-garde. In 1903, he founded the *Verein für Kunst* and married poet Else Lasker-Schüler. In 1910, he founded the magazine *Der Sturm*, which was followed in 1916 by the art school of the same name. His musical works include *Zehn Gesänge zu Dichtungen der Else Lasker-Schüler* and *Dafnislieder* for voice and piano, the opera *Die Nachtwächter* to text by Theodor Körner and the musical pantomime *Die Vier Toten der Fiametta*. In 1918, he joined the German Communist party. Facing the spread of Nazism and antisemitism, he left Germany, in 1932, and moved to Moscow, where he worked as a language teacher and publicist. Walden's predilection for the avant-garde aroused the suspicions of the Soviet authorities, and he was consequently arrested in 1941 and sent to the Saratov gulag, where he died on 31 October 1941.

Paul Marcel (Pavel) Rusakov was born in Marseille, in 1908, to Jewish immigrants from Rostov-on-Don who had been expelled from Russia because they were considered untrustworthy, although the family returned to the USSR to take part in Soviet propaganda. He studied at the Leningrad conservatoire and graduated in piano and composition. In 1925, he set to music poems by Alexander Blok and Vladimir Mayakovsky. On 2 February 1937 he was arrested, charged with being a member of an anti-Soviet organisation and sentenced to be shot, but the sentence was commuted to ten years' imprisonment, which he served in Gulag K-231 (Vyatlag) in Kirov.

In Vyatlag, he organised musical theatre sessions. Rusakov attempted suicide on several occasions. Released in 1947, he worked as music director of the Leningrad Circus, and died in that city in 1973.

TWENTY-TWO

Aliens

Émigrés

In the wake of the Nuremberg Laws, musicians with a German or Austrian passport, including Hans Gál, Peter Gellhorn, Franz Reizenstein, Mátyás Seiber, Leopold Spinner, Vilém Tauský and Egon Wellesz, obtained political asylum in Great Britain. They were referred to as '*émigrés*', a French word with political connotations that had previously been used for the Huguenots, forced to leave France in 1685, and for the couriers of Louis XVI's courtiers who had fled Republican vendettas during the French Revolution.

When the Second World War broke out in 1939, these musicians were interned on the British mainland and on the Isle of Man, or else transferred to Commonwealth countries and classified as 'Enemy Aliens'. Huyton was essentially a transit camp for transfers to the Isle of Man, while Ramsey, on the Isle of Man, had the Mooragh Civilian Internment Camp, opened by Britain on 27 May 1940, among other camps on the island, including Peel Hutchinson Camp Douglas, Onchan and the Rushen women's camp.

Born in Nuremberg in 1911, Franz Reizenstein studied composition with Paul Hindemith and piano with Leonid Kreutzer at the Berlin Academy of Music. In 1934, after the Nazis came to power, he emigrated to Great Britain. When war broke out, he was interned in the Central Camp in Douglas, where he wrote various works. On 8 December 1940, his *Ballet Suite* for small orchestra was performed at House No. 29. He died in London in 1968.

The German pianist and composer Fritz Grundland, known as Freddie Grant, was born in Berlin in 1913, relocated to London in 1934 and enrolled at the London School of Music. He wrote the famous song 'You'll Get Used to It' to text by Gordon Victor while interned at Huyton from May to July 1940, and was later transferred to the Farnham internment camp in Quebec.

At least eleven pianos were available at the Peel Hutchinson Camp, and an orchestra was formed, conducted by Rudolf Kästner. There were also Italian internees who held recitals and shows at the camp auditorium. A production of *Romeo and Julian* – a homosexual take on *Romeo and Juliet* – was staged. The German artist Kurt Schwitters gave readings and Dadaist performances.

The Austrian Jewish composer and musicologist Egon Wellesz engaged in research on Eastern music and, in 1920, wrote the first biography of Arnold Schoenberg. In 1938, he emigrated to Britain, worked for the *Grove Dictionary of Music and Musicians* and, in 1939, was appointed a Fellow at Lincoln College, Oxford. In 1940, however, he was interned at the Peel Hutchinson Camp. He went back to work at Oxford after his release and died on 9 November 1974.

In Kraków, the Polish pianist Marjan Rawicz met Walter Landauer. They became a renowned piano duo and emigrated to Britain in 1935. In 1940, they were interned in the Peel Hutchinson Camp. After the war they embarked on an international career and became very popular thanks to BBC radio broadcasts with the British-Italian conductor Mantovani.

Born in Breslau in 1912, Peter Gellhorn studied piano, composition and conducting at the Berlin Hochschule für Musik. Following the Nuremberg Laws, he emigrated to Great Britain in 1935, settled in London and began working at Toynbee Hall. As a foreigner with a German passport, he was interned at Warth Mills in Bury, Lancashire, in 1940, and subsequently transferred to the Mooragh Civilian Internment Camp in Ramsey, on the Isle of Man. He wrote *2 Studies* for violin, *The Cats* for string orchestra without double bass (probably unavailable in Ramsey), *Mooragh* for male chorus and strings, Andante for string orchestra without double bass (or string quartet) and Serenade for string orchestra without double bass (missing). Released in 1941, he was summoned by the British Government in 1943 to work for the war effort. In 1946, he became assistant musical director and conductor at the Royal Opera House, Covent Garden. He died in Kingston in 2004.

From Great Britain to Australia

The Austrian Jewish pianist and composer Peter Stadlen has gone down in history as the first performer, in 1937, of the Piano Variations, op. 27, by Anton Webern. He took refuge in Great Britain and, in 1940 was classified as an Enemy Alien. He was, like several thousand other refugees, sent to an internment camp in Australia, although he returned to Britain after the war. He gave the European premiere of Schoenberg's piano concerto. As a musicologist, he specialised in studying and playing Beethoven. However, because of a neurological problem in his left ring finger, he had to give up his piano career.

On 10 July 1940, 2,545 German and Austrian refugees resident in Britain, classified as Enemy Aliens, as well as 200 Italian prisoners of war, sailed from Liverpool aboard the HMT *Dunera* under the watch of 309 British guards of the Pioneer Corps. Crammed to the rafters, with deplorable hygiene conditions and in constant danger of an enemy attack, the ship finally reached Darling Harbour, in Sydney. The following day, the prisoners – subsequently called 'Dunera Boys' – were taken on four trains to the civil internment Camps Nos 7 and 8 in Hay, New South Wales, 400 kilometres west of Sydney;

in November, Camp No. 6, for the internment of Italian and Japanese civilians, became operational.

In May 1941, German and Austrian internees were transferred to Tatura and Orange under the supervision of the Australian army. Seven camps under the control of the Australian army and intended for civilian and military internment were opened, including Rushworth, Murchison and Tatura; about 2,000 Enemy Aliens were interned in Tatura.

Using makeshift materials and petrol jerrycans, the internees put up a theatre and staged musicals during their internment: *Hay Fever* was performed in Camp No. 7 and *Hay Days are Happy Days* in Camp No. 8. The musical accompaniment was provided by the musicians, who created a make-believe jazz ensemble by imitating the sound of musical instruments with their mouths.

The composer and conductor Ray Martin (born Kurt Kohn) was one of those on board the HMT *Dunera* bound for Sydney and the Hay camp. He wrote various ironic pieces about internment. In 1941, he was released and formed a band for the radio entertainment of British troops, returned to Britain, and devoted himself to composing and created the BBC Northern Variety Orchestra, which he conducted until 1951. He then moved from Britain to the US, where he signed a contract with RCA Records. Later, in Paris, he also recorded with Polydor, but returned to Great Britain for health reasons in 1972, before finally relocating to South Africa.

Boaz Bischofswerder, a rabbi at the Brunnenstrasse Reform synagogue in Berlin, wrote religious hymns with organ or piano accompaniment. He left Germany in 1933 and took refuge in London, but when the war broke out he was interned and, in 1940, sent aboard the HMT *Dunera* with Felix, one of his sons. On his way to Australia, he wrote *Phantasia Judaica* for four tenors. Interned at the Hay camp, he rewrote *Phantasia Judaica* for violin and piano (the only instruments available in the camp). He was subsequently transferred to Tatura, where he wrote mainly arrangements of music by Louis Lewandowski, including 'Jir'u Eynenu', 'En Kelohenu' and 'J'hi scholom b'chelech' for male chorus and 'Mi Addir' and 'Sheva B'rochoth' for baritone and piano. Freed in 1944, he remained in Australia and died two years later. We have two cassettes with recordings of traditional Jewish music sung by Bischofswerder himself ('El Male Rachamim' and 'Lehu Nerann'no'), transcribed as a score at the Archive of Australian Judaica at the University of Sydney.

Felix Werder (Bischofswerder), Boaz's son, was interned and travelled to Australia with his father on HMT *Dunera*. In 1943 he wrote *Ac tomos* for violin and male voice, which was reworked for string orchestra after the war. In 1944, he completed his Symphony No.1, op. 6 (revised in 1952), *Off and Running* for clarinet and orchestra, and Psalm 127, op. 32, for mixed chorus, two horns, vibraphone, percussion and double bass, works that are orchestrally complex, in an avant-garde idiom that reaches beyond Webern's pointillism. Liberated in 1944, he also remained in Australia.

In 1955, the Sydney Symphony Orchestra, conducted by Eugene Goossens, performed his symphonic poem *Balletomania*. His stage works include *Kisses for a Quid*, *Agamemnon*, *The Vicious Square* and *The Conversion*. In 1988, he was honoured with a doctorate in music by the University of Melbourne. He died in Melbourne in 2012.

Felix and the missing page

I went through every inch of Sydney and Melbourne's libraries and universities, and finally unearthed Felix Werder's address. I was fascinated by this man, the son of a rabbi, who severed the first part of his family surname, and thanks to the German musicologist Albrecht Dümling – the creator, with Peter Sarkar and Guido Fackler, of the Berlin research project *Musica Reanimata*, and an expert on the Bischofswerders, father and son – we know a fair amount about the journey that brought the two already exiled musicians from Britain to their further forced exile on the other side of the planet.

In the Hay camp, Felix Werder studied Nietzsche's *Also sprach Zarathustra*, while in Tatura he discovered the works of the German poet and philosopher Herder. His reading of philosophy and literature radically influenced his composing idiom. His Symphony No. 1, written in Tatura, is surreal in its unbridled pointillism: sudden physical absences of bars appear, conveying still unoccupied cosmic spaces.

Werder was fully immersed in German culture and his internment did not weaken but strengthened the ancestral bond with his country of birth; yet, paradoxically, while many other former internees quickly left Australia after the war to go back to their native countries, the deeply German Werder remained in Australia until his death.

In 2005, when Werder was already elderly, I wrote him a letter asking him to send me the scores he had written in Tatura. They arrived, six months later, from an Australian music centre – Werder's nicely bound scores and, in another package, his typewritten letter with photocopies of Psalm 127, op. 32, for mixed chorus, written in Tatura. However, when I checked the score attentively, I noticed there was a page missing from Psalm 127, probably skipped while being photocopied. There was a chance I might not have Werder's entire internment camp repertory.

I took the liberty of writing to him again, but, a few months later, I received a letter from Werder telling me he was too old and tired. Unfortunately, my story with Werder ended there. A year later, however, I went to see my friend, Robert Foah, in Atlanta and, luckily, a colleague of his had easy access to Australian libraries, so I asked him to get me Psalm 127, and it arrived together with the songs of Australian prisoners of war in Changi. Australians Ray (Raymond Arnold) Tullipan and Clifford Frank 'Slim' De Grey were both members of the Australian Imperial Force (AIF) Concert Party there.

Once again, there were two recurring situations: on one hand the delicate relationship with a very elderly composer and the overriding, reverential respect towards these extraordinary men and their advanced age; and on the other hand, an inexplicable mechanism by which, if you lose one piece of music, you end up finding two or three hundred others. By some magic, this research multiplies whatever it touches.

Shanghai

From 1937 to 1941, and in particular after *Kristallnacht*, 24,000 Jews chiefly resident in the Reich's metropolitan territory found refuge in Shanghai, at that time a kind of international free city administered by the Republic of Nanjing. A collaborationist Chinese political entity founded in 1940, it recognised the independence of Manchukuo (a puppet state of Japan in Manchuria, 1932–45) and, in 1936, signed the Anti-Comintern Pact with Japan and Germany. On 9 January 1943, the Republic of Nanjing declared war on the US and Great Britain.

In the wake of the Japanese bombing of the US naval base at Pearl Harbor, on 7 December 1941, Japanese troops occupied European settlements in Shanghai. On 18 February 1943, they instituted a ghetto in the Hongkou quarter, where Jewish refugees ended up, placed under the generic classification of 'stateless'. A safe haven where it was possible to land without a visa, Shanghai was a welcoming place for Jewish refugees thanks to the action of Feng Shan Ho, Chinese general consul in Vienna, and to the Japanese government's basic indifference to the Third Reich's racial and antisemitic policies.

One such refugee was pianist, operetta composer and entertainment musician Siegfried Sonnenschein, who was informed in Dresden by a Nazi Party member friend that he was about to be arrested, so he sailed to Shanghai instead. He wrote songs and operettas – his famous *Sag, bist du mir gut* was staged in April 1946 at the Eastern Theater in Hongkou. He gave piano recitals as a soloist and accompanist of singers and was musical director of variety shows.

German and Austrian Jewish composers, concert musicians, conductors, singers, actors and cabaret artists created a substantial amount of artistic activity in Shanghai, partly thanks to institutions such as the Shanghai City Council Symphony Orchestra (formerly the Shanghai Symphony Orchestra, founded in 1879) – and the Guoli yinyue zhuanke xuexiao (now the music conservatoire). From August 1939 to November 1946, a hundred or so plays and operettas, including thirty-two world premieres, were staged there. Musicians favoured entertainment and deliberately avoided making artistic choices with political undertones

A wave of Viennese repertoire, from Johann Strauss, Jr and Imre Kálmán to café music, pervaded Shanghai's halls and cinemas. Siegmund Rodman formed a jazz band. Among the most prominent musicians emigrating to Shanghai were the aforementioned Sonnenschein, Wolfgang Fraenkel, Julius Schloss, and Gino Smart, the Austrian pianist and composer who wrote the hit songs 'Ein Kleid aus dunkelgrüner Seide' and 'Barbara' to text by the Austrian Jewish playwright Hans Morgenstern.

After Pearl Harbor

In 1943, at the Weihsien compound (present-day Weifang/ Shandong in China), the Japanese opened a civilian internment camp for a total of 1,800 people, mainly British, US and Australian citizens resident in the territory. Prolific musical activity developed thanks to a Salvation Army orchestra, a symphony orchestra and the jazz band of Earl Whaley, the American saxophonist and band leader.

Whaley was in Shanghai during the Japanese attack on Pearl Harbor. Subsequently, he was sent to Weihsien on a train with three hundred prisoners and brutally tortured, his fingers broken; he somehow survived, while some of his band members lost their lives in the compound.

On 15 February 1942, Japan occupied Sumatra and other islands in the Dutch West Indies (present-day Indonesia) and captured numerous civilians, mainly Dutch and British women who were then transferred to the Palembang internment camp, on the southeast of the island. Thanks to help from conductor and composer Norah Chambers, who had graduated from the Royal Academy of Music in London, the Presbyterian missionary Margaret Dryburgh – who was well-versed in music and endowed with a phenomenal memory – put together women's choir arrangements of music by Bach, Handel, Mozart, Beethoven, Chopin, Dvořák, Ravel and Grieg. This music was performed by a vocal orchestra made up of about thirty women, who sang syllables, not actual words. In 1942 Dryburgh wrote 'The Captive's Hymn' for female chorus. It was first sung by Dryburgh, Shelagh Brown and Dorothy MacLeod at a Sunday service, and from then on the hymn was sung by the women every Sunday. The concerts took place from 27 December 1943 to early 1945; however, exhausting transfers to other camps in Sumatra (Muntok, Loeboek Linggau, Belalau), malnutrition, tropical disease and cruelty on the part of the Japanese decimated the prisoners and the choir. It undermined the already precarious health of Dryburgh, who died in April 1945 on Bangka Island.

In Tangerang, a city in the province of Banten, west of Batavia (present-day Jakarta in Indonesia), Japan opened an internment camp for Jewish civilians, Masonic Lodge members and colonial administrators. The Dutch women there produced the *Tangeranglied* for female chorus and piano, texts intended for singing and a copious amount of poetry.

During the Japanese occupation, the prisoners of war and civilian internees in Western Java were brought together in camps in Batavia, Cimahi and Bandung, while others were transferred to labour camps outside Java, where treatment was brutal.

In 1942, during a tour of Asia, the Hungarian pianist Lili Kraus and the Polish violinist Szymon Goldberg, former leader of the Berlin Philharmonic – were arrested by the Japanese and interned in Java. Kraus and her family were interned until 1943, while Goldberg was transferred to various other camps and finally to Cimahi, 180 km southwest of Jakarta.

After the war, Kraus moved to New Zealand, resumed her career and obtained British citizenship. She taught at the Texas Christian University in Fort Worth and settled in Asheville, North Carolina. She died in 1986.

In 1953, Goldberg became a US citizen; he taught at Yale, the Juilliard School in New York, the Curtis Institute of Music in Philadelphia and the Manhattan School of Music in New York. He moved to Japan and died in Toyama in 1993.

Bandung-born Theodor 'Theo' Smit Sibinga was interned, until 1945, in a Japanese camp on the Celebes Islands (present-day Sulawesi, Indonesia). During his internment, he wrote *Kantjil-Fantasie* for piano and orchestra and *Indische Nocturne No.3 [Toradja]* for orchestra; the latter was performed for the first time in New York by Arturo Toscanini. Similarly, Indonesian-born violinist Will Eisma, who had studied at the Rotterdam Conservatory and the Royal Conversatory in The Hague, was interned at the Japanese camp at Bandung, where he wrote Sonate, op. 6, Scherzo, op. 8, for three violins and Bagatellen for violin and piano. Other musicians forced into prison camps in the Far East include composer, pianist and conductor Paul Seelig and painter and composer Walter Spies.

TWENTY-THREE

Roads that Separate and Unite

The Dead Sea Scrolls

Wherever conditions of imprisonment and suffering are produced, there music is created. After all, the Afro-American Blues – a forefather of gospel and jazz – produced on US cotton plantations, is, arguably, concentrationary music. Jazz, which still harbours the African tribal spirit of percussion, was played in protests against denied rights and disappointed expectations. Entire generations have used jazz in their battles, giving us an unforgettable lesson in history.

Concentrationary music also includes a wide body of songs written by Italians in the open camps of the Austro-Hungarian Empire before the First World War, the Republican songs in Franco's prisons during the Spanish Civil War, the songs of political dissidents in the Soviet gulags and those by US prisoners of war during the Vietnam war.

The musicologist Peter Stadlen – interned in Australia – spent many years searching for Beethoven's metronome, certain that the weight fitted on it was defective and that this explained some of the metronomic speeds in his sonatas, which were probably incorrect. At long last, he found the metronome, but discovered that the weight was missing. This anecdote shows us that research does not always yield the intended fruits; a hyper-digitalised society has lost its way in a world that revolves around the delicate balance between the researcher, the witness (or their heirs) and the sheet of music withered by time or damaged by worms and dust.

These musicians were not behind us but ahead of us.

According to statistical calculations by the ILMC Foundation, if you put aside musicians and singers and take into account the collective music created in captivity by various nations during the Second World War and in post-war Communist regimes, the number of composers of material produced in civilian and military captivity from 1933 to 1953 (composers, arrangers, band leaders, parodists and authors of light music and other popular genres) amounts to a number somewhere between 110,000 and 130,000. An impressive fact that not only gives us an idea of the work still to be done, but also of the vast historical, musicological and documentary task already accomplished up to now by Alexander Kulisiewicz, Shmerke Kaczerginski, Bret Werb, Guido Fackler, Jana Belišová and only a few others.

The cosmic lack of financial support for research on concentrationary music is worrying, and there are still many unanswered questions, not to mention a great regret: this musical literature could have been spared a delay of at least fifty years. If it is true that – to paraphrase Gustav Mahler – memory is not the worship of the ashes but rather the fuelling of the fire, our generation has reached a turning point. The daily discovery of works written in captivity involves us all, confronting each other with one of the most important conquests of human talent. This means that in music nothing is where it is supposed to be and that logic starts almost always from the absurd.

Going back to concentrationary music, those who wrote

their last scores in Prague then concealed them in Leningrad, those who filled music notebooks in Westerbork then left them in Bergen-Belsen, those who created songs on a train from Thessaloniki to Birkenau, orally passed on the tunes in the lager to someone who emigrated to São Paulo after the war, and those who composed music during the construction of the Death Railway took their music diaries with them and now live in Brighton or Canberra. Like in a wonderful jigsaw puzzle, we are piecing together every tessera, completing pentagrams, sewing places of captivity to places of origin and return, slotting in fragments with as much patience as if they were the Dead Sea Scrolls, but with the risk that we could be sent back to the beginning if something goes wrong.

It is a risk worth taking.

Jon's violin

In early 2020, film producer Donatella Altieri and I decided to go to the US, not in order to retrieve scores or manuscripts nor to meet survivors, but for the sake of a violin used in a lager.

It began with an email from Bay City, Michigan: someone wrote on behalf of Hanna Grazyna Hillenbrand, the widow of the Polish violinist Jon Stanisław Hillenbrand, who had played in the Auschwitz I orchestra. Mrs Hillenbrand had seen the report on 'The Lost Music' on *60 Minutes* on CBS, which had featured a piece about my research. Her dream was that her husband's violin should find a better home and also that it should be played again. Why, indeed, not?

Naturally, I seized this opportunity, but a complex, not to mention expensive trip had to be organised, which included intercontinental flights, accommodation and inland travel, and Sabina Castelfranco, the Italian journalist from CBS, was going with us.

First stop, New York, where we spent the night in a hotel near JFK; the next day, a stopover in Detroit, then a flight to Saginaw, where, at the exit of the small airport, we took a taxi to Bay City. Saginaw and Bay City were covered in snow. We arrived to find not only Hanna Hillenbrand, but a CBS crew sent from the New York head office, as well as a warm, welcoming home.

Jon Hillenbrand was only seventeen when he was sent to Auschwitz I Stammlager. He was allowed to take his violin with him and, in the camp, he covered it with fabric taken from clothes worn by the deportees. A talented musician, Jon was co-opted into the *Lagerkapelle*, the orchestra that played at the Auschwitz I gates and which, thanks to the baton of the Polish conductor Adam Kopyciński, reached an excellent standard.

Because Hillenbrand was very young, he did not play in the front row, which was reserved for his elders. He survived, but the Communist regime in Poland made his life difficult, and he emigrated to the US and settled in Bay City, in Michigan, where he worked with the choir and musicians of a local Evangelical church. He took his wonderful instrument with him.

I opened the case and carefully took out the violin. The strings had snapped, the bridge was wobbly, there were marks on the wood, and my first thought was to restore life to it. Just as the music composed in the camps must live again, so must a musical instrument tormented by the same imprisonment and deportation; the only way to give life back to a musical instrument is not by displaying it in a museum but by playing it. I promised Mrs Hillenbrand that I would take the violin to a good luthier and have it restored as soon as I could.

We spent that night in Bay City, then resumed our American journey from the Michigan cold to warm Miami, where we would hug the legendary Polish Jewish musician and percussionist Saul Dreier, who had become a naturalised American.

Saul Dreier

At the age of ninety-five, Saul Dreier still brims with energy and enthusiasm. Some time ago, he founded, with other survivor musicians, the Holocaust Survivor Band and still plays percussion at sold out concerts to an auditorium of young people who sing popular songs in Yiddish, at the top of their lungs, to the beat of his drums.

Born in Kraków in 1925, the young Saul and his family were sent to the Kraków ghetto when the Second World War broke out. Like most Jews in that ghetto, he was then deported to the nearby labour camp in Płaszów. Subsequently transferred to Mauthausen and, finally, to Linz, Dreier was liberated by US troops and sent first to Salzburg, then on to the Apulian refugee camp in Santa Maria al Bagno.

In 1946, he was transferred to Barletta, to the refugee camp in Casermette. Saul distinguished himself as an excellent football player in one of the Jewish refugee teams; he even considered staying in Barletta and playing for the local team. Except his fate lay elsewhere. Sent to Bari with other refugees in 1947 (he organised ship boardings to Mandatory Palestine), he sailed from Naples to the US.

Saul sat next to me, remembering and singing songs created

in Płaszów and Mauthausen: a priceless musical treasure. For thousands of men and women stripped of everything, music provided a parallel life made of beauty.

I wrapped Hillenbrand's violin in several cellophane bags and parcel tape. On every flight we took, I asked for it not to be stored in the overhead locker but in a safe place, and the violin thankfully made it in one piece through the check-ins at Saginaw, Detroit, New York, Miami and Fiumicino.

There was still Bari to go.

It was late February 2020, and they were beginning to take the passengers' temperatures because of Covid. A guard stopped Donatella and me as we were exiting Arrivals. He asked us to run our suitcases and the violin through the scanner and asked: 'Is this your violin?'

It was not mine, but stating the truth would have complicated things, so I said: 'Yes.' Even now, when asked a similar question about an instrument or music, usually I reply without hesitation: 'It belongs to everybody.' *Everybody* conveys a general involvement.

Thanks to the advice of my violinist friend Fabrizio Signorile, I gave Hillenbrand's violin to the Apulian luthier Bruno Di Pilato to be restored.

Off the train to Treblinka

During the first half of 2021, thanks to a project in partnership with the USC Shoah Foundation in Los Angeles, I was able to access video-phonographic documents from Steven Spielberg's monumental project, which contained a wealth of musical material created in the lagers and performed by survivors. Hearing them sing especially touches the heart of someone like me who has been working on such material for decades. Their interrupted singing is a human imprint on the stone of history.

In 1942, shut in a train carriage taking Jews from Lublin-Majdanek to Treblinka to be gassed, two sisters grabbed their nine-year-old younger brother by the belt and hurled him out of the train through the small air vent – only he could fit through it: to love sometimes means to push those we love away from us to save their lives. That little boy's name was Hershel Taichman and he survived. A few years ago, he gave his testimony, kept at the USC Shoah Foundation, and, during the interview, sang 'Lublin, Lublin', created in Lublin-Majdanek by an anonymous composer.

During the German occupation of Latvia, the Nazi regime opened a labour camp in Strasdenhof (present-day Strazdumuiža, in the Riga district), technically a sub-camp of Riga-Kaiserwald. Operational from early August 1943, Strasdenhof consisted of 1,200 Jews from the liquidation of the Vilnius and Riga ghettos.

In Strasdenhof, forced to carry out brutal forced labour, the fifteen-year-old Lithuanian Jew Masha Rolnikaite wrote two songs in Yiddish: 'Der Shtrasdenhofer hymn' and 'Sport'. In 1966, she published her diary, later published as a book, *I Must Tell*. She died on 7 April 2016 in St Petersburg. With regard to 'Der Shtrasdenhofer hymn', Rolnikaite wrote, 'We worked half days on Sundays, so had the afternoon free. The Jews in the camp couldn't accept the idea that they were free, so we'd march in the camp, singing this hymn.' The words were, '*We were the masters of the world and now – if you'll forgive me – we're the lice of the world.*'

'Der Shtrasdenhofer hymn' was recorded by the Lithuanian singer Sarah Kogan and is currently available at the sound archive of the Ben Stonehill Collection (Hebrew University of Jerusalem); it is also recorded in the audio-visual material of the USC Shoah Foundation, performed by the Lithuanian-Jewish survivor Esra Jurmann. The music and lyrics were published by Shmerke Kaczerginski in *Lider in di getos un lagern* (1948), and in a late recording of his Argentinian period, kept at the Ben Stonehill Collection, 'Kaczerginski sings "Shtrasdenhofer hymn"'.

Unfortunately, Kaczerginski misunderstood the name of the camp and identified it as Strassenhof, near Vienna, intended for the detention of 25,000 Hungarian Jews put there thanks to a pact between Hungarian humanitarian organisations and Adolf Eichmann. In this recording, Kaczerginski sings 'Strassenhof' instead of 'Strasdenhof' and repeats this error in his book, using the Yiddish word 'Shtrasnhof' (in Hebrew script).

The song begins with a worrying couplet: '*Mir zaynen di shtrasdnhofer yidn / Dos 'naye eyrope' boyen mir*' – 'We're

Strasdenhof Jews / We're building the New Europe'. The '*Neue Europe*' coincided with the Third Reich's continental and ideological vision of a new Europe from the Pyrenees to the Caucasus, yet in the lyrics sung out loud by the Strasdenhof Jews, the *Neue Europe* was practically liquefied and pulverised to the rhythm of music by a three thousand-year-old prophetic sense of the war's events, which, at the end of 1943, actually marked the irreversible military and strategic defeat of the Nazis and its 'neo-European' delirium. The Jews were literally destroying the Nazi regime from within, at the cost of their own lives. That was what the 'building' in the hymn referred to.

From the Strasdenhof of the Jews who marched in the lager to the Ventotene of the Manifesto to the Ravensbrück of the monumental hymn 'Žalm vdov po národních zen mučednících r.1945 v Ravensbrücku', written by Ludmila Peškařová, men and women looked to a Europe that would not be properly reborn from Nuremberg, but from the great libraries and the diverse and integral cultures in an anthropocentric vision capable of resurrecting an entire continent from the ruins of the war. This was not exactly how things turned out, but there is nothing to stop an umpteenth, giant collective effort: a utopia, a waking dream, a legend?

Legend is the road that connects fantasy and history; something becoming fantasy or history does not depend on the thing per se, but on the direction we mean to take down that road. The Strasdenhof Jews, as Masha Rolnikaite reports, marched in the direction of history.

The music written in deportation, internment and civil and military imprisonment is neither history nor fantasy – it is the road that separates and unites. Like the Strasdenhof Jews, this music is now legendary.

That kibbutz with the name of a lager

In late July 2021, I was in Israel with Donatella to meet musicians who had survived the war; the pandemic situation in Israel was extremely critical, so the trip required the joint intervention of the Italian Embassy in Tel Aviv and the Israeli Embassy in Rome.

Hilde Zimche Grünbaum, a violinist and copyist in the Birkenau women's orchestra, lived in the Netser Sereni kibbutz. My Israeli director friend Gady Castel told me that this kibbutz was originally called 'Buchenwald', because many of its founders came from that camp. If it is true that the mind creates what is real, we can repair the unstable bridges and beams of human thinking and even call a kibbutz 'Buchenwald'.

In 1975, in the Givat Chaim kibbutz, former internees of the camps started the Beit Theresienstadt, with a library, an archive and a learning centre: by this process, names and places gradually regenerate.

When, on the eve of Shabbat, the members of the Chabad Lubavitch sing the *Marseillaise* with Hebrew lyrics, they simply redeem it and bring it back home (part of the French national anthem comes from the Second Temple). Names like 'Ravensbrück' and 'Buchenwald' in song lyrics created in deportation, instead of evoking the tragedy, are almost pleasant to the ear. Thanks to the miraculous power of music, singing the name of Auschwitz brings us so close to that reality that we can correct it.

On the ruins of the great German theatres destroyed by the bombings, as well as on the hecatomb caused by the war and Nazism, Richard Strauss wrote: 'The most terrible period in human history is coming to an end, a twelve-year reign of bestiality, ignorance and anti-culture enacted by the greatest criminals, during which the fate of two thousand years of cultural evolution has been put at stake.'

If twelve years of the Third Reich destroyed two millennia of cultural heritage in Germany, how many years will it take to restore to the human race the treasures created under Nazism and Stalinism, which sank into a seven-decade oblivion and are far from being fully recovered?

There is no more time to answer: we have to act.

'I don't come from Auschwitz . . .'

The Austrian-American Jewish writer Susanne Ruth Klüger, a Birkenau survivor, wrote, 'The name Auschwitz exercises a kind of negative influence because it strongly determines our thoughts about a person the moment we realise this person has been there. But that's not true, because no matter what you may think, I don't come from Auschwitz; I come from Vienna'.

'I don't come from Auschwitz; I come from Vienna' – we will etch to infinity and in all its versions this neo-Biblical verse on the marble of contemporary history.

The truth that emanates from these words is elusive; the human mind cannot hold its immensity and its coordinates are equal to the earthly plane. It is the watermark which, as on a banknote, makes our lives genuine and valuable – and not just those of the witnesses.

From 1995 to 2006 in Şanlıurfa, Turkey, archeologists unearthed the site of Göbekli Tepe, a discovery that compelled historians to rewrite the history of humanity. The carbon dating of the site proves that it was built over twelve thousand years ago, much, much earlier than Stonehenge, the pyramids of Giza and the Babylonian ziggurats.

In 2003, at the Tibetan monastery of Sakya, behind a great wall, a huge library was discovered, containing 84,000 scrolls and books with ancient texts on Buddhism, mathematics, astronomy, literature, art, philosophy and human history dating from over ten thousand years ago.

On the shelves of an imaginary library of the history of music and musicians, the books on concentrationary music were missing until now, as though they had been eaten by a monster. Musical literature, specifically of the twentieth century, will have to be completely revised because of the rediscovery of the musical output created in captivity from 1933 to 1953, just as a huge amputated limb reattached to the body restores the circulation of blood, and so of life.

It is the end of a thousand years of mourning, and we are casting into the atmosphere the seeds of better times; this music draws, or rather carves in the air, incredible new intellectual and artistic coordinates.

We have not yet realised the conciliatory extent of such immense musical literature; commemorating is useful and necessary, but we need more if we want to make blueprints, build dams and bridges and, thereby, channel the overflowing rivers of music produced in captivity.

We are still in Pompei (the archeological phase) and must get to Alexandria (the library phase).

We are waiting to give the masterpieces of this musical literature the just, awaited and deserved stage.

Epilogue

The first gulag, opened in 1919 on the Solovetsky Islands, and the first lager, opened in 1933 in Dachau, displayed similar inscriptions, inspired by work, over their entrances, '*Trud ukreplyayet dushu i telo cheloveka*' ('Work strengthens the body and soul') and '*Arbeit macht frei*' ('Work makes us free'). This is not the only resemblance between gulags and lagers, but, in the tragic senselessness of the concentration camp world, these inscriptions paradoxically concern everyone.

A multidimensional abyss has cracked open before us, originating from the recovery of music written in captivity in the time between the first lager being opened and the last gulag being closed; an expert process of artistic creation will be restored and fully operational in this multidimension.

On the stone and iron remains of Barletta's former distillery, the Citadel of Concentrationary Music will rise – oceans of music, thoughts, stories and the distress of entire nations, which the researcher has swept towards Barletta and which have been transformed into lines, graphics, trusses and spaces for libraries and museums. We are waiting for the whole project to become concrete, marble, iron, shelving, rooms, stage, doors and gates, which will be open to all those who will love this world hub of the most dramatically brilliant music of the twentieth century.

This immense artistic and human heritage is currently looked after by the Istituto di Letteratura Musicale Concentrazionaria, created in Barletta in 2014 as a natural progression from the Institute for Jewish Music that my wife Grazia and I founded in 2003.

The Citadel of Concentrationary Music will be the home of the music of people who believed in a better world. With public financial support, it will stand on an area of about 10,000 square metres and will be completed by 2026. This is more than a promise; it is an obligation towards institutions, a guarantee of good construction, the territorial conquest of a decaying zone, the challenge to a certain widespread feeling that many promises have been made but few kept.

Once it is fully operational, the citadel will embrace scholars, researchers, musicians, technicians, choirs and orchestras. For this, and so many other reasons, in the name of thousands and thousands of composers who extracted living music from dead matter like a sword from a stone, for the sake of millions of people belonging to the most diverse nations who experienced persecution, discrimination, genocide and human disasters, we must now declare with unwavering certainty that we will succeed.

A dream cultivated courageously and a clear vision of the future firmly rooted in the present is turning stones and iron into flowers and jewels. Lead into gold.

In addition, 2027 will be the year of completion of a no less demanding project: the publication of the *Thesaurus Musicae Concentrationariae*, a comprehensive twelve-volume, historical and scholarly encyclopaedia of research into concentrationary music from 1933 to 1953. The *Thesaurus Musicae*

Concentrationariae involves research staff and an editorial team that includes researchers, scholars, university lecturers, historians, historiographers, musicians and musicologists of international fame, who are working on publications and recordings. It will include the history, historiography, theory and aesthetics of concentrationary music in this period, a dictionary of the camps where this musical output matured, biographies of the composers, six hundred scores of works written in civilian and military captivity, synoptic tables, a bibliography, discography, filmography and crucially important texts written by Kulisiewicz, Werb, Fackler and others.

The mission to achieve such a rescue operation has become especially onerous in addition to requiring increasingly tight deadlines. Up to now, the cost of travel, research and recovery of concentrationary music has been met by me personally and by the limited resources of the foundation. This has been a significant sacrifice based on the certainty that, if this music were not saved, time would have easily condemned most of it to deterioration and the disappearance of paper and sound records, thereby nullifying the act of brilliance and resistance these works meant for their authors.

Goodwill, a missionary spirit and shared moral objectives are worthy but not sufficient for an achievement on an international scale. We need adequate resources to match the situation and, up to now, the institutions in charge have not been overly swift or always able to share the task.

Jewish institutions and foundations, although constantly appealed to, have not come forward, each believing the others will step in. Consequently, no one has done anything.

The researcher's optimism has become the perfect alibi. An excuse for not helping him, for doing nothing when the work-load is becoming almost unsustainable.

The volume of musical material is more than we had dared imagine, and there are still as many scores to recover as there are elderly survivors to contact. As time is running out, this research risks hitting a dead end, just like a car that has run out of fuel.

This is the moment in history when we need to pick up the pace to win the race against time. In 2018, the foundation launched the 100 Viaggi project: to search for survivor musicians, put musical works in a safe place and make sound recordings in order to reconstruct, among others, the concentrationary music of the Roma people and Ukrainian bandurists. If we had adequate financial support, we could undertake a large number of trips worldwide. This project, created by Donatella and supported by the Apulia regional administration, is finally taking off.

The trips are lengthy and costly, digitalising every single page is equally demanding and restoring musical instruments is also laborious and very expensive, as Jon Hillenbrand's violin shows, but all the necessary and sufficient elements to make donations and help support this research financially exist.

It is worth quoting a line from a splendid song, 'Kolysanka oświęcinska', written in Gusen by Henryk Leszczyński: 'Who is this song for nowadays?'

It is a question addressed to posterity. I think I can say that this and all the songs written between 1933 and 1953, from Mauthausen and Treblinka to Kolyma and Vorkuta, are forever ours.

Concentrationary music is a literature. It has developed its own prerogatives and must be elaborated, studied and promoted by artistic and musical institutions, from universities to conservatoires to schools of art and history. In other words, we must disengage this literature from memory: Italian literature is not there to commemorate Dante and Foscolo, but to study them.

The humanitarian tragedy of the twentieth century is the engine room of this research; it is to concentrationary music what the engine is to the car. Only dissemination of this literature on an academic, concert and publishing level will produce the proper immune defences and the appropriate weapons to fight denialism, reductionism of any kind and antisemitism.

Despite the unhappy times, in the end something will save us and will concern everybody without distinction. The writer Jorge Luis Borges said that it would simply be common sense; some rely on science, others prefer to go up a few steps and trust in the Transcendant, but whatever the chosen vehicle, they will be saved.

Noah, his family and the animals who survived the Flood were on board an ark, while Moses was saved from the waters while in a papyrus basket; it does not matter if we are saved on a ship as large as three aircraft carriers or in a basket, the Torah uses the same word for both: *tevah*.

The music written in captivity has stood the most severe tests of inexorable time and history. Few other bequests like this literature will make us immune to any intellectual disaster and ferry us to an era that will put human beings, their dignity and their unequalled creative and constructive ability at the centre of individual and collective interests.

In the Talmud Yerushalmi, Sanhedrin 4:12, it is written that '*kol hamatzìl nèfesh ahàt keìllu itzil 'olàm umlò*': whoever saves a soul, it is as if they saved a world and its fullness. If the life we still have of these musicians is what pours out of their music, then it is right to let ourselves be saved by it. A song will save the world; an uninterrupted, ancestral song that smells of polished stone, intense like a rainbow after a downpour, with melodies that stand out over our cities.

That is what the substance of this music will be made of,

closer to real dreams than to unsubstantial reality. There will be nothing left of ghettos, lagers or gulags, there will just be music.

Help me bestow this heritage on every man and woman; the Earth will become more welcoming. And we will make this music into a universal heritage.

A song will save the world.

Acknowledgements

This book is the tip of the iceberg of work carried out for over thirty-five years, and which would never have been possible without the help of my mentors and, effectively, fathers of concentrationary music research: Bret Werb, Guido Fackler and the pioneer of this research, Aleksander Kulisiewicz, whom I have never met, although I am familiar with every act of his life and his mission thanks to his son Christof, my great friend and a tireless champion of his father's work.

I wish to thank the members of the Institute of Concentrationary Music Literature, who have contributed significantly to my research, and without whom this book would not have been possible: Grazia Tiritiello, to whom I dedicate this book, Donatella Altieri, Paolo Candido, Ottavio Di Grazia, Enzo Garofalo, Luciana Doronzo, Nannette Del Carmen, Roberto Malini, and Dario Picciau.

My thanks also go to those who have made this result possible through their work. These include Vicki Satlow, Katherine Gregor, Anna Hervé, Dominique and Isabelle Losay, Claude Torres, Alexandre Valenti, Sabina Castelfranco, Giovanna Grenga, Angelo De Leonardis, Andrea Bartošová, Rino Daloiso, Tanja Jörgensen-Leuthner, Viviana Kasam,

Marilena Citelli Francese, Danielle Morali, Guido Regina, Natale Pagano, Werner Grünzweig, Peter Konopatsch, Hannah Abrahamson, Martin Anderson, Geraldine Auerbach, Fietje Ausländer, Jana Belišova, Linda Berry West, Loïc Bouchet, Michel Welterlin, Patrizia Citeroni, Lucia Rampazzo, Salvatore Giannella, Michele Pentrella, Martine Michon, Tonio Bernardini, Rocco Dileo, Raffaele Di Candia, Magda Widlak-Avolio, Lena Makarova, Andrea Di Betta, Marco Visalberghi, Piero Piergiovanni, Antonio Parisella, Eleonore Philipp, Johannes Pickers, Albrecht Dümling, Peter Sarkar, Mozes Heinschink, Ursula Hemetek, Elizabeth Herbin, Martin Hummel, André Laks, Ruth Levin, Marie Paule Libert and Lysianne Dancsa, Martina Šiknerová, Roberto Stringa, Peter Kreitmeir, Minako Waseda, Heidy Zimmermann, Joanna Alexander, Susan Cohn, and Eric Gombert.

Moroeover, I wish to thank the survivors and their families, who have enriched concentrationary music literature by donating manuscripts, photographs and letters. These include Giancarlo Coppola, Alberto Guareschi, Frédéric De Foucaud, Giovanni and Deborah Frisone, Jean-Louis Haguenauer, Ivan Karel, Jean-Christophe Lannoy and Sabine van Lerberghe, Peter and Cordelia Koppitz, Waldemar and Iwona Kropiński, Elisa Longarato, Paolo Orsolino, Riccardo Pacifici, Orlane Paquin and André Letourneur, Nelly and Mario Quercia, Maria Santa Savino and the Marinelli family, Claudio and Eros Capostagno, Adrian and Valerie Blair, Eva Fox-Gál, Friedrich and Christine Gürtler, Elisabeth Thiriet, Patrizia and Pia Maggioli, Frédérique Andrée Soret, Rod Beattie, Sears Eldredge, Laura Foster, and Aviva Bar-On.

It is impossible to list all the cultural institutions that have contributed to this research, so I will mention only Akademie der Künste and musica reanimata in Berlin,

Gedenkstätte in Buchenwald, Gedenkstätte in Sachsenhausen, DIZ Emslandlager in Papenburg, the University of Sydney, the National Library of Australia in Canberra, the Auschwitz Museum, Centralne Muzeum Jeńców Wojennych in Opole, the Imperial War Museum in London, King's College, Cambridge, Beit Lohamei HaGetaot, Beit Theresienstadt in Givat Haim-Ichud, Yad Vashem and the Hebrew University in Jerusalem, Bibliothèque nationale de France in Paris, Goetheanum in Dornach, Paul Sacher Stiftung in Basel, Densho Encyclopedia in Seattle, the US Holocaust Memorial Museum and the Library of Congress in Washington DC, the US Army Combined Arms Center in Fort Leavenworth, Národní knihovna in Prague, the Moravian Museum in Brno, Památník Terezín, and Joods Historisch Museum in Amsterdam.

I would like to pay homage to those – the survivors or their relatives, scholars and benefactors – who have helped me in my research and are no longer with us; the list is endless, so I will mention only Chaim Refael, Blanka Cervinková, Petr Pokorný, Esta Kramer, Hanuš Weber, David Bloch, Dov Freiberg, Jack Garfein, Bernard and Nirmala Goué, Carlotta Guareschi, Eliška Kleinová, Robert Kolben, Milan Kuna, Gabriele Mandel Khan, Rosa Nardone, Josef Bek, Zuzana Růžičková, Paul Aron Sandfort, Heinz Jakob "Coco" Schumann, Milan Slavický, Alice Herz Sommer, Piero Terracina, and Felix Werder.

Last but not least, my heartfelt gratitude for the memory of my parents Concetta and Giuseppe.